Landmark Visitors Guide

Lake District

Norman Buckley

llowing more than forty years as a frequent visitor, Norman Buckley s lived in the Lake District since 1990, indulging his enthusiasm for this unique area, its history and its landscape.

r the past sixteen years he has been a prolific writer of guide books various kinds; this is his fifth and most comprehensive Lake District ide, previous books having concentrated on routes for walkers and exploring the towns and villages.

partnership with wife June, Norman has also written several books king recommended walks and tea shops in various parts of Britain, more to come. He is a keen environmentalist, holding post-graduate mas in Environmental studies from the Universities of Liverpool and Lancaster respectively, and an M.A from Lancaster University.

Young lambs on hills side high above a cumbrian village

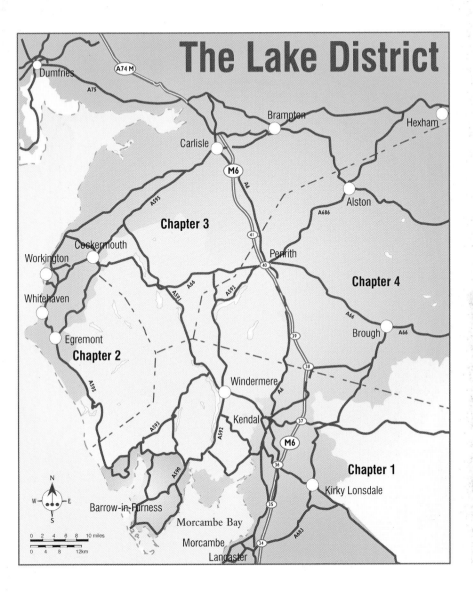

The Lake District

Dumfries

A74 M

A75

Brampton

Hexham

Carlisle

M6

A6

Alston

A595

A686

Chapter 3

41

Cockermouth

Penrith

Workington

40

Whitehaven

Chapter 4

A591

A66

A592

A66

Egremont

39

Brough

A66

Chapter 2

A595

Windermere

A6

A593

Kendal

37

A592

38

N

W—E

S

Chapter 1

M6

36

A590

Kirky Lonsdale

35

Barrow-in-Furness

0 2 4 6 8 10 miles

0 4 8 12km

Morcambe Bay

Morcambe

34

A683

Lancaster

Note on the maps

The maps drawn for each chapter, whilst comprehensive, are not intended to be used as route maps, but rather to locate the main towns, villages and points of interest. For exploration visitors are recommended to use 1:50,000 (approximately 1¼ inch to the mile.) Ordnance Survey 'Landranger' maps.

Contents

Welcome to the
Lake District

Top Tips

Beatrix Potter: The life and works of Beatrix Potter has been of enormous interest to Lake District visitors since her death in 1943, much intensified at the beginning of 2007 by the release of the film *Miss Potter*. **Hill Top** at Near Sawrey, the **Beatrix Potter Gallery** at Hawkshead and the **World of Beatrix Potter** at Bowness are the three focal points for visitors.

Lake Steamers: The scheduled 'steamer' service on Windermere carries thousands of visitors between the landing stages at Waterhead (Ambleside), Bowness and Lakeside during the season. Smaller launches operated circular trips, particularly from Bowness, and maintain the scheduled services out of season. Similarly, on Ullswater the historic 'steamers' operate between Glenridding, Howtown and Pooley Bridge. On Coniston Water, the Coniston launch operates a round the lake service, calling at several intermediate jetties, particularly that serving John Ruskin's home at Brantwood. The beautiful National Trust owned *Gondola* operates cruises from Coniston. Derwentwater has the Keswick launches, traditional wooden boats, providing a timetabled service around the lake. Alternately clockwise and anti-clockwise, they start from the base at Keswick landings.

Rheghed: A comprehensive modern visitor centre attraction, set into the landscape, a little way to the south of Penrith. Home to the National Mountaineering Exhibition, visual presentations, giant cinema screen, children's play area, shops and restaurant.

Sellafield Visitor Centre: A very popular centre with wide ranging exhibits, particularly of scientific interest.

Ravenglass and Eskdale Railway: Long established and much loved narrow gauge railway line connecting Ravenglass and Dalegarth, in Eskdale, with several intermediate stations. Beautifully maintained steam locomotives. Catering and other facilities at both terminal stations.

Cumberland Pencil Museum: Devoted to the long and fascinating history of the pencil, an excellent all-weather attraction. A journey through a 'graphite mine' is included.

Wordsworth–Dove Cottage, Grasmere: Of the four houses in the Grasmere/Rydal area which William Wordsworth occupied at different stages of his life, Dove Cottage is probably the favourite. Adjacent exhibition centre.

The Lake District is one of the most popular areas for visitors in the country. In all seasons, people come to explore its fells and valleys, whether in spring when wild daffodils may be seen in many areas, in the balmy days of summer, or autumn when the changing foliage brings a richness to the colours of the fells and lakes. Even in winter, a dusting of snow on the fells creates scenes of memorable beauty.

In addition to the fells, valleys and lakes, there are the literary attractions which draw visitors from all around the world who come in large numbers to see for themselves the homes of Beatrix Potter and William Wordsworth.

There is much to see and much to do, all of it set against a backdrop of magnificent scenery protected by the National Park and the area's major landowner, the National Trust. The Lake District attracts visitors back time and time again, often several times a year. The Lakeland experience endears and endures despite the passage of the years.

Yes, there is always a welcome in the Lake District, to new visitors and old friends alike. Even if it pours down while you are there, your enthusiasm to return will not be dampened. In that sense, the Lake District can readily claim to be the complete holiday destination.

Very short answers to the above key questions might be given as follows:-

It is a compact area, roughly circular and about fifty kilometres (thirty miles) in diameter, situated in the far north-west of England. Within this area is a unique and outstandingly beautiful combination of lakes, mountains, woodland, small towns and villages, the great majority of the area being accessible to visitors.

The answer to the boundary question could be and has been debated at great length. The only official boundary is that laid down when the area was created a National Park in 1951, which many feel to be too restrictive. For the purpose of this guide that boundary has been generally adopted but has been stretched a little in places to include towns such as Kendal and Cockermouth, leaving many attractive fringe areas, with their towns and villages, to be recommended as car excursions from bases within the district.

Within its modest and manageable size this book sets out to provide all the information about the Lake District which the modern visitor will need, with colour photographs to give a sample preview of this wonderful area.

The introduction to the book gives an outline history of the district together with a balanced view of some of the more important aspects of Lakeland life today, perhaps whetting the appetite for further reading.

For the busy or short term visitor the introduction can, of course, be ignored. After all, the heart of the book is the place by place guide and the associated 'Factfile'. However, referral back to the historical material, possibly after a visit, could well be rewarding in giving depth or context to some feature or other which has been encountered along the way.

The main part of the guide divides the district into four large geographical areas, each with an introductory map.

Highlights

The main highlight has to be the scenery; the mountains and lakes are spectacular, no matter from where you view them; on foot, bike or from a vehicle.

Good food and local beers.

Plenty of accommodation for all tastes and plenty to do.

Close to a motorway network.

Within each area there are sub-divisions, each dealing with one or more valleys and/or linked towns and villages to make a chapter of manageable size, but dealing comprehensively with everything of potential interest to visitors, from ancient monuments to car parks and public conveniences. Suggested walks (including well-known mountain ascents), cycle rides and motor car excursions are given.

Separate short chapters on particular Lake District subjects such as William Wordsworth and Beatrix Potter are provided for those with more specialised interests, for example, in seeking out every Lake District property associated with Wordsworth.

The chapters on accommodation and eating out are, of necessity, very selective in an area so devoted to catering for visitors. Examples across the range are given for each section, listed in order corresponding to the chapters of the main part of the guide.

'Factfile' includes in list format a vast amount of information which could be of use to visitors, with addresses and telephone numbers where appropriate. Again, each part is in the same order as the chapters of the main guide.

How the Lake District was formed

Since geologist Jonathan Otley produced, in 1820, the geology of the Lake District the subject has always attracted interest. For the layman it is probably enough to know that the formation of the district involved a complex mixture of the laying down of marine sediments and volcanic activity, with later compressive movements forcing the land above water and into a great dome-shaped mound.

The oldest rock, about 470 million years, is the **Skiddaw Slate**, forming the northern part of the district from Loweswater to Blencathra, with an isolated mass at Black Combe in the far south-west. Next came the lava and ash from the volcanic eruptions, forming the **Borrowdale Volcanic Series** of the rough, craggy, central core. A covering of **Coniston Limestone** followed, now seen only as a very narrow, occasionally outcropping, band running south-west to north-east from the Duddon Estuary almost to Shap. Much more important in relation to the present landscape is the next sedimental phase, the variety of rocks formed during the **Silurian period**, present right across the southern part of the district and responsible for the comparatively soft, gentle, countryside seen around Hawkshead and Windermere.

Repeated earth movements took place and another sinking beneath the sea resulted in thick coverings of carboniferous limestone and, later, sandstone. During the time of this latter covering, desert conditions prevailed for a few million years. Erosion has removed the limestone from all except a rim around the area, best seen at Scout Scar near Kendal or Whitbarrow Scar, well to the south. Likewise most of the sandstone has gone; the fringe remains are very impressive in the cliffs at St. Bees and have also been used in the construction of Furness Abbey and much of the town of Penrith.

Further uplifting, perhaps 60 million years ago, eventually produced the dome shape now recognisable, with fissures which became the origins of the present valleys spreading out like the spokes of a wheel. During the last one million years, recent times by geological standards, the repeated southerly extension of the polar ice cap has resulted in great moving sheets of ice overtopping the Lakeland peaks, with intervening periods of milder climate during which the ice retreated. The grinding, scouring and plucking of the moving ice has had a profound effect on the landscape, producing the classic glacial features such as U-shaped valleys (Great Langdale, Langstrath) with hanging valleys (corries) high up the valley walls, moraines and drumlins. It is a mere 10,000 years since the final retreat of the ice left the area ready for the first appearance of man.

Human Occupation

To our eyes this **Palaeolithic Age** (Old Stone Age) landscape would have seemed intolerably dreary and desolate. It has been compared with parts of Norway as they exist today; vary sparse fauna and flora, with much reindeer moss and a few stunted birch trees slowly creeping in around the fringes. Human activity was confined to a few wandering hunter/gatherer bands, probably following the herds of reindeer known to be present at the time.

As the climate improved between 8,000 and 5,000 B.C., during the **MesolithicAge** (Middle Stone Age), diversified forest gradually took over, covering the mountains to a high level. There is evidence of a more settled form of occupation in favoured areas such as the fringes between mountains and coast, where there was a comparatively plentiful and diverse supply of food, including fish. By about 3,500 B.C., in the **Neolithic Age** (New Stone Age), transformation of the hunter/gatherers into the first farmers, again on the margins of the district, was taking place and forest clearance, increasing the area of grassland, had commenced. The first cultivation of cereals started a few hundred years later.

By the time of the **Bronze Age**, from about 2,200 B.C., the higher ground was without tree cover and it is during this period that most of the surviving **prehistoric monuments** were constructed. Most noteworthy are the avenue of standing stones at Shap, the large stone circles at Castlerigg, near Keswick and at Swinside, the array of small stone circles on Burnmoor, Eskdale, and the henge monuments at Eamont Bridge, south of Penrith.

The axe factory in the scree-filled gully beside Pike of Stickle in Langdale, **Lakeland's first industry**, came into use at this time. A particularly hard band of Borrowdale Volcanic rock produced a flint-like stone which could be shaped

Ancient stones old Castlerigg stone circle

by rough chipping on site, followed by a final polish with coarse sandstone particles on the coast. The axes were produced in large numbers and exported for long distances.

Many hut circles from the late **Neolithic** and the **Bronze Ages** can still be identified; some of them in remote high situations were probably the first of the seasonally occupied 'sheilings' or summer dwellings, a pattern of farming whereby livestock was taken to high pastures for summer grazing under supervision, being moved to more sheltered lower areas during the winter. This practice continued in Lakeland into medieval times. Similar farming activities continued throughout the **Iron Age**, ebbing and flowing to some extent with changes in climate, and with a more coherent tribalism evidenced by the construction of hill forts, the largest of which is found on Carrock Fell.

The Romans

The Romans arrived in an area which had been farmed for 3,000 to 4,000 years, the resident population at the time being part of the huge Brigantes tribe. As this tribe was loosely spread over most of northern England, local chieftains must have wielded considerable power. Initially, in AD. 79, Agricola subdued only the eastern part of the district, by-passing the remainder on his way to and from Scotland. Full Roman control was imposed gradually over the next 50 years or so, when most of the forts and other known sites were constructed. Apart from a little mining and the use of the port of Ravenglass, Roman occupation was very much a military presence having minimal effect on the lives of the indigenous people who carried on as before with the essential struggle to keep body and soul together by farming this harsh area.

The Dark Ages

Following the Roman departure early in the fifth century came the so-called **Dark Ages**, very important in the formation of today's Lakeland landscape.

The examination of fossilised pollen preserved in the sediments of lakes and tarns has yielded valuable information about the trees, wild plants and cultivation from prehistory onwards. In the 6th century, cultivation and its associated settlement spread higher into the uplands than at any time before or since, resulting in over-exploitation and consequent soil erosion. Coupling this with the arrival of a wetter climate, the inevitable result was abandonment of marginal settlements and a retreat to the valleys, leaving the hilltops largely as we see them today. Covered with large blanket bogs. In lower areas there was some regeneration of woodland at this time.

Merger by **local tribal chieftain**s formed the Celtic kingdom of Rheged, probably centred on Carlisle. As Rheged declined in the latter part of the sixth century, the Anglian kingdom of Northumbria expanded westwards and there was a relatively bloodless take over as incomers merged with the existing population. From the seventh to the tenth centuries the district remained under Anglian influence. As Northumbria itself collapsed under the pressure of Danish invaders, the British kingdom of Strathclyde pushed southwards from its Scottish heartland, absorbing much of what is now Cumbria. At about the same time sea-borne Norse invaders, ('Vikings') who had been living in Ireland and the Scottish Western Isles, arrived in considerable numbers, soon infiltrating and settling wherever they could find unoccupied land capable of being farmed. A later Scottish invasion in 1061 desecrated large parts of what later became Westmorland and north Lancashire.

Landscape

With the Normans in control, the stage has now been reached when the impact of man on the landscape can be more accurately assessed. The examination of fossilised pollen preserved in the sediments of lakes and tarns has yielded valuable information about the trees, the wild plants and the cultivation from pre-history onwards. In the sixth century, cultivation and its associated settlement spread higher into the uplands than at any time before or since, resulting in over-exploitation and consequent soil erosion. Coupling this with the arrival of a wetter climate, the inevitable result was abandonment of marginal settlements and a retreat to the valleys, leaving the hilltops largely as we see them today, with large blanket bogs. In lower areas there was some regeneration of woodland at this time.

Place Names

The subsequent colonisation by Anglians from the east, Scots from the north and Norse from the sea may be traced by the examination of place names. Most important are those names of Norse origin which indicate: a summer pasture – words ending in 'er; ergh; scale; set; side', a clearing in woodland – words ending in 'thwaite' or a farmstead – words ending in 'by'. Progressive colonisation of the dales by the Norse can often be traced, early sheilings (summer pastures) being later converted into permanent farmsteads.

Christianity

Not surprisingly, there is a scarcity of evidence of very early Christianity in the Lake District although church dedications do give clues about the activity of well known saints in the area. No less than eight churches in the northern part of Cumbria are dedicated to St. Kentigern (or Mungo), who moved south from his Strathclyde homeland to convert the heathens of this mountainous area. Included is the important church at Crosthwaite, Keswick. Another early saint active in the area was St. Ninian, whilst St. Wilfrid also has the odd dedication. Standing lonely by the shore of Bassenthwaite Lake is the small church dedicated to St. Bega; the great sandstone cliff of St. Bees' Head is close to the spot where she allegedly landed after leaving her home in Ireland. In all these cases of church dedications the present buildings are, of course, of much later date than the saints themselves.

The names of **ancient wells** also provide clues to early Christianity although, as with St. Patrick's at Glenridding, subsequent folklore is usually unsupported by any real evidence of origin or of involvement with a saint. Very few of today's churches have structural elements which pre-date the Norman conquest, although a circular or oval shape to a churchyard is very often significant in indicating an **early Christian site**. The most notable structure is a little way outside the Lake District at Morland, south-east of Penrith, where the tower is a fine example of Anglo-Saxon architecture. Several **Anglo-Saxon monastic sites** have been identified, those at Dacre and Heversham having documentary evidence. Other sites have produced **carved stones**, generally parts of crosses. The best surviving example is at Irton, north of Ravenglass; other fragments have been found in the vicinity of later churches, in some cases built into the fabric of the church, tending to indicate that the site was originally monastic.

The arrival of the Vikings disrupted the Anglo-Saxon monasteries, although the incoming settlers were quickly converted to Christianity. Subsequent **Viking sculpture** was widely distributed throughout the area and, unlike the Anglo-Saxon, was not confined to monastic sites. The cross at Gosforth is a wonderful example of the transitional period, combining the Crucifixion with Norse pagan mythology. Other important Norse survivals are the '**hogback' gravestones**, well seen in the churches and churchyards at Dearham, Lowther and Penrith.

Farming

Following the Norman conquest and the establishment of the feudal overlords, the great 'forests' were established as their hunting preserves. At the same time, farming settlement was pushed further into the remote parts of the district, setting the basic pattern with which we are familiar today. Large **dairy farms** ('vaccaries') were established by the overlord himself on land retained in his direct control towards the heads of several of the valleys, that at Gatesgarth, Buttermere being documented from very early times. **Population growth** in the twelfth and thirteenth centuries coincided with much conversion of summer pastures into **permanent farms**, with more grazing being wrested from the rough hillsides.

Not surprisingly, woodland dwindled, largely due to the intensive grazing of the flocks of sheep and herds of pigs. Trades such as charcoal burning, iron smelting, tanning, mining and weaving all flourished. In the south of the district Furness Abbey became the dominant landowner, playing a leading role in many of these developments.

Further expansion was, however, curtailed by Scottish raids, by the arrival of the Black Death in 1348 – 9, and by later outbreaks of plague, livestock diseases and harvest failure, collectively producing deserted settlements and impoverished inhabitants, with fields reverting to the wild over a period of a hundred years or so.

Recovery from the mid fifteenth to the late sixteenth centuries was largely related to the development of the **woollen cloth industry** based on Kendal. Land was once more in demand and fell side was again taken into small, hard-won 'intakes'. With recovery of the **woodland industries**, particularly the demand for charcoal for the smelting of iron and other ores, areas were fenced to exclude livestock and coppicing was developed as a means of managing and

Female kayaker paddling on Lake Windermere

retaining surviving forest

Particular to the Lake District farming environment was the rise of the '**statesmen**' (estates men) from the mid sixteenth to the mid eighteenth centuries. In most essentials these largely independent farmers were similar to the yeomen of other parts of the country. Their customary tenure of the land, usually quite small in extent, gave them near freehold status and thus great power over the development of that land and, collectively, on the evolution of the landscape. Townend, at Troutbeck, in the care of the National Trust, is a good example of a statesman's house which remained in the same family for more than three hundred years.

In valley bottoms '**town fields**' were shared between several farmers. Oats and barley were extensively grown on the better quality land, whilst on the unfenced fell sides grazing was shared in accordance with rules laid down and enforced by Manor Courts. Towards the end of the period the numerous farms in each valley were already being amalgamated into larger units; the process accelerated in the nineteenth and twentieth centuries. Some of the abandoned farmsteads can still be identified.

The valley bottom open fields were gradually partitioned and enclosed by the dry stone walls which are such a feature of the present day landscape. '**Parliamentary' enclosure** whereby large areas of open common grazing land were divided to create individually – owned fields – reached the district in the latter half of the eighteenth century, firstly on low moorland fringing the district proper, but reaching many more central areas of high ground by the mid

Looking out over Tarn Hows

nineteenth century. Scarcity and inflated grain prices of the period of the Napoleonic Wars brought more land under the plough than ever before or since. No land which is truly Lake District is now used for arable crops, but the '**ridge and furrow**' undulations remain as evidence of previous ploughing in many places.

Gentrification

Whilst the farming landscape has remained, with continuous but subtle change to field shapes and to farm buildings, a few **grand houses**, with extensive park land, have been superimposed, largely contemporary with the 'discovery' of the scenic attraction of the district in the late eighteenth century. Notable examples are the Round House on Belle Isle, Windermere (1774), followed by Lyulph's Tower, Ullswater, and several beside Derwentwater. From the mid nineteenth century the **cotton magnates** and other successful tycoons of Man-chester and its district were following this lead by building lesser but often still impressive villas in favoured positions, particularly close to Windermere, where the **newly arrived railway** provided swift communication to and from their businesses. Many of these houses are now used as hotels; examples are the Belsfield, Bowness, the Langdale Chase and the Merewood, both between Windermere and Ambleside.

The 'Discovery' of the Lake District

The previously virtually unknown Lake District was 'discovered' by some discerning and intrepid travellers of the latter half of the eighteenth century, who became **the first tourists**. There had been one or two earlier visits, for example by Daniel Defoe, who described the landscape as 'barren and frightful' and 'of no use or advantage either to man or beast'. This set the tone for the tours by, *inter alia*, Dr. John Brown, a local vicar who wrote *Description of the Lake and Vale of Keswick* in 1767, Thomas Gray (of *Elegy* fame) and William Gilpin. Their writings promoted considerable interest among the leisured classes of the time. Mountains continued to be described as 'horrid' or 'dreadful' by these sensitive souls, but the more gentle vales and lakes were regarded as 'delicious views', to be analysed piece by piece and described in meticulous detail. Thus was born the **'picturesque' movement**, the refined tourists viewing the scenery through a Claude glass, a device in which scenes were framed in order to create the best picture.

Thomas West published the first *Guide to the Lake District* in 1778, advocating 'viewing stations' from which visitors could admire the best views in each area. Inevitably, many painters and engravers of the time flocked to Lakeland, often regarding it as their duty to rearrange the natural features sufficiently to achieve an improved balance for the picturesque or to exaggerate the mountains in order to emphasise the horror. Not surprisingly, J.M.W. Turner painted what are probably the finest pictures of the district. However, there are many others which are of great interest, not least in illustrating the attitudes of these early visitors themselves.

Industrial History

Quarrying

Apart from the production of the stone axes in Langdale, early industry in Lakeland comprised the extraction of various minerals and the localised quarrying of stone for building purposes.

Over the centuries quarrying has continued into modern times in many parts of the district. The particular qualities of some of the Borrowdale Volcanic Series rocks, notably the cleavage into thin **slates** and the range of attractive colours, resulted in great expansion of this industry in the nineteenth century, with the development of sizeable quarries in comparatively remote places such as Kentmere, Troutbeck, Kirkstone and Langdale. The latter two quarries are still worked. Although, as quarries become worked out, nature eventually provides some cover, the landscape impact of the digging, blasting and tunnelling has been, and remains, considerable. The Tilberthwaite area, near Coniston, shows the greatest concentration of scars from generations of quarrying.

The geological intrusions of granite have been extensively quarried for building blocks and roadstone, still providing a major industry at Shap. Others at Threlkeld and in Eskdale have closed down.

The ring of carboniferous **limestone** which surrounds the district has also been of industrial importance. Blocks from Scout Scar near Kendal and from Whitbarrow Scar in the south have provided the large runner stones for gunpowder mills and, more importantly, the former has provided the building material for much of Kendal, in consequence locally known as the Old Grey Town. Lime for agricultural use, for mortar and for limewash, was produced by burning the stone in small kilns, the ruins of some of which can still be seen. A few kilns can also be found on or adjacent to the narrow band of Coniston limestone which crosses the district.

Quarrying of the remains of the red **sandstone** was confined to the coastal strip near St. Bees and the vicinity of Penrith. It can be seen in the buildings of these areas, often as lintels, quoin stones and decorative blocks. The long disused quarries have generally blended into the landscape.

Mining

The varied rocks of Lakeland contain a wealth of minerals including iron, copper, lead and small amounts of gold and silver. The extraction of these minerals from such difficult terrain has ebbed and flowed over several centuries. Early workings were always from the surface the 'stopes' still apparent above Coppermines Valley near Coniston – with tunnels or 'levels' later being driven into the hillsides to follow the mineral veins underground. The levels provided drainage and ventilation in addition to access and many can still be found. It goes without saying that the harsh climate, the rough mountain country and the hazards of primitive working underground, compounded the difficulty, danger and expense of extraction.

German miners were brought to the Keswick and Coniston areas in Elizabethan times by the Company of Mines Royal. **Copper** was the main objective and large smelters were constructed at Brigham on the River Greta near Keswick. Early to mid nineteenth century revival of the copper industry brought Cornish miners to the Lake

District, the Coppermines Valley becoming a huge industrial complex, of which abandoned workings, levels, shafts, pit wheels, mill races and buildings remain as evidence. The Coniston branch railway line of 1859 was constructed to meet the need to transport large quantities of ore to a smelter at St. Helens in Lancashire.

Lead was also worked by the German miners of the sixteenth century, particularly in the Newlands Valley, south-west of Keswick. Again, this industry was intensified in the second half of the nineteenth century, coinciding with the enormous demand for lead for roofs and plumbing systems in the rapidly expanding towns of the northern industrial areas. There were smelters at Stoneycroft near Keswick and near Hartsop Hall, south of Patterdale. The scars of former lead mining are still widespread in the Caldbeck area, in Newlands and, most notably, at the large Greenside mine above Glenridding, closed as recently as 1962. The toxicity of the waste from lead mining ensures that spoil heaps remain largely free of masking vegetation.

Iron ore (haematite) is present in most of the types of Lake District rock and has been extensively worked since well before the arrival of the Romans. **Smelting** was carried out in primitive 'bloomeries', tiny clay and stone furnaces where the necessary temperatures were achieved by the use of hand operated bellows, with charcoal as the fuel. As charcoal was bulky and fragile to carry, the ore was carried to bloomeries sited close to the woodland which produced the charcoal. A later development was the 'bloomsmithy',

17

with water power and mechanical hammers much increasing the output. Many of these early smelting sites have been identified by the deposits of slag and by associated place names e.g. Cinder Hill and Smithy Beck. Early in the eighteenth century the first **blast furnaces** were set up at several sites in the district including Cunsey on the western side of Windermere, Backbarrow near Newby Bridge and Duddon Bridge. The increased output of these furnaces consumed vast quantities of charcoal. With a late conversion to coke firing, the Backbarrow furnace continued in use until 1966. The remains of the Duddon Bridge furnace have been taken into the care of the National Park Authority as a scheduled ancient monument.

Rich deposits of the ore were concentrated in the carboniferous limestone of West Cumbria, where the extensive abandoned nineteenth and twentieth century workings have been filled and re-graded, changing much of the landscape over a large area inland from Workington and Whitehaven. In the nineteenth century this area, together with the Millom district, became covered with excavations, factories, workers' houses, mineral railways and spoil heaps. Despite the modern improvements, many of these industrial remains are still very evident. Millom is a Victorian town built on the wealth created by iron, whilst villages such as Pica are typical of the mining era. The Florence Mine at Egremont is open to visitors.

The still thriving **pencil industry** of Keswick was founded on the graphite extracted since Elizabethan times from a mine near Seathwaite, in Borrowdale. Today, the graphite used in the factory is imported.

Woodland Related Industries

Woodland related industries have long flourished in Lakeland. The south of the district in particular has large areas of deciduous woodland rich in oak, beech, ash, hazel, birch, alder and sycamore, providing raw material for the building of houses and ships, with an array of other traditional uses which included the brushwood and the bark of the trees. Particularly important was **coppicing** – the cutting down of a tree in such a way that re-growth is encouraged in the form of multiple shoots. After fifteen years the shoots are about six metres (20 feet) long and twelve centimetres (5 inches) in thickness, ready for cutting and use. The tree's root system is stimulated into further growth to repeat the process and the wood has become a renewable resource for use in **charcoal** production for smelting, brewing, tanning and a variety of constructional purposes. The charcoal burning has left large numbers of 'pitsteads' – circular clearings or platforms of about six metres (20 feet) diameter on which a mound of coppiced timber was carefully constructed and then fired. Controlled combustion, with air largely excluded, and constant attention by the burners was needed to produce good quality charcoal in a few days.

Charcoal was also an essential ingredient of **gunpowder**, in great demand in an area with so many mines and quarries. By the mid nineteenth century there were five gunpowder mills in operation within or close to the district, that at Elterwater being the most central and probably the best known. It is now the site of the Langdale time-share holiday complex. These large industries also needed copious supplies of water to power the many water wheels and large sites to accommodate the wheel pits, the tramways, the storage buildings and the blast walls. As accidents were not uncommon with such a volatile substance, the works were well spaced in order to reduce the damage resulting from such an occurrence.

More gentle woodland-based trades included the making of woven baskets or 'swills', besom brushes and clothes pegs. Many towns and villages had tanneries using tree bark.

Mills

Most characteristic of Lakeland was the bobbin mill, more than sixty being in use early in the nineteenth century,

Footpath near Seathwaite

providing the **wooden bobbins** required by the million for the booming Lancashire cotton industry. The concentration of these mills in the south of the district resulted from the combination of abundant water power,

Gt Calva in the distance and Blencathra to the right

coppiced woodland providing the right type of wood, ready access to Lancashire and many existing buildings capable of modification for the purpose. The bobbin turning lathes and associated machinery were also made locally, by Fell at Troutbeck Bridge (now the Royal Mail sorting office) and Braithwaite at Crook. The decline of the cotton trade and the introduction of plastic bobbins soon decimated the mills, that at Stott Park between Newby Bridge and Lakeside being the last to close, in 1971. Happily, this mill has been preserved as a working museum.

From medieval times, sheep farming and the consequent woollen industry centred on Kendal, meant that small scale **fulling mills** were common in Lakeland by the sides of the rivers and larger streams, often close to the equally small **corn mills**, serving the local communities. Hand spinning and weaving of the wool was a contemporary domestic craft. Ambleside has an obvious former mill area by the side of Stock Ghyll, close to the main street. A little further upstream another, larger, mill area has been redeveloped with modern housing. As the **industrial revolution** reached the district, the spinning and weaving of wool, cotton and flax were carried out in larger factories, often on the site previously occupied by a fulling mill. Because of the geography, such large mills were on the fringes, at Staveley, Kendal, Ulverston and Cockermouth. The fine late eighteenth century example at Barley Bridge, Staveley has a typically varied history of cotton, wool, bobbins and paper packaging. These larger mills became the centre of mill communities, with terraced housing for the workers close by.

Paper mills developed from the late seventeenth century, the scale much increasing after the middle of the following century, with the banks of the River Kent between Staveley and Kendal being particularly noted for this trade. The huge mill at Burneside is the surviving example.

Transport

Roads

The mountainous countryside and the limited importance of the Lake District to the Romans restricted even these doughty engineers to comparatively few routes, the lines of most being only partially confirmed. A particular puzzle is the famous route over the summit of High Street, reaching an altitude of more than 610 metres (2,600 feet). The much more obvious parallel route over the present day Kirkstone Pass is better in all respects and is now known to have been used by the Romans. The central section of the road from Galava (Waterhead, Ambleside) via the Hardknott Pass and fort to Ravenglass is obvious and well-confirmed, but most of the remainder of this road and its eastern continuation to Watercrook, south of Kendal, is still conjectural. From Papcastle (Cockermouth) the lines of the roads to the north-east to Carlisle and north-west to Maryport are confirmed, but to the south-east the road heading for Troutbeck, Whitbarrow and Penrith has long sections which rank only as 'probable line'.

After the Romans, although there was no actual road construction until comparatively modern times, the routes in use today were gradually established by the movements of people, livestock and, importantly, **packhorses**, for trade purposes. In such a mountainous area there was no incentive to establish major highways and these 'roads' remained narrow and unimproved for many centuries. The geography ensured that the chosen routes would use exactly the same high passes as are used today, some now having surfaced carriageways, some still being for foot traffic only. Zig zags eased the most severe gradients for the packhorses, with bridges being constructed at important river and stream crossings. Many have survived, some being widened and strengthened for present day traffic.

Not dissimilar are the '**corpse roads**' along which coffin bearers travelled from outlying communities to the parish church where burial would take place. Notable examples are the track from Wasdale Head by Burnmoor to Boot and that from Rydal to Grasmere. Coffin roads fell into disuse as churches and chapels were built in the more remote places.

From 1739 the **first turnpike roads** were constructed around the outside of the district, including what became the A6 trunk road over Shap, but it was not until 1762 that the road from Cockermouth to Keswick and Penrith and that from Keswick to Windermere and Kendal were made subject to the Turnpike Acts, as the first true 'modern' highways in Lakeland. With some realignment, that of the A6 being considerable, these have remained the only major roads in the district.

Although roads are, of necessity, the only means by which residents and visitors travel throughout the district, very few new roads have been constructed since the turnpikes. The difficult terrain and the need to protect the environment both militate against road construction. Widening and other improvements have been carried out, major in the case of a few selected roads such as the A66 and A591, both former turnpikes, and minor roads such as the Hardknott Pass have been surfaced. With these exceptions, the prevailing philosophy is that the environmental damage of road construction and improvement is not acceptable in an area of such outstanding but fragile landscape beauty. In recent years the M6 motorway has, of course, relieved the A6 of most of its long distance traffic and now provides access for the great majority of Lakeland visitors from both north and south, whilst the Kendal by-pass has diverted visitor traffic away from the streets of that congested town.

Canals

The Ulverston and the Lancaster Canals served the Lake District fringe and, for a while, were of economic importance to Ulverston and Kendal respectively. For obvious reasons no canal penetrated into the Lake District proper.

Railways

The main line from London to Glasgow, now known as the West Coast Main Line, was opened in 1846, skirting the eastern fringe of the Lake District as it climbed laboriously over Shap summit. In the same decade, the

Gate at Rydal Wate in winter

rich industrial wealth of the coastal area attracted railways, linked first to Carlisle, and then to the Furness area in the south by 1850. In 1857, Furness was connected to the Scottish main line at Carnforth by which time, like the earlier roads, the railways virtually surrounded the district. In 1847, however, one important line did penetrate, when the Windermere branch, leaving the main line at Oxenholme, reached a terminus at Birthwaite, two kilometres (1.5 miles) from the lake, opening up the district to **mass tourism** across a wide social spectrum for the first time. The hamlet grew spectacularly over the next few years, eventually coalescing with the much older village of Bowness on Windermere to form Lakeland's most comprehensive and busiest holiday resort. Violently opposed by William Wordsworth and, later, by John Ruskin, a proposed extension of this line to Ambleside and, possibly, to

Keswick was abandoned.

The opening of the Coniston branch of the Furness Railway was opened in 1859, was followed by the only through line in 1865, when Cockermouth, already linked to Workington, was connected to Keswick and Penrith. As with the Coniston branch the original motivation was industrial, bringing coke from Durham to the ironworks of West Cumberland, but the chosen route was also intended to maximise tourist traffic to the Keswick area. Yet another branch of the Furness Railway was opened from the Furness main line near Ulverston to Lakeside at the foot of Windermere in 1868 – 9. A station provided interchange facilities with the lake steamers, but the route by Backbarrow ensured that the line had commercial traffic in addition to the tourists.

The final railway into Lakeland was a line constructed to the curious gauge of three feet, running from Ravenglass to Boot in Eskdale, the primary purpose being to carry iron ore to the coast. After the failure of the mines the line was converted to fifteen inch gauge as a tourist attraction, with the upper terminus moved to Dalegarth. In the latter part of the nineteenth century the mineral railways in the Workington/Whitehaven area proliferated as rival companies competed for the then lucrative iron and coal related trade.

The decline and closure of most of these railways has mirrored that of railways in Britain generally. The West Coast Main Line survives, as do the links across Furness to Barrow and along the coast north to Whitehaven, Workington and Carlisle, albeit with a

Ravenglass & Eskdale Railway, Dalegarth Station

Thirlmere

mediocre service in the latter-case. The Windermere branch still plays a considerable part in carrying visitors to and from the district and the Ravenglass and Eskdale is a very active and attractive little line. Part of the Lakeside branch has been restored as the Lakeside and Haverthwaite Railway, with a steam depot at Haverthwaite. But the rest is silent.

The multiplicity of lines between mountains and sea is now nothing more than a tangle of overgrown cuttings and embankments, sadly neglected bridges and former stations in a derelict industrial landscape. The terminus station at Coniston is a car park and, even on the operational Windermere branch, the fine old station has been incorporated into a supermarket. Perhaps saddest of all is the Cockermouth to Penrith line, now largely covered by asphalt in improvements to the A66 road, and with Keswick station standing forlorn, without apparent purpose. If the line had survived for just a few more years, a more enlightened attitude might well have prevailed and this line could then have continued to form a useful and attractive link across the northern part of the district.

Architecture

With exceptions such as Sizergh and Muncaster Castles. the Lake District is not an area noted for stately homes. Much more interest for visitors lies in the evolution of the widespread **vernacular buildings** which are, collectively, of great landscape importance. The rough terrain, the climate and proximity to raiders from across the Scottish border have, from early times, all played a part in shaping the siting, the layout and the construction of buildings.

Locally quarried stone is seen throughout the district as the natural material, skilfully sited farms and their outbuildings blending with the environment to achieve a satisfying sense of rightness. A few of the oldest farms, such as those at Burneside Hall and Kentmere Hall, are founded on a defensive 'pele' tower of the fourteenth or fifteenth centuries. The area is famous for the **dry stone** construction whereby walls were built without mortar in the joints. Better quality buildings did, however, have clay mortar, internal wall plaster and several coats of limewash forming an external protective rendering against the weather. Early thatched roof coverings gave way to slate or thin cut stone late in the eighteenth century, some ridges being finished with interlocking 'wrestler' slates as a local substitute for properly shaped ridge tiles.

Most characteristic are the **chimney stacks,** massively cylindrical, at first limited to larger houses, but later being added to more modest dwellings. The chimney tops were initially without protection, but often had a pair of inclined slates added later; chimney pots are comparatively recent.

The variations of internal layout of traditional Lake District houses, often linking family accommodation with the housing of livestock are, in themselves, a fascinating study. As farming has changed and as living standards have risen over the centuries, modifications to these layouts can often be traced by external observation, noting the positioning both of existing and of blocked-off doors and windows, changes to roof lines and other variations. Some of the older buildings are of cruck construction but this is usually impossible to detect from outside.

In the later part of the seventeenth century and the early part of the following century, the prosperity of the woollen trade resulted in a period of quite intensive new building and the improvement of older buildings. Fortunately, many buildings of this era are dated externally. A walk through Troutbeck (near Windermere), as set out in the author's *Town and Village Trails of Cumbria and the Lake District* is highly recommended for the average visitor and Townend should certainly be visited. Those with a deeper interest in Lakeland architecture should read Brunskill's and Denyer's books which are a mine of information on all aspects of local vernacular architecture.

Among the many types of farm outbuilding, the **bank barns** are most characteristic, using the slope of the ground to give level access both to the lower floor housing livestock and to the upper floor normally used for threshing grain. Very common in Lakeland, Norway and the Black Forest of Germany, these barns are rare elsewhere in Britain. Much admired by visitors are the 'spinning galleries provided in some farmhouses and outbuildings to give shelter from the elements, but with as good light as possible for the home-based woollen craft industry. However, use of these galleries was more likely to involve the drying and storage of the yarn than the actual siting of spinning wheels.

Traditions

Not surprisingly in an isolated area like the Lake District, entertainments and sports developed on a very localised basis, the catchment area usually being the valley. These festivities have ebbed and flowed over the centuries but many, generally in a modified form, have survived.

First mention must go to **fox hunting**; not the horse-riding, rather class bound version common to the rest of England, but a hard grafting no nonsense following of the hounds on foot, across mountains and valleys, doing what the sheep farmers believe is a vital job of work. Indeed, the farmers themselves make up a large proportion of the hunters, convinced that the fox is the prime predator of their flocks and that control by hunting is the best method of countering this threat. They do, of course, enjoy the chase and particularly successful huntsmen have long been celebrated locally. Who has not heard of John Peel, almost rivalling William Wordsworth in his world wide fame and his instant identification with Lakeland? Active over a long period in the north of the district and buried at Caldbeck, ironically his enduring pre-eminence is due to a song of dubious merit. Equally celebrated locally are Tommy Dobson of Eskdale and Joe Bowman of Ullswater.

Fortunately, other once common animal related 'sports' such as cock-fighting and bull baiting are long gone, although a few traces of former cockpits do remain.

During the late eighteenth and the nineteenth centuries, **lake regattas** were a popular pastime for the leisured classes. Eccentrics such as Joseph Pocklington, who then owned Derwent Island, staged elaborate mock naval battles, with cannons and muskets contributing to what must have been an incredible spectacle.

These regattas were the extravagances of 'offcomers', but the truly indigenous population held shepherds' 'meets', combining daytime business with evenings of simple rustic merry-making and fairs permitted by ancient charters, such as Egremont Crab Fair and, a little distant, Appleby Horse Fair. Both are still held although, in the case of Egremont, the nature of the fair has changed a good deal over the years. The twice yearly hiring fair was another important local custom. At Kendal, Cockermouth, Keswick,

Penrith and Ulverston, farm labourers and domestic servants were hired for a six month period. The system lasted until World War I and is described in Melvyn Bragg's '*The Hired Man*'.

Local **annual sports meetings** have long been popular, with sports such as the skilful Cumberland/Westmorland wrestling, guides races and **hound trailing** providing the basis for a day of all round entertainment. The hounds follow a laid trail of aniseed and oil along a route over rough mountain ground, including walls and other obstacles, starting and finishing in the sports arena. Competition is very keen and the dogs are carefully reared and trained by their proud owners. The best known Lakeland sports meeting is held at Grasmere, closely followed by Ambleside, Hawkshead and Eskdale. In recent years **sheep dog trials** have also become popular, both with competitors keen to show the abilities of their dogs which are, after all, an important part of the livelihood of the sheep farmer, and with spectators.

Quite different are the annual church ceremonies of **rush-bearing**, again best known at Grasmere and Ambleside.

The dates and places of the fairs, sports meetings and trials are included as 'events' in the relevant chapters of the main part of the guide, with a quick reference list in the Factfile.

Flora and Fauna

In an area with the rich diversity of the Lake District, flora and fauna are topics worthy of substantial books in their own right or of chapters in more general books such as Pearsall and Pennington's *The Lake District*.

Derwentwater and Skiddaw from Ashness Bridge

The remaining semi-natural broad leaf woodlands are an important scenic and wild life asset but, at least in scenic terms, the same cannot be said of many of the conifer plantations, such as those planted by the former Manchester Corporation around Thirlmere and the much maligned Forestry Commission planting in Ennerdale. However, as felling takes place in these commercial woodlands, the opportunity is being taken to diversify the species, using native trees such as oak, ash and birch wherever appropriate. This must be an improvement. There are important **forest visitor centres** at Grizedale and Whinlatter. Although, historically, forest covered much of the mountain area, the present day view is that the largely bare fell sides contribute greatly to the beauty of the landscape as we have known it for generations and attempts at re-afforestation will not be made.

Associated with the different woodlands are distinct flora and fauna, for example bird populations such as pied flycatchers, redstarts and wood warblers in the oak forest. The **red squirrel** is the most characteristic Lakeland creature, Sadly, despite efforts at containment, the advance of the grey squirrel from the south seems to be inexorable and, as the two species never seem to co-exist for long, the demise of the red in the district is being forecast. Sightings of this lovely but shy creature are, therefore, to be treasured. Also associated with the woodland is the **roe deer**, plentiful, but elusive to the casual observer, its natural camouflage making it difficult to see when standing still. In the Martindale area there is a famous herd of the larger red deer.

Not surprisingly, the majority of the district is covered by grass, predominantly poor acid grass including much mat grass (*Nardus*) on most of the uplands, but with species richer grassland on the fringe limestone areas.

The lakes and tarns support an exceptional variety of plants and animals, including comparatively rare types of fish such as char, schelly and vendace. Many shores have important wetland habitats and, because of the large differences in altitude from the rushing headwaters of mountain streams to the placid flow in valley bottoms, the streams and rivers also feature a wide span of wildlife.

High on the eastern mountains the once common eagle has reappeared, under protected breeding conditions, joining the more common buzzards, ravens and birds of prey such as the peregrine in its soaring flight.

The delicate natural balance in the area has long been recognised and is protected by the creation of Nature Reserves and Sites of Special Scientific Interest, some very large and other tiny. These sites are listed in the FactFile; all can be visited, in one or two cases subject to first obtaining a permit.

The Lake District Today

Finally, in this introduction we can stand back and look at the Lake District as it exists today, a compact area of thrusting mountains, serene lakes, farms and woodlands, colourful and characterful at all seasons of the year, with an overall allure which brings back so many visitors time and time again throughout their lives. An area easy to think of as **timeless** but which, as we have already seen, has changed a great deal overall during the last few thousand years and, in some popular parts, even more during the present century. An area with the landscape largely determined by the **ebb and flow of farming**, yet in which the farming is, economically, entirely marginal and now dependant on constant subsidies. An area in which the **rough terrain and harsh climate** has bred tough, characterful, people from the mixed Celtic, Anglo-Saxon and Viking stock, their farming and their industries having shaped what we now see. An area in which **major tourist centres** such as Bowness on Windermere, Ambleside

and Keswick sometimes rub shoulders uneasily with **outstanding scenic beauty**.

So, how do we, as its temporary guardians for a few decades, keep this earthly paradise in a fit condition to hand on proudly to future generations?

Recognition of the need to protect the area came late in the nineteenth century, following the formation of the **National Trust** in 1895 by the great philanthropist Octavia Hill, Rev. (later Canon) Rawnsley, and Robert Hunter. From its first Lakeland property at Brandlehow on the Derwentwater shore, the Trust, an independent charity, has gone from strength to strength in the district. It now owns, for the benefit of the nation, something of the order of thirty percent of the land area, including many working farms and other properties. The Trust is much the largest landowner, with a high proportion of

Great Gable and Kirk Fell from near Blackbeck Tarn with Scafell in the distance

the land holdings in the central, most spectacular area. Rawnsley in particular was an incredibly active Lake District enthusiast and was a close friend of Beatrix Potter and her brother. On her death in 1943, Beatrix left her vast estate to the Trust.

Ownership of mountain land by the Trust is a guarantee of access in perpetuity by fell walkers. Likewise, Trust ownership of working farms is the best possible protection of rights of way across the farmland and of resistance to unsuitable alterations to the buildings or developments on the land.

The National Park

In 1951, an area which includes the great majority of what is generally regarded as 'The Lake District' was designated as a National Park, as were several other outstanding areas of the country. Not parks in the accepted sense, in that they contained towns and villages as working communities, and not National because they are not controlled centrally, the main purpose of the designation of these areas was to achieve strong, unified, planning control over proposed development of all kinds. Like other planning authorities, the National Park Authority publishes a structure or development plan setting out its aims and objectives for the area, against which individual planning applications will be judged. Overall, the Authority is charged by the constituting Act to preserve and enhance the natural beauty of the Lake District and to ensure that people can continue to enjoy the Lake District'. A tall order indeed!

Subsidiary duties include the securing of public access to open country, securing the provision of visitor accommodation, camping sites, car parks and toilets, the making of Byelaws to control activities on the lakes and for better control of land owned by the Authority or over which it has access agreements and the provision of information and warden services.

All in all, considering the history and the character of the area, as outlined in this introduction, and the commercial pressures, the Authority has an awesome responsibility; on the one hand to preserve the beauty of the landscape, including its flora and fauna, on the other to facilitate the public enjoyment of that beauty, accepting that more public presence, particularly in motor vehicles, puts pressure on limited road capacity and car parking facilities and also results in problems such as severe erosion of popular footpaths on the mountains. On the whole it is fair to say that the Authority has been successful although the balance between environmental/ ecological concerns and commercial interests is often uneasy, occasionally breaking into open warfare as in the case of the speed limit on Windermere. Brockhole, three kilometres (two miles) north of Windermere village, is the Authority's principal information and visitor centre.

The appearance of the unsightly 'draw down' areas around the sides of Thirlmere and Haweswater serves as a useful reminder of the environmental damage caused by large scale water abstraction by the then Manchester Corporation in the 1890s and 1930s respectively. More recent proposals for further abstraction have been opposed by the Park Authority and many other organisations including the Friends of the Lake District and local farmers, saving Ullswater, Wastwater, Ennerdale Water and even Windermere from similar official vandalism. Without this kind of vigilance and concerted action it is difficult to imagine how the Lake District would look, left to the pressure of commercial and economic forces. What is certain is that it would be a much less attractive place for the visitor seeking the 'quiet enjoyment', which must remain the fundamental characteristic of England's finest landscape and which is written into the constituting Act of Parliament.

One other official body which must be mentioned is the **Cumbria Tourist Board**. Visitors during peak season must surely doubt the need for an organisation with a strategic role of encouraging visitors to come to the district. Most people know about the Lake District and need no such encouragement. However, tourism is undoubtedly Lakeland's major industry and the Board plays a valuable role in overseeing the provision of the whole range of visitor accommodation and in assessing, grading and publicising that accommodation. The Board is also active in encouraging a wide range of improvement in visitor services generally, public transport being an area of major concern.

Food & Beverage

Cumbria Foods (outlets in Grasmere and Keswick) offer a range of speciality and regional foods including fresh meats, smoked fish and meats, traditional bacons, hams, sausage, pies; speciality beers, breads and cheeses. Available through their outlets or by mail order (www.cumbriafoods.co.uk). Visitors to the former Whigs tearoom in Hawkshead will no doubt remember the management starting to produce local preserves, chutnies etc. Well, Whigs is no longer there as the jars needed more space! The Hawkshead Relish Company is doing well and gaining prizes for its produce. Situated opposite Henry Roberts' bookshop. www. hawksheadrelish.com.

For local beers, Jennings has been around since 1828, moving to Cockermouth in 1874. Brewery shop and tours also available (tel: 0845 1297190, admission charge). Buy on line: www. jenningsbrewery.co.uk. The area has now three relatively new breweries: Hesket Newmarket Brewery, originally established in 1988, has over 50 outlets (look for the leaflets). Now a village co-operative, employing professional brewers, some of their brews are really good. Their Haystacks beer is 'Refreshing Ale for Fellwanderers'. That is one claim that is spot on! Brewery tours followed by a meal at the pub next door (The Old Crown) need to be pre-booked. Tel: 016974 78288. www. hesketbrewery.co.uk

Another one is Tirril Brewery, now brewing at Brougham Hall, near Penrith. It (currently) produces three different beers.

Over in Coniston and founded in 1995, is Coniston Brewery located at the Black Bull, a 400-year-old coaching inn. Its Bluebird Bitter was Supreme Champion Beer in 1998.

Look out for Kendal Mint Cake and take it onto the fells (if you can take the sugar in it). Sarah Nelson's shop in Grasmere has been making gingerbread for over 150 years which is well worth buying. Cumberland sausages are now a nationally known dish. See p108 for Woodall's Sausages, which hold the Royal Warrant.

Family/Rainy Days

Whilst the Lakes has memorable sunny days and warm weather, Seathwaite does have the highest rainfall in England (3.65m/144inches). Visitors should always be prepared for wet weather. Having the gear or knowledge of where you can take the children if its wet can keep everybody smiling! Some indoor attractions that are good for families whatever the weather are:

Rheghed, south side of the A66 west of the Penrith Junction on the M6. It is an exhibition centre with shops, food bar and a giant I-max cinema. The complex has a grass-covered roof. One of the best attractions in the area. Films include some with a bearing on Lakeland heritage.

Aquarium of the Lakes, Lakeside, at the southern end of Windermere, recreates river and marine habitats for fish. If you go by car, you can also visit Stott Park Bobbin Mill nearby. Alternatively, take the Windermere steamer to Lakeside.

Brockhole National Park Visitor Centre, between Windermere and Ambleside is well worth a visit, with lots of displays and estate walks by the lake.

Beatrix Potter attractions fascinate the young at heart of all ages, such is the appeal of her books and characters. These are: World of Beatrix Potter Attraction, Bowness; her home at Hill Top,

Near Sawrey; The Beatrix Potter Gallery, the former offices of her husband, now a National Trust site in Hawkshead.

Two attractions with a connection with William Wordsworth are Dove Cottage, Grasmere and Rydal Mount, Rydal. The latter is opposite Rydal Hall that has a tearoom (house is private).

The Cumberland Pencil Museum, Keswick; The Abbot Hall Art Gallery/Museum of Lakeland Life, Kendal and Sellafield Nuclear plant offer a lot to see and cater for completely different tastes. All can easily take up an hour or two, whether wet or not outside.

Local country houses offer an alternative. Don't overlook these in the south – Holker, Levens and Sizergh, plus Townend at Troutbeck, northeast of Windermere (town). It dates from 1626 and is a National Trust property.

The Windermere steamer has been mentioned above. There is another on Ullswater and smaller ones on Con-

Watendlath

iston, but the Windermere one is the longest (and best) if it is raining, because of the time on the boat and choice of activity if you go south to Lakeside.

Finally, don't forget the cinema in Ambleside (it has a restaurant attached if you need to feed the children while out), Bowness and Keswick.

There are good shopping centres in the main communities and no shortage of outdoor-wear shops. Also, Hayes Garden Centre at Ambleside has much more than plants; a large outlet with an equally large tearoom. Great if it is raining, great for the children, but expect a big dent on your bank balance if you are not firm enough. If you are just looking for a park for ball games, Keswick, Ambleside and other larger towns have the facilities.

Lakeland Products

Local Herdwick sheep, bred by Beatrix Potter on her farms produce a good quality wool. Look for local products that help to sustain this local species of sheep and the hillfarmers who breed them. The local agricultural-type shows often sell locally produced goods, eg: Lakeland walking sticks.

Lakeland Plastics in Windermere, adjacent to the railway station, are now nationally known and worth a visit.

There are lots of local crafts, working out of small sites all over Cumbria. Several are grouped together at Brougham Hall near Penrith (where Tirril Brewery may be found). Jan Burgess runs Mill Pottery at Unit 1, Goosewell Farm, near Keswick, only 5 minutes walk from Castlerigg Stone Circle. Making stoneware products, Mill Pottery may be found on Kes-

Buttermere, with Haystacks beyond

wick's Craft & Local Produce Market on Thursdays (March-December). Tel: 017687 80123.

Look out for sites such as Plumgarth's Farm Shop and Lakelands Food Park, Crook Rd, Kendal, LA8 8QJ. At the large roundabout where the A591 (Kendal bypass) crosses the Kendal-Bowness road (B5284) turn for Bowness and it is on the left. You can purchase all sorts of Lakeland produce here on an out-of-town site, including award winning Cumberland sausage, Cartmel sticky toffee pudding, Lakes ice-cream, chutnies etc. There are

31

several shops here in a farmyard setting. Tel: 01539 736300.

Out and About

Walks

In the Lake District walking is a prime activity. Ranging from the gentle amble around Bowness or Grasmere villages to the scaling of mountain tops by tough, demanding, routes, a high proportion of visitors will use their feet to a greater or lesser extent as an essential part of the enjoyment of the district.

Inevitably, there are many specialised books (refer to bibliography) which will assist walkers, ranging from the author's *Town and Village Trails of Cumbria and the Lake District* and *Lakeland Walking on the Level* – in two volumes – to the late Alfred Wainwright's celebrated mountain guides.

Whilst dealing more comprehensively with the features of towns and villages, a general guide can act only to whet the appetite in the case of the hundreds of country and mountain walks which are available. However, all the highest and really famous mountains are included, as are such unmissable easier walks as Orrest Head, Tarn Hows and the Ullswater lake shore.

But, first a word of warning! Although no Lake District mountain ('fell' in local parlance) reaches a height of 1,000m (3,282 feet) and by world or even European standards they are small, do not underestimate them, particularly in winter. Steep and dangerous cliffs abound, there are often wet, sometimes icy, conditions underfoot and the weather can change from benign to severe with great rapidity.

Always carry extra clothing and food and be well-shod. In Lakeland there is no substitute for strong waterproof boots with well formed semi-rigid soles. Cloud is often low, reaching well down the valley sides and in these conditions the mountain tops are confusing and **potentially dangerous places**, needing the correct use of a compass for safe descent.

There are Mountain Rescue Teams covering all parts of the area but the volunteer members are certainly not looking for extra work; for example the Ambleside and Langdale team answers about 100 distress calls each year; some of these are fatalities. **You have been warned!**

If you are not an experienced hill-walker but would like to climb a mountain or two and feel sufficiently fit so to do, by all means go ahead. The rewards of Lakeland mountain views and the sense of achievement will make all the hard work worthwhile. But do choose a fine day and stick to the well used routes, not being tempted to cut across country. It is better not to walk alone and to allow more time than you really expect to take.

Guided walks organised by the National Park Authority are widely available. The extensive programme is set out in the free 'Out and About' magazine, issued annually. Details are available at all Tourist Information Centres, from which many of the walks start. Refer to the FactFile p219 for addresses and telephone numbers.

Most areas of Great Britain now have designated medium and/or long distance footpaths; the Lake District is no exception. For example, Wainwright's famous **Coast to Coast** has its start (or finish) at St. Bees' Head near Whitehaven, crossing the middle of the district on its way to Robin Hood's Bay in Yorkshire. More local to the district is the **Cumbria Way**, starting at Ulverston and crossing Lakeland in a south to north direction. The **Dales Way** is generally walked from east to west, starting at Ilkley in Yorkshire, crossing part of the Yorkshire Dales, keeping well to the north of Kendal and finishing at Bowness on the Windermere shore. Modest in length and without mountains is the **Cistercian Way** across the Furness district in the south of the county. From Grange over Sands to Roa Island, this 53km (33 mile) ramble has a strong historic interest. Also without mountains and shorter is another 'coast to coast', from Askam on the Duddon Estuary to Rampside on Morecambe Bay, visiting Dalton and Furness Abbey en route, with a total distance of about 20-25km (12-15 miles) Visitors considering tackling one of these footpaths will no doubt obtain detailed information from an appropriate Tourist Information Office, probably supplemented by one of the specialised books/maps available.

Cycle Rides

As it is assumed that keen visiting cyclists will have their own itineraries for substantial rides, the routes suggested in this guide are aimed at the more casual or occasional cyclist and are, on the whole, comparatively short. For obvious reasons many such cyclists will not enjoy climbing long, steep, hills, so the recommended routes tend

to concentrate on the towns, villages and countryside of the attractive areas which surround the Lake District.

The places to be visited duplicate to some extent those included in the motor tours but, for cyclists, country lanes and other minor roads are always given preference over main roads. Apart from **Grizedale Forest**, no suggestions are given for off-road cross country cycling using bridleways and other tracks; these are very mush a matter of personal choice for the users of mountain bikes. These machines can be hired locally; refer to the FactFile.

The Lake District National Park Authority operates cycling events, led by a park ranger. Free, but it is necessary to book in advance. (015394 46601).

Car Tours

Apart from the obvious drives to the Lake District towns and villages featured in this guide, visitors have a wealth of choice of destination in the very attractive areas which surround the district. Stately homes, wildlife centres, working restored mills, historic market towns and sea coast are only some of the features which will contribute to a rewarding excursion. Compared with the Lake District roads in high season, the comparative lack of traffic is an added bonus.

It is obvious that several of the suggested circuits have enough visitor attractions such as stately homes and museums to fill several days and the intention of the guide is to offer wide choices, with something to suit all the family or, perhaps, to encourage more than one visit to a particular area. The generally short distances in driving

Sarah Nelson's Gingerbread shop

places of historic interest can be identified with certainty.

For generations the Ordnance Survey has produced fine maps; their Lake District Tourist 1-inch map was the mainstay for walkers and other visitors for a long number of years after World War II. Subsequent metrication has brought diversity and, with it, the very fine Outdoor Leisure series, covering the Lake District in four sheets, nos. 4 – 7 inclusive, at a scale of 1:25,000 (roughly 2.5 inches to the mile). For those who want the ultimate in geographical features, with rights of way, bridleways and footpaths, and with other information useful for visitors, at a generous scale, these maps are

terms allow for viable half day excursions. Conversely, with plenty of time available and no wish to spend hours at a particular property, two or more of the routes may be combined to provide a longer drive through good countryside.

Whilst road suggestions in each case are limited to the more major roads, giving the basic direction and shape of the tour, in virtually all cases there are permutations of minor roads which enterprising drivers with time to spare may wish to substitute.

Maps

For the great majority of visitors a suitable map is not only a great help in finding one's way around a district, but also considerably increases the appreciation and enjoyment of that district. Names can be given to lakes, tarns, mountains, woodlands and farms;

A female hiker descending the path from Loughrigg with Grasmere in the background

wholeheartedly recommended.

Mountain walkers will probably use these maps in conjunction with a mountain guide book. Mention must, therefore, be made of the series of eight books, covering the area geographically, written and illustrated by the legendary late A. Wainwright. Despite being up to forty years out of date these books are still in print and are cherished as the most comprehensive guides to every route on every mountain. They include large scale maps and are widely regarded as minor works of art.

For visitors whose primary interest is to tour around the district by car, cycle or public transport, smaller scale maps are perfectly adequate. The Ordnance Survey Landranger series at a scale of 1:50,000 (roughly 1.25 inches to the mile) has superseded the old 1" maps. At this scale it might be expected that the district could be covered by a lesser number of sheets. Unfortunately, as this series is not tailored to the shape of the district, four maps are needed for full coverage: nos. 89 – West Cumbria; 90 – Penrith and Keswick; 96 – Barrow in Furness and South Lakeland; 97 – Kendal to Morecambe. Possession of these four sheets does, however, have the advantage of including a great deal of the Lakeland fringe which features largely in the cycle and motor tours.

For an economical, one map, coverage adequate for general tourism, the *Leisure Map of the Lake District*, by Estate Publications, highlights most of the visitor attractions in a clear format at a scale of 1:75,000 (a little less than 1" to one mile). Another one map solution is Tourist Map no. 3, published by the Ordnance Survey, reverting to the old pre-metric one inch to the mile scale.

Place names

The names of towns, villages, farmsteads, mountains, rocks and streams have long been a valuable resource, in same circumstances the only resource, in tracing the history of human occupation of the Lake District through

Sheep on Sheffield Pike

the phases before documentary records began in the 12th and 13th centuries. Place names must, however, be treated with care. By no means all of today's names can be confidently interpreted, as spelling changes and other mutations have taken place over many centuries.

The first identified settlers in the area, well before Christian times, were Celtic people or Cymrl, from whom the present name Cumbria is derived. The linguistic link with Celts in Wales is obvious. Relatively few names from this era have survived, but a few such as Blencathra, Glenderamackin and Penruddock have an authentic Celtic/ British ring.

From the later period of Anglian domination, from the 6th to the 10th centuries, the typical place endings of 'tun' (ton), 'ham', and 'lea' are, overall, much less dominant in Lakeland than in the rest of the country. Their concentration around the Lake District fringe, on the better quality land, tends to indicate that the earlier Celts had been pushed inwards towards the core area of mountains and steep sided valleys. Examples of Anglo-Saxon names include Bampton, Workington and Clifton. There are more of the Celtic/British names remaining in the north of the area.

From the 10th century the invasion of Viking settlers superimposed Norse place names, particularly in the more mountainous part of the district, where they named lakes, tarns, rivers, mountains and rocks, Particularly important are those names which include, possibly in a modified form, one of the word endings indicating a summer pasture or shieling – 'ergh', 'side', 'saetr' – Ambleside, Sizergh. Even more commonly

found are names ending In 'thwaite' – a clearing in woodland – Stonethwaite, Rosthwaite, Flnsthwaite.

This list glves a selectlon of components of place names with their interpretations:

Band	ridge of hill
Beck	stream
Bield	shelter, animal's lair
Berg	hill, mountain
Bothy	hut
Brant	steep
Byre	cowshed
Cald	cold
Cot	cottage
Derw	oak
Dodd	rounded hill
Dub	deep pool
Earn	eagle
Elter	swan
Esk	water
Fell	mountain
Force	waterfall
Gate	road, path
Gill, gyil, ghyll	stream in narrow ravine
Grange	outlying farm (usually monastic)
Gimmer	yearling sheep
Hause	narrow pass
How	small hill
Kirk	church
Lind	lime tree
Mere	lake or pool
Mire	swamp or bog
PIke	peak, sharp summit
Rake	path up hill
Scar	crag, precipice
Whin	gorse

Place names, with their likely meanings:

Ambleside summer pastures by river sandbanks

Askham among ash trees

Borrowdale valley of the fort

Bowness bull's headland

Brockhole badger's hollow

Buttermere lake by dairy pastures

River Caldew cold river

Cartmel sandbank by rocky ground

Coniston the king's farm

Dovedale valley of the doves

River Derwent many oak trees

Dunmail Raise the memorial cairn of King Dunmail

Elterwater lake of the swans

Esthwaite Water lake by the eastern clearing

Grasmere lake with grassy shores

River Greta rocky river

Grizedale, Grisedale valley of the pigs

Hawkshead shieling belonging to Hauk (family name)

Kendal village with church in the valley of the River Kent (formerly Kirkby Kendal)

Keswlck cheese farm

Kirk Fell mountain above the church

Langdale long valley

Ling Mell heather covered hill

Loweswater leafy lake

Patterdale St Patrick's valley

Pike O'Stickle peak with sharp summit

Rosthwaite clearing with heap of stones

River Rothay trout river

Rydal Water lake in valley where rye Is grown

Scales Tarn tarn (small lake) by shepherd's hut

Steel Fell mountain with steep path

Styhead Tarn tarn at top of path

Troutbeck trout stream

Uillswater Ulfr's (personal name) lake

Windermere Vinandr's (personal name) lake

For the great majority of visitors Kendal has long been the 'gateway to the Lake District', although this is less apparent nowadays with the by-pass whizzing motorists well away from the crowded streets of this bustling old town.

Kendal

Nevertheless it is still entirely appropriate that Kendal should have first consideration in any Lake District guide.

Standing astride the River Kent, Kendal is a good sized ancient market town situated in a basin several kilometres south-east of the mountains of the Lake District proper, but with more gentle hills to the north, east and west. Immediately to the west, Scout Scar and Cunswick Scar, both facing away from the town, display some of the best surviving features of the limestone which once covered the whole district.

The strong north/south axis of the town, with the main street named, from the south, Kirkland, Highgate and Stricklandgate, in total well over one kilometre (three quarters of a mile) in length, is a reminder of the communications importance of the town from Roman times, when there was a fort at Watercrook, just to the south. The main road to Scotland, first a turnpike road, then becoming the A6, was along this main street. Later came the main railway

line from London to Glasgow which passes a little way to the east, with a junction at Oxenholme. Last came the modern M6 motorway, again passing to the east of Kendal as it heads for the Lune Gorge and Shap as the easiest crossing of the high moorland.

The consistent use of local stone for the buildings gives Kendal a uniform, characterful, but at times rather dull, appearance, hence the nickname '**Old Grey Town**'. As would be expected in the centre of an ancient barony, there is a medieval castle (of about 1180), its ruins standing high on a knoll to the east of the town centre from which it is not visible. This is, in fact, Kendal's second castle. An earlier structure, probably of wood, stood on another elevated site, which can still be identified to the west of the main street. One owner of the present castle was the father of Katherine Parr, sixth of King Henry VIII's wives.

The town itself grew from two early settlements, one around the present Market Place and the other some distance to the south by the parish church. The two later coalesced. Very distinctive in the development were the many close knit residential 'yards' reached through narrow openings off the main streets. Claims that the tight packing of these small dwellings was for defensive protection against Scottish raiders are unfounded, as construction was long after hostilities had ceased. As in northern industrial towns generally, it was advantageous to pack as many workers as possible close to the mills and factories, in Kendal's case largely along the banks of the adjacent river. Many numbered yard entrances can still

be seen but the houses were, inevitably, demolished and cleared as living standards rose and proper sanitation became obligatory during the later nineteenth century onwards.

As an industrial town, Kendal has long been famous for **woollens** and other textiles such as carpets (there is a reference in William Shakespeare's *King Henry IV part I* to knaves dressed in Kendal Green clothing), tobacco and snuff, leather goods and water turbines.

Fortunately, many of the better old buildings have survived, at least in a modified form, largely along the main street where, above the mainly modern shop frontages, some fine old structures are apparent. Several old inns are included. For those with an hour or two to spare, Kendal lends itself well to the 'Town Trail' approach; two admirable *Discover Kendal* leaflets published by the Civic Society are available at a small charge at the Tourist Information Centre.

The one-way traffic system in Kendal is notorious and is likely to be perplexing to visitors.

Most of the car parks are towards the northern end of the town. Space can usually be found in the multi-storey attached to the Westmorland Centre or at the car park behind the library, close to Marks and Spencer. Both are convenient for the main shopping area and the northern half of the main street. As befits a country centre with a considerable 'catchment area', the town is well provided with shops both traditional and modern. Unlike the smaller settlements in the Lake District proper, there are relatively few of the more gimmicky gift, Lakeland wool and so-called 'factory clothing' shops.

Burneside

An industrial settlement by the River Kent dominated by the large paper factory of James Crooper & Co. It has a railway station on the Windermere branch line. Burneside Old Hall has more recent buildings grafted on to a fourteenth century pele tower, but is not open to the public.

Staveley

A large village well equipped with shops and inns and with a considerable industrial history, the River Kent and its tributary the River Gowan having powered several mills making bobbins and processing textiles. The village is much improved since the by-pass was constructed a few years ago.

Upstream of Staveley the valley of Kentmere becomes progressively hemmed in by the mountains of the two arms of the Kentmere Horseshoe, rising to High Street.

Woodcraft Workshop – Peter Hall and Son. Visitors can see craftsmen at work on a variety of new and antique furniture. Open throughout the year, Mon to Fri, 9.00 to 17.00, Sat and Bank Holidays, 10.00 to 16.00 (show-room only).

Railway Station on the Windermere branch line.

Kentmere

Kentmere hamlet has the fifteenth century church of St. Cuthbert and the Old Hall nearby, and a fourteenth century pele tower incorporated into more modern farm buildings.

Events

1) Westmorland County Show

Lane Farm, Crooklands, near Kendal. Comprehensive agricultural show with lots of events. Second week in September. ☎ 015395 67804

2) Lake District Sheep Dog Trials

Ings near Staveley. Early Aug. ☎ 015394 33721

Walks

1) Scout Scar

Easy, almost level walk with wonderful views.

By car, from the main street in Kendal turn left into Allhallows Lane, at the traffic lights directly opposite the town hall; continue up Beast Banks, soon forking right into Greenside. Heading for Underbarrow and Crosthwaite, the road climbs out of town to cross the main by-pass. In about 2km. (1.3 miles) from the town centre the signposted car park is in a former quarry on the right.

Walk across the road, go through an old metal gate and ascend quite steeply to the right to reach the top of the scar. The length of the walk is now optional; the long flat top extending to the south for several kilometres. Make your own circuit. Most people head for the prominent shelter building, where a rather worn frieze sets out the highlights of the view which is the crowning glory of this pleasant little walk. To the south is the estuary of the River Kent, merging into Morecambe Bay, with the knoll of

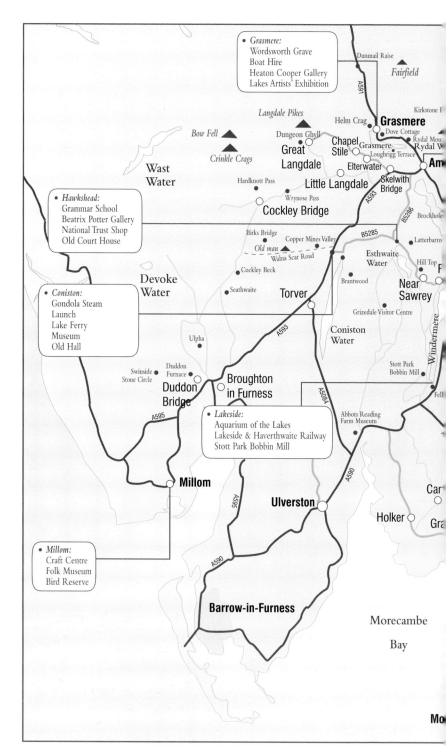

Grasmere:
Wordsworth Grave
Boat Hire
Heaton Cooper Gallery
Lakes Artists' Exhibition

Dunmail Raise

Fairfield

A591

Kirkstone P

Langdale Pikes

Helm Crag

Grasmere

Bow Fell

Dungeon Ghyll

Dove Cottage
Rydal Mou

Crinkle Crags

Great
Langdale

Chapel
Stile

Grasmere

Rydal W

Loughrigg Terrace

Wast
Water

Elterwater

Am

Hardknott Pass

Little Langdale

Skelwith
Bridge

Hawkshead:
Grammar School
Beatrix Potter Gallery
National Trust Shop
Old Court House

Wrynose Pass

Cockley Bridge

B5286

Brockhole

Birks Bridge

B5285

Latterbarro

Copper Mines Valley

Old man

Walna Scar Road

Esthwaite
Water

Hill Top

F

Cockley Beck

Devoke
Water

Brantwood

Near
Sawrey

Seathwaite

Coniston:
Gondola Steam
Launch
Lake Ferry
Museum
Old Hall

Torver

Grizedale Visitor Centre

Windermere

Coniston
Water

A593

Ulpha

Stott Park
Bobbin Mill

Swinside
Stone Circle

Duddon
Furnace

Broughton
in Furness

A5084

Duddon
Bridge

Fell

A595

Lakeside:
Aquarium of the Lakes
Lakeside & Haverthwaite Railway
Stott Park Bobbin Mill

Abbots Reading
Farm Museum

Millom

A595

A590

Ulverston

Car

Holker

Gra

Millom:
Craft Centre
Folk Museum
Bird Reserve

A590

Barrow-in-Furness

Morecambe

Bay

Mo

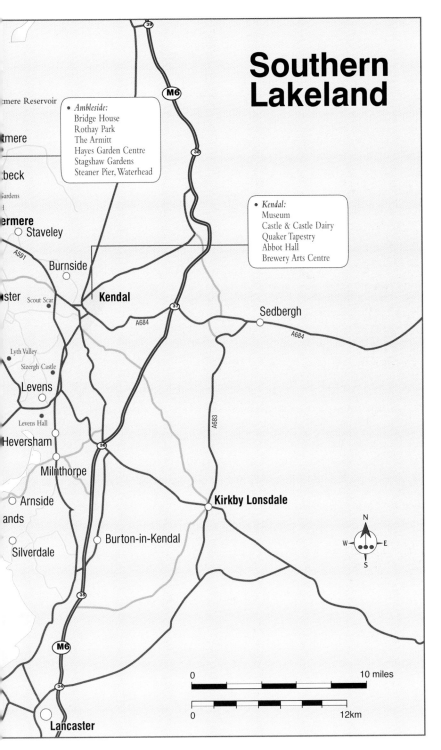

Southern Lakeland

• *Ambleside:*
Bridge House
Rothay Park
The Armitt
Hayes Garden Centre
Stagshaw Gardens
Steaner Pier, Waterhead

• *Kendal:*
Museum
Castle & Castle Dairy
Quaker Tapestry
Abbot Hall
Brewery Arts Centre

mere Reservoir

tmere

beck

Gardens

ermere

○ Staveley

A591

Burnside

ster   Scout Scar

Kendal

A684

Sedbergh

A684

Lyth Valley

Sizergh Castle

Levens

Levens Hall

Heversham

Milnthorpe

○ Arnside

ands

○

Silverdale

A683

Burton-in-Kendal

Kirkby Lonsdale

N
W — E
S

Lancaster

0   10 miles

0   12km

Arnside Knott beyond. To the west and north a great panoply of Lake District mountains beckons, with the Langdale Pikes as the most instantly recognisable, whilst away to the east the long chain of the Pennine Hills includes the Howgill Fells above Sedbergh and the well-known peak of Ingleborough.

As this walk is on limestone, it is very dry underfoot and is one of the few walks in the district which does not really need proper walking boots.

2) Kentmere reservoir

Almost level walk on good tracks. 8km. (5 miles)

From the small car park at Kentmere hamlet continue along the surfaced road and keep right at a junction in 400 m or so. Where the road ends, by-pass Hartrigg Farm and continue along a good track beneath the steep slopes of Rainsborrow Crag to the reservoir at the head of the valley, a very pleasant spot ideal for family picnics.

Cross to the other side of the valley, either at the dam or about 400m. downstream. The return path passes through the ruins of Tongue House; there is the site of an ancient settlement at the rear. At Overend Farm keep right to pass below Hallow Bank hamlet, continuing along a walled lane (Low Lane) which angles up to join a surfaced roadway (High Lane).

At the first road junction turn right, downhill, then right again to return to the car park.

Cycle Rides

1) Sedbergh and Kirkby Lonsdale

57km. (36 miles) A ride over low hills to visit two attractive old towns and the valley of the River Lune.

Leave Kendal to the north, turning right from Stricklandgate at the Sandes Avenue traffic lights, passing the railway station, then forking right on the A685 towards Tebay. In about 5km. (3 miles) turn right into a minor road towards Dockray. Keep left, then straight on to cross over the M6 motorway in 4km. (2.5 miles).

Turn right then left to follow a hilly little road past Fox's Pulpit. The beautifully shaped hills across the valley are the Howgill Fells. Join the A684 and turn sharp left to ride into Sedbergh, crossing the River Lune on the way.

Sedbergh is an attractive small town in the Yorkshire Dales National Park, with a well-known public school and a Tourist Information Centre.

Leave Sedbergh by the same road, but fork left to take the A683 to Kirkby Lonsdale, heading south never far from the River Lune. In 8km. (5 miles) turn left into a minor road which stays parallel with the main road, passing through Barbon before rejoining that road. Continue through Casterton, heading for Kirkby Lonsdale. Close to the junction with the main A65 is Devil's Bridge, high over the river, but now superceded by the modern road bridge. This is a pretty area, excellent for picnics. Continue to Kirkby Lonsdale, another fine old town, with a famous viewpoint over the Lune Valley, acclaimed by John Ruskin. Pass by the church and carry on for 100 metres or so to reach the viewpoint.

Leave Kirkby to the north, by the B6254 to Old Town. It might be old, but it certainly is not a town – nothing more than a few dwellings by the road-side. Ride on through Old Hutton, past the railway station at Oxenholme, and return to Kendal at the south end of town.

2) Arnside and Silverdale

57km.(36 miles) A moderately level route to the estuary of the River Kent, part of the Morecambe Bay shoreline and Leighton Moss Nature Reserve, noted for waterfowl.

Leave Kendal to the south, initially by the A65, Endmoor, road, forking right into the more minor Natland road soon after passing the K Shopping Village. Ride through Natland and Sedgewick, then over the M6 to Hincaster and Woodhouse before turning right at Ackenthwaite, into Milnthorpe.

Go stright across at the traffic lights and along the side of the estuary by Sandside to Arnside, a quietly attrac-tive little place with the Kent railway viaduct prominent. Turn left to go up through Arnside, bearing right, between Arnside Knott and Arnside Tower, then turn right at a junction, into Silverdale.

From Silverdale head inland, cross the railway, and pass Leighton Moss Nature Reserve. At Yealand Redmayne turn left to the A6. Go straight across, over the main railway line and the M6 and turn left at the A6070 junction into Burton in Kendal.

Continue along this road; Farleton Fell is the impressive hill immediately to the right of the road. Cross the A65 at a roundabout, then go under the M6, to Crooklands.

Turn left here, cross the Lancaster Canal, and turn right into a lane just before a bridge over the major A590.

Follow this lane to the north, back to Natland, then return to Kendal by the outward route.

3) Lyth and Winster Valleys

39km.(24 miles) A ride through lovely, undulating, countryside, with the two traverses of Scout Scar as the only significant hill climbing. Levens Hall and/or Sizergh Castle can be visited.

From the traffic lights opposite the town hall, ride up Allhallows Lane, then Beast Banks. At the junction fork right, go over the main A591, and continue to Underbarrow then, broadly straight on in an area of many lanes, to Crosthwaite.

Bear left, reach the main A5074 in 1km., turn right and, in less than 0.5km, turn left on a minor road to Bowland Bridge.

The well-known Mason's Arms is a little further, on the right at Strawberry Bank. From Strawberry Bank head south for 2km.along a little lane then turn sharp left to Cartmel Fell where there is a fine little church. After the church, rake back again, this time to the right, to continue south along the foot of Newton Fell for almost 5km.

Turn left to head for Witherslack. Turn right in Witherslack to Town End, then turn right again, then left to ride along a minor road parallel with the main A590. Join the A590 briefly then, just after the junction with A5074, turn left into a lane leading to Levens village. Head north to Brigsteer, then turn sharp right to climb back over Scout Scar to Kendal.

The entrance to Levens Hall is from the A6, about 1km.south-east of Levens village.

Sizergh Castle can be reached by

turning right in Levens village. The distance is almost 2km. From Sizergh Castle the direct (and lower level) route back to Kendal is by Sedgewick and Natland.

Windermere

Possibly the best known place name in the Lake District, **Windermere** can mean either the lake or the small town/large village which grew around the terminus of the railway line some 2km. (1.3miles) from the lake.

Windermere: The lake

At nearly 17km. (10.5 miles) in length the biggest in England, Windermere is a fine sheet of water with numerous, mainly small, uninhabited, wooded islands. Largest is the only inhabited island, **Belle Isle**, close to Bowness, which has a villa of 1774, the first truly circular residence in Britain. There is

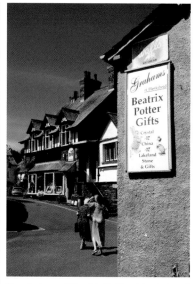

Reminders of Beatrix Potter, Hawkshead

no public access to Belle Isle. From its southern foot in comparatively low lying countryside the lake reaches close to high mountains at its northern end, the ring forming the **Fairfield Horse-**

Weir and Willow tree on the river Kent, Kendal

Watersports on Windermere, one of many attractions around the lakes

shoe above Ambleside and Rydal providing a wonderful panorama. Along much of the west shore the well-wooded **Claiffe Height**s plunge steeply towards the water, whilst the gentler east shore has been more built up with individual residences and the settlements of **Bowness** and **Waterhead**. The lake is extremely popular for boating, several thousand craft ranging from tiny dinghies to substantial cruisers being registered as users. From the west side at **Ferry Nab** the road leads to **Far** and **Near Sawrey** and **Hawkshead**.

Timetabled boat services ply between Lakeside, Bowness and Waterhead (for Ambleside), with some calls at **Brockhole,** the Lake District National Park visitor centre. In season attractive powered 'steamers' are used, the late nineteenth century '*Tern*' being particularly elegant. In winter much reduced services are operated by smaller motor launches. In addition to the scheduled services, during high season there are frequent and varied circular trips from Bowness and Waterhead. At **Lakeside** connections may be made with the steam hauled trains of the Lakeside and Haverthwaite Railway, for which

Late evening, Windermere

combined tickets may be purchased. A 'Freedom of the Lake' ticket allows unlimited cruising for a period of 24 hours, whilst a combined ticket for boat and the 'Aquarium of the Lakes' is also discounted.

Rowing and small motor boats are available for individual hire at Bowness and Waterhead. Water skiing and similar sports may be pursued at the Low Wood Hotel, by the side of the main road to the south of Waterhead and at Sport Aquatic at Windermere Quays, Glebe Road, Bowness. Hire of yachts, with a skipper, is possible at the Spinnaker Club, Windermere Marina Village, 1km. south of Bowness on the A592 road to Newby Bridge. At Shepherds Boat Yard, Glebe Road, Bowness, cruises on a modern luxury cruiser *Spirit of the Lake* are available. This boat may also be chartered by the hour.

Most important is the **Windermere Ferry**, which for centuries has crossed the lake at a narrow part between the landing stage just to the south of Bowness and Ferry Nab. The present vessel, successor to several more primitive ferries, is fixed to a submerged chain, plying to and fro every 20 minutes from 0700 until 2200 in summer, but terminating at 2100 in winter. Three hundred years ago a ferry sank, with the loss of more than 30 lives. Eighteen average size vehicles are carried each journey, together with foot passengers. Services are suspended in very windy weather. Operated on behalf of Cumbria County Council.

Windermere Village

Windermere village is basically a nineteenth century settlement of rather austere solid stone buildings, with a small shopping centre and several inns and restaurants. Large car park for shoppers at Booth's supermarket. Pay and display public car park in Broad Street.

Bowness on Windermere

Although it is very much the holiday part of the Windermere/Bowness built-up area, with a good deal of modern development, ironically **Bowness** claims what is much the oldest portion of the settlement The narrow streets clustered behind St. Martin's parish church include buildings 300 years or more of age; many houses were lived in by boatmen/fishermen.

The large number of shops includes a high proportion catering for visitors and there are inns and restaurants to suit virtually all tastes. Worth a special mention is the 'Hole in t'Wall', formerly the New Hall Inn, tucked away in the old part of the village.

By the lake shore, the promenade is a bustling place in high season, with all kinds of boating activity contributing to the holiday atmosphere. The characteristic boatmen's huts, replacements of nineteenth century structures, are known locally as 'cushion huts'.

Sitting high above the promenade is the Belsfield Hotel, one of the early mansions built in a commanding position to provide fine views over the lake. The second owner, in the later part of the nineteenth century, was the industrialist H. W. Schneider, whose wealth was founded on iron/steel and armaments at Barrow in Furness. Each day Schneider walked down through the garden to his waiting steam launch, *Esperance*. His butler followed close behind with breakfast on a silver tray, for consumption during the sail down the lake to Lakeside. Here a private train (Schneider was a director of the Furness Railway Co.) took the great man on to his business at Barrow.

Car parking – small – Crag Brow near the cinema. Large – Rayrigg Road (short and long stay sections). Largest – Follow Glebe Road, passing a small car park, to reach Braithwaite Fold, near the caravan site. Some way from the village, but served in season by a 'road train'.

Troutbeck

Troutbeck is very much a linear village, a series of hamlets losely strung together along the valley side well above the Trout Beck from which its name is derived. The best feature is the fine array of traditional vernacular Lakeland buildings, largely dating from the 17th century. Brunskill's *Vernacular architecture of the Lake Counties* (Faber) sets out a fascinating trail from one end of the village to the other, with detailed descriptions of more than thiry of these buildings. Included is one of the 'spinning galleries' on a building across the road from the post office/stores. There are two inns, one of which – the Mortal Man – has a famous sign.

The views across the valley to the ridge which, from the right, includes Yoke, Ill Bell and Froswick, are very fine.

Town End

At the south end of the village, a former 'statesman's (yeoman farmer) house

of 1626 which was the home of the Browne family for more than 300 years. Since 1943 in the care of the National Trust, the interior has been kept as it was during occupation by the family. Charge. Open late March to the end of October, Tuesday to Friday, Sundays and Bank Holiday Mondays.
☎ 015394 32628

Jesus Parish Church

On the site of an earlier church by the side of the main Windermere to Patterdale road (A592) in the valley bottom, the present structure dates from 1736, with restoration in the nineteenth and twentieth centuries. The churchyard is noted for its daffodils. Inside, most notable is the large east window by the pre-Raphaelite painter Burne-Jones, allegedly assisted by his friends William Morris and Ford Maddox Brown who happened to be on a fishing holiday nearby at the time.

Holehird Gardens

To the right of the Windermere to Patterdale road (A592) about 1km. (1.5 mile) north of the mini roundabout on the fringe of Windermere village. Entered by a drive past an obvious lodge. Holehird is a grand house of the mid nineteenth century, twice rented as a summer holiday home by Beatrix Potter's family and now in use as a Cheshire Home. A large area of the garden has been taken over by the Lakeland Horticultural Society and is beautifully maintained by the members. The national collections of hydrangeas and astilbes are housed here. Open to visitors. Car Park. No charge, but donation requested.

Walks

1) Orrest Head

2.25km. (1.5 miles). A very short but quite steep little walk, often a revelation for first time visitors as the views from the top, at 239m. (784 feet), include much of the glory of southern Lakeland.

Cross the main A591 road close to the NatWest. bank in Windermere. A signboard points the way along a broad, surfaced, roadway, rising steeply as it weaves around substantial properties. There is soon a view of the lake. With more open country on the right, the surfaced road ends at Ellerey Wood Cottage. Continue along a broad, stony, track, straight across at a junction of paths, now more level and possibly muddy.

Bend right along the side of a wall to rise again towards the summit, now visible to the left, above. Go left through a kissing gate to reach the summit, where identification of the mountains

Crinkle Crags

is helped by a view board.

Return to the kissing gate and down by the wall. Return either by the same route or make a circular walk as follows. By an arrowed post leave the outward route by continuing down by the wall

A country lane near Staveley

Ambleside Youth Hostel by the side of Windermere at Waterhead with lots of small family rooms. Once three seperate hotels

Jetty from lakeside path, Windermere

to meet another track. Turn left, then right at another yellow arrow, along a broad, unsurfaced track, descending more gently.

Masses of wild growing rhododendron cover this hillside. Go right as the track forks, bear left at a junction by a high stone wall, and rejoin the surfaced road, turning right to go back to the village.

2) Cockshott Point

Less than 2km. (1.25 miles). A very easy level stroll, partly by the edge of the lake, with good views of Belle Isle

and across to Claiffe Heights

From the Tourist Information Centre in Bowness walk along Glebe Road, diverting on to a path on the right "Cockshott Point" signpost. As the road bends to the left. Follow this path by the lake shore. On joining another path close to the marina and landing stages by the ferry terminus, turn left to head back towards Bowness. Pass the former Rectory to reach Glebe Road. Go straight across and continue along the narrow road by the cemetery to return to the start.

Fell Foot, Windermere

3) Windermere shore and Rayrigg Wood

6km. (3.75 miles). A well varied short walk combining woodland with a very attractive section of lake shore. Views across the lake to Claiffe Heights.

From Crag Brow, Bowness, set off down Longlands Road, close to the cinema. Bear right to pass the rugby club and continue along the broad track into and through the woods, ignoring any side tracks. Emerge at Beemire Road, soon reaching Birthwaite Road. Turn left, then right at a signposted footpath. Follow this path to the main A591, reached close to St. Mary's Church.

Turn left, then left again at once into another signposted path. Stay with this path as it descends steadily to Rayrigg Road. Cross the road to a gate and continue down by the side of an attractively rushing stream to the lake shore at Low Millerground, the site of a ferry many years ago. The housing for the call bell can still be seen. Turn left and take the delightful lake shore path, soon passing the landing stages and barbecue/picnic area at Rayrigg.

As the path ends, turn left to cross a meadow, back to Rayrigg Road. The ancient Rayrigg Hall is to the right. Turn right at the road, and walk by the roadside towards Bowness. Close to the Steamboat Museum turn left up a broad roadway to rejoin Longlands Road. Turn right to return to Crag Brow.

4) Troutbeck village and church

A short, easy, walk passing a wonderful array of traditional buildings and the parish church. 3.5km. (2.25 miles)

Park in a small, informal, parking area close to Church Bridge in the valley bottom. From Windermere turn left into a lane immediately after crossing the bridge and before reaching the church. The parking area is on the left.

Walk up the lane to the road junction in the village. The former bank barn with the spinning gallery is on the left, before the stores.

At the road junction turn left to walk a short distance to Townend. Return to the junction and continue along the road, passing various connected hamlets, each with its fine old buildings. After passing the 'Mortal Man', turn right at a building with a clock on the wall and descend back towards the 'Mortal Man'. This is High Green hamlet.

Keep to the left of the inn to follow a footpath which heads in a fairly straight line towards the church. At the church join the main road, turning right to return to the parking area.

Cycle Rides

1) Fell Foot, Lakeside and tour of the lake

25km. (15.5 miles) or 48km. (29.75 miles). No real hills, pleasant countryside, lake views and plenty of interest.

Leave the Bowness promenade by the road towards Newby Bridge (A592), continuing by the lake side almost to the foot of the lake. At Fell Foot the National Trust has reorganised the country park which now includes a formal garden, adventure playground, picnic areas, rowing boat hire, toilets, tea room and shop. A foot ferry crosses to Lakeside.

Carry on along the A592. Turn right at the A591, then right again to cross the

River Leven by the Swan Hotel.

From this point the Haverthwaite terminus of the Lakeside and Haverthwaite Railway is just 3km. (2 miles) further along the A590. Visitor facilities include engine sheds, cafe and shop.

Keep right towards Lakeside to reach the other terminus of the steam railway, boat landings and aquarium.

From Lakeside continue north. Stott Park Bobbin Mill is 1km. (0.75 mile) further. The road stays roughly parallel with the lake. Fork right after passing Graythwaite Hall, quite steeply downhill, to Low Cunsey and High Cunsey, forking right again to join the B5285 approx. 1km (0.66mile) from the Windermere ferry. Turn right to descend and return to Bowness using the ferry, with its superb along the lake views.

For an extended ride completely circumnavigating the lake, keep left at High Cunsey, into Near Sawrey (Hill Top, Tower Bank Arms) and keep left to Hawkshead. Continue north to Outgate and join the A593 at Clappersgate, turning right, then right again at Borrans Road, to reach Waterhead (Roman fort). Turn right at the traffic lights to return to Bowness along A591. The shortest route is to turn right at the mini roundabout into Rayrigg Road.

2) Ride to Fell Foot

As above then, in less than 0.5km, (0.3 mile) fork left into a minor road passing through Staveley in Cartmel before reaching the A590 main road. Go straight across and follow another minor road for several kilometres to Cartmel, turning right into the village. Cartmel is noted for its fine Priory,

delightful little square with inns, book shops and a surviving gate-house, and occasional race meetings.

Leave Cartmel by returning to the semi main road on the edge of the village. Turn right then left and climb a little to a junction in about 1.5km. (1 mile). Turn left to descend to Grange over Sands. In Grange, turn left to follow the main road (B5277) to Lindale. As this road kinks right in Lindale, go straight ahead into a very minor road which passes under the main A590 and then meanders along the bottom edge of Newton Fell to Cartmel Fell, with its little church (ref. Kendal cycle rides).

Watch the route carefully here but, basically, left then right turns will continue towards Strawberry Bank (Masons Arms).

Left, then right, at Strawberry Bank will continue towards Ghyll Head reservoir and the main A592. Turn right to return to Bowness.

3) Modify the Lyth Valley/ Winster Valley

Ride listed under Kendal on p49. Just a few kilometres longer than from a Kendal start and finish but otherwise similar in all respects.

From a Bowness start, take the A5074 through Winster (signposted 'Kendal' in Bowness). In about 6km. (3.75 miles) from Bowness join the Kendal cycle route by turning right to Bowland Bridge.

Towards the end of the Kendal route, at Brigsteer, keep straight on to Underbarrow and then the B 5284 at Crook. Turn left to return to Bowness.

The Windermere 'Steamer' arriving at Waterhead Pier, Ambleside

Ambleside

Situated close by the River Rothay 1.5km. (1 mile) from the north end of Windermere, the stone-built market town of **Ambleside** has a fine scenic backdrop of mountains. Understand-ably popular with visitors, but still a thriving community in winter, the town seems large by Lake District standards; its truly compact size can best be appreciated by climbing a little way up one of the surrounding hillsides.

The oldest part of the town rises steeply to the east of the main street,

The Bridge House, Ambleside

from North Road by the Salutation, an old coaching inn, up to Smithy Brow and Chapel Hill, with narrow streets and old stonework making an attractive combination. How Head, close to a converted chapel, dates in part from the fifteenth century, almost certainly the oldest building in town.

Stock Ghyll, a tributary of the River Rothay, tumbles down a famous waterfall, **Stock Ghyll Force**, signposted along the road behind the Salutation. The fall is just a few minutes walk away. Between the foot of the fall and the town centre an impressive array of water-powered mills produced bobbins, processed fabrics and ground corn. Although the mills are long closed and most have been demolished or converted, the view from the main street bridge upstream along the beck still gives some impression of those industrial days.

The modern town has many shops, both for basic needs and for visitor requirements. Particularly plentiful are those selling climbing, mountain

Rydal Hall

walking and general outdoor activity clothing and gear. Similarly, there is no shortage of inns, cafes and restaurants. The combination of cinema and vegetarian restaurant at Zeffirelli's in Compston Road is unique in Lakeland.

All in all, Ambleside is a pleasant place in which to wander. Many will continue, either on foot or by car (an unusual electric passenger vehicle operates from the town centre in season), along Lake Road or Borrans Road to Waterhead, an outpost where hotels and boat landings contribute to the holiday atmosphere. The steamer pier is the northern terminus of the scheduled services. Close by are lakeside gardens and the first century Roman fort of

Grasmere Lake and village

Galava.

On Lake Road, the striking Hayes Garden Centre has expanded into a considerable all-weather visitor attraction.

The largest car park is by the side of the main A591 road to Grasmere and Keswick, just north of the town centre, opposite the attractive Charlotte Mason College, now part of the University of Cumbria. Smaller car parks are found in Kelsick Road, opposite the library, and off Lake Road just south of the Kelsick Road junction. Further out of town along Lake Road, there is usually space at Low Fold car park. Waterhead has its own large car park.

Events

Ambleside Daffodil and Spring Flower Show

Mid March. Details from Tourist Information Office.

Ambleside Rush Bearing

St Mary' Church. First Saturday in July. Ceremonial renewal of the rushes which covered the earth floor in medieval times.
☎ 015394 33205

Ambleside Sports

Rydal Park, by the A591 Grasmere and Keswick road, just north of the town centre. Includes traditional Lake District events. End of July/beginning of August.
☎ 015394 45531

Ambleside Flower Show and Craft Fair

Early August.
☎ 01539432252

Lake District Summer Music

Major music festival and summer school held during the first two weeks of August each year at a range of venues throughout the district. ☎ 08456 442505

Rydal

With a picturesque setting between the steep face of Nab Scar and the placid Rydal Water, the scattered village of Rydal is by the side of the A591 Ambleside to Grasmere and Keswick road. Were it not for Rydal Mount and Rydal Hall the village would scarcely warrant a mention.

However, the small lake is very beautiful and there are attractive walks linking it with the better known Grasmere. The start (or finish !) of the Fairfield Horseshoe mountain walk is at Rydal and a very good, but more modest, ramble is along the former 'coffin track', starting near Rydal Mount.

Rydal Hall

A large building largely of the eighteenth and nineteenth centuries, but with older portions. The home of the LeFleming family for about 300 years, now used as a conference and retreat centre by the Diocese of Carlisle. The house is not open to the public. The formal gardens were laid out by Thomas Mawson in 1909 and the park land extends almost to Ambleside. There are large camping areas and a youth centre used by organisations such as Boy Scouts and Girl Guides.

Rydal Beck cascades through the grounds, with two good waterfalls; the oldest 'viewing house' in the country

(1669) is carefully sited below the lower fall, but is not open to the public. This fall has been painted by many artists, including Joseph Wright of Derby.

A right of way runs behind the house and on through the park land and there is access to the gardens. Tea shop behind the house.

Rydal Mount – Home of William Wordsworth

At the top of the cul de sac road, a substantially extended old farmhouse rented and occupied by William Wordsworth and family from 1813 to 1850, the last thirty-seven years of his life. Pleasant gardens and lake views. The house belongs to descendants of Wordsworth and contains some of his furniture and belongings. Car Park. Charge (Reciprocal discounted tickets with Dove Cottage and Wordsworth House at Cockermouth are available). Open March to October 9.30 to 17.00; November to February 10.00 to 16.00 (closed Tuesdays in Winter and most of January).

☎ 015394 33002.
Fax. 015394 31738.

Events

Rydal Sheep Dog Trials

Ambleside showground field. Early/ mid – August.

Grasmere

A major and readily accessible visitor attraction, Grasmere village sits by the head of the lake in a broad vale at the foot of Dunmail Raise, where the main A591 road climbs over a low pass to Keswick. The village is overlooked by mountains. Silver Howe, the sharply pointed Helm Crag and Stone Arthur are most prominent, but the greater heights of Helvellyn and Fairfield are also close by.

Until comparatively recent times the vale was a centre of farming, mainly sheep, with a rural tranquillity which was highly acclaimed by the distinguished tourists of the eighteenth century. Thomas Gray, one of the earliest of these literary visitors, waxed eloquent – 'Not a single red tile, no flaring gentleman's house, or garden walls, break in upon the repose of this little unsuspected paradise; but all is peace, rusticity, and happy poverty in its neatest, most becoming attire'. Whether Gray had any evidence of the happiness or otherwise of those suffering the poverty is not recorded. Anyway, whilst the vale is still beautiful, Grasmere itself is now a much more sophisticated place, with tourism replacing farming as the main local occupation.

The village is large, with separate hamlets at Town End and Town Head, and is well served with shops, hotels and a number of cafes/tea shops. The lake is of medium size, almost 1.5km. (1 mile) in length, with a wooded island adding to its charm. Rowing boats may be hired from a site close to the village. Fittingly for a place which has so excited literary figures over the years, this is very much Wordsworth country, with three residences, a dedicated museum and his family grave all to be seen.

Likewise, it is hardly surprising that painters have also long had an interest in this rather special place. The long established Heaton Copper Gallery offers some original works and a large choice of prints for purchase. A car and coach

Rydal Hall with a formal garden designed by Thomas Mawson

park is prominent by the southern entrance to the village. There are more car parks a little way along the road which turns off to the left, opposite the church, and at the far end of the village, beside the village hall.

Dove Cottage

A former inn, the Dove and Olive Branch, at Town End hamlet on the east side of the A591 main road. Home of William, Mary and Dorothy Wordsworth from 1799 to 1808, when the increasing size of the family necessitated a move to larger accommodation. Much of William's best and most youthful work was done at Dove Cottage. Many of the great literary figures of the day, including Samuel Taylor Coleridge, Thomas DeQuincey, Sir Walter Scott and Robert Southey, were hosted here. The cottage is still much the same as it was in Wordsworth's day. An agricultural building at the rear has been converted into a Wordsworth museum and display centre, whilst the impressive Jerwood Centre, recently constructed on an adjacent site, now houses the William Wordsworth Trust's large collection of manuscripts, books and paintings. Special exhibitions each year.

Events

Grasmere Sports

On the large field adjacent to the main public car park/coach park. Largest and most popular of the traditional Lake District sports days, with a very comprehensive programme of events, including hound trailing and Cumberland and Westmorland wrestling. Held on the third Thursday after the first Monday in August. ☎ 015394 32127

Grasmere Rush bearing

St. Oswald's Church. Held on the Saturday nearest to St. Oswald's Day (5th. August). Rush bearing goes back to the days when churches had earth floors, made more tolerable by a covering of rushes, which were ceremonially renewed each year.

Lakes Artists Exhibition, The Hall, Grasmere

Open daily from late July to early September each year.

Walks

1) Wansfell Pike

484m. (1588 feet) Circular walk of 8km. (5 miles) with a steep climb but no real difficulty underfoot. Ambleside's own mountain, with good views over the town and surrounding countryside.

Start up the road behind the Salutation, towards the waterfall, Stock Ghyll Force. After passing the fall, turn right at a junction of paths to head uphill towards the top of Wansfell Pike, visible ahead. The path is well used and has been much repaired to counter erosion. The way is never in doubt.

Continue over the top, along a path heading towards Troutbeck. Reach a cross wall in less than 1km. (0.5 mile) and turn right on the far side. For about the same distance this path is a little vague but there is intermittent way marking. By an attractive little stream bear left to follow a rough roadway (Hundreds Road).

At a junction by the foot of this roadway, turn sharp right through a gate and descend to High Skelghyll Farm, continuing into Skelghyll Wood, where the celebrated Jenkin Crag viewpoint is passed. On reaching a major junction of paths, turn left, downhill to Waterhead or carry straight on to reach the main A591 road close to Hayes Garden Centre in Ambleside.

Rowing boats on Grasmere

2) Fairfield Horseshoe

A classic circular mountain walk of 17km. (10.5 miles) over the peak of Fairfield – 873m. (2,865 feet) – and several lesser heights. Broad ridges all the way without any scrambling. May be walked either way round; a start and finish at Rydal allows the steepest ground to be part of the ascent. Superb views, including Ullswater. The top of Fairfield is a confusing place in low cloud/mist and a compass is a great advantage.

Cars may be parked along one side of the cul de sac road leading to Rydal Mount. Start up the roadway, passing Rydal Mount, soon climbing steeply up the side of Nab Scar, heading for the first peak, Heron Pike. The way along the ridge, over Great Rigg, to Fairfield is unmistakable.

After enjoying the views, turn right from Fairfield summit, almost due east and then south-east, towards the next summit, Hart Crag. Ignore any paths going to the left and continue to Dove Crag. Fork right to head due south towards Ambleside.

The ridge descends over High Pike and Low Pike, with the path close to a wall most of the way down. The well-known High Sweden Bridge is below to the left, soon after the path wriggles among Brock Crags, and may be visited by making a small diversion along a connecting path.

The direct path continues to Low Sweden Bridge and a roadway behind Charlotte Mason College. Turn right and right again in Ambleside and walk beside the main road to the gate leading into Rydal Park. Finish the circuit along the broad trackway, passing behind Rydal Hall to regain the cul de sac road.

3) Rydal Park and Under Loughrigg

A gentle stroll of 6km. (3.75 miles) which can be enjoyed at all times, even without boots!

From Ambleside set off along the side of the main A591 Grasmere and Keswick road. Turn right at a gate which gives access to Rydal Park and follow the broad trackway across this attractive park land. At Rydal Hall, the right of way passes between the buildings, to the rear of the Hall itself. Short excursions to view the gardens and the waterfall may be possible. There is a tea shop.

On reaching the cul de sac road close to Rydal Mount, turn left to descend to the main road. Turn left for a short distance, and then right to cross the River Rothay by a road bridge. Follow the minor Under Loughrigg road for nearly 2km. (1.3 miles).

Turn left to cross the river by a bridge. There is now a junction of paths. Go ahead to return to Ambleside by the main car park, or turn to the right to cross another bridge and return by Rothay Park and the church.

4) Loughrigg Terrace and the 'Coffin Road'

A circuit of 8 km (5 miles) (shorter version available), which embraces all the best of Rydal and the Vale of Grasmere. A fair amount of comparatively gentle up and down, but no hills or mountains.

From the cul de sac road at Rydal, cross the main road, turning right for a short distance. Turn left to cross the

River Rothay on a footbridge. Turn right after the bridge to follow a good path rising gently above Rydal Water.

After passing the far end of the lake there is a major junction of paths.

For the shorter version, turn right here, to descend through woodland to a bridge across the River Rothay. Cross the river and turn right to reach part of the White Moss car parking area, with public conveniences. Go up to the main road, cross, turn right for a few metres, and ascend a stony track to the left. At the top, join another track and turn right. This is the 'Coffin Road', clear on the ground all the way back to Rydal.

For the full circuit go straight on at the junction. This is now the famous Loughrigg Terrace, giving wonderful views over the Vale of Grasmere. At the far end of the Terrace a path to the left gives direct access to the summit of Loughrigg Fell (335m. (1,099 feet).

Bend slightly right to go through woodland, angling towards the road which comes over Red Bank from Elterwater. Join the road and descend to Grasmere.

Turn right by the church, walk to the main road, and take the minor road opposite. Pass Dove Cottage as this minor road climbs towards a tiny tarn. Leave the through road to keep uphill, then bend right by a seat. This is the 'Coffin Road' which loses its surface to become a rough trackway and then a bridleway as it keeps close under Nab Scar on its return to Rydal.

5) Helm Crag

A challenging and well-shaped little peak of 398m. (1,306 feet) overlooking Grasmere village and dominating

all the views over the Vale from the south. The ascent is steep but is not too prolonged, and the circuit is barely 5km. (3 miles) in distance.

Park in the village centre and walk to the junction of Easedale Road with the main road, by Sam Read's bookshop. Continue along Easedale Road, keeping straight on at the junction by Goody Bridge. At the end of the road go across a field towards a small hamlet, bending right, uphill, to a gate to start the ascent proper. The well-used path is initially to the left but then zig zags a little as it gains height rapidly. The top is soon reached. Here, there are two great rocky outcrops on which many feel impelled to test their rock climbing skills.

Continue over the top and descend to the saddle between Helm Crag and Gibson Knott. Turn left to take a fairly vague path which goes steeply down the hillside until it joins the main Far Easedale path at the bottom. Turn left to return to the hamlet and Grasmere. *If you don't like the look of this path you can always return by the outward route. Alternatively, if you want a longer walk, continue over Gibson Knott and along the rather vague ridge. There is a path all the way. At the far end, bend left until the Far Easedale path is met. Turn left to descend the long valley back to the hamlet and Grasmere.*

6) Helvellyn

One of the great and the most frequently climbed peaks of Lakeland, rising to a height of 950m. (3,118 feet). Much better ascended from the east – Patterdale/Glenridding – but, if you must climb from Grasmere, the route is straightforward.

Elterwater

Fell Foot Farm, at the southern end of Windermere

Elterwater

Park your vehicle in the long layby on the west side of the main A591, Keswick road, north of the Swan Inn. Walk along the roadside past the Travellers Rest Inn and turn right at a bridleway by Mill Bridge. A good track climbs steadily to Grisedale Hause (pass)

before falling a little to the tarn of the same name. Turn left by the far end of the tarn to tackle the steep zig zags up the side of Dollywaggon Pike. From the top, the gently rising broad ridge leads via Nethermost Pike to Helvellyn itself, a distance of about 2.5km. (1.5 miles).

Langdale

Easily reached from the M6 motorway and the railway station at Windermere, for the great majority of visitors **Great Langdale** provides the readiest access

Helvellyn

to the heart of Lake District mountain country. The head of the valley is dominated by the great bulk of the Crinkle Crags and Bowfell, whilst the ice scraped sides embrace a fine example of a textbook U-shaped valley. Most characteristic, and visible from far away on the approach to Lakeland, are the Langdale Pikes, by no means the highest of the mountains but unmistakeable in their uncompromisingly rocky outline. Rock climbers have long practised their skills on buttresses such as Gimmer Crag.

The lower reaches of the valley are altogether more gentle, with woodland and with the rather elusive Elterwater as its comparatively small lake. Below Skelwith Bridge the Great Langdale Beck becomes the River Brathay for its short remaining journey to the head of Windermere.

The whole of this area is prime walking country, ranging from a gentle

Salter's Bridge, Little Langdale

stroll between Skelwith Bridge and Elterwater village to the hard day's march to Scafell Pikes and back.

The two villages in Great Langdale are Elterwater and Chapel Stile. Elterwater sits attractively at the foot of its

Lancrigg, Grasmere, one of the many lovely small country hotels

great common, surely on a fine day one of the best picnic sites imaginable, with the immensely popular Brittania Inn providing snug comfort in less clement weather. The Langdale time share complex is behind the Brittania on the site of the historic gunpowder mill. South of the village an immense quarry provides the fine, highly esteemed, green Lakeland slate.

Chapel Stile is also well situated below the wide bulk of Silver Howe, with the solidly built parish church prominent. By the side of the main road, a little way short of the village, is Wainwright's, a hotel/bar managed by the Langdale timeshare group.

Skelwith Bridge is merely a hamlet at an important road junction, with hotel/bar and the Kirkstone Gallery. Each village has a general store.

Car parks are to be found: 1) in a former quarry on the right, a little way past Skelwith Bridge; 2) opposite the Brittania Inn, Elterwater village; 3) on the lower part of Elterwater Common; 4) opposite the New Dungeon Ghyll Hotel; 5) on the right just beyond the New Dungeon Ghyll Hotel; 6) at the Old Dungeon Ghyll Hotel.

As the valley road in Great Langdale seems to be heading for a dead end by the Old Dungeon Ghyll, a sudden left twist takes it past Wall End Farm and then steeply (25%) uphill to Blea Tarn, where there is another car park and wonderful views back to the Langdale Pikes.

The subsequent descent is into **Little Langdale**, another fine valley, less dramatic than its bigger neighbour but with its own little tarn and with mountains such as Wetherlam, Pike of

Blisco and the Crinkle Crags all close in view. From the junction at the foot of the hill, the road to the right climbs over one of the great passes, Wrynose, to the Duddon valley. The beck from Little Langdale Tarn tumbles down Colwith Force (waterfall) on its way to Elterwater. The valley has no villages but the Three Shires Inn, with a hamlet including a part-time post office, is a focal point.

Events

Langdale Show

Traditional Lakeland country show held in mid August.

Walks

1) Scafell Pikes

At 978m (3210 feet), the highest mountain in England, Scafell Pikes has an obvious attraction for those with the necessary strength and determination. Often climbed from Great Langdale by a quite long – 17.5km. (11 miles) – return walk, but is more easily reached from Wasdale. No particular difficulty, but the ability to walk safely on rough rocks of all shapes and sizes is required.

Set off from the Old Dungeon Ghyll Hotel along the broad track up Mickleden, now part of the Cumbria Way. At a junction of paths by a footbridge keep left and tackle the prolonged and rugged ascent of Rosset Gill. There are path variations here, but all emerge at the same place at the top, just above Angle Tarn.

Drop a little, pass the tarn, and climb again, with Great End impressive ahead.

Turn left at a cross paths and rise to Esk Hause, another junction of routes. Turn right here to climb up Calf Cove and gain the Scafell Pikes summit ridge, a broad, stony, wilderness. Bear left along the ridge, passing Broad Crag on the way to the summit.

After due admiration of the extensive view, the easiest return by far is by re-tracing the outward route.

2) Langdale Pikes

Harrison Stickle – 736m. (2,416 feet) – and Pike of Stickle – 709m. (2,327 feet) – fine mountains rising abruptly from the Great Langdale valley floor. A circuit of only 6km. (3.75 miles) takes in both peaks but this is a prime example of the horizontal distance greatly under-estimating the time and effort required. Despite the formidable appearance, there are no problems other than the prevailing steepness.

Park in either of the car parks close to the New Dungeon Ghyll Hotel and start up the engineered footpath beside the rushing waters of Stickle Ghyll, climbing remorselessly up to Stickle Tarn, a former reservoir which provided the abundant water power needed by the gunpowder mills at Elterwater. Bear left here and take the obvious path up the flank of Harrison Stickle. Across the tarn the great cliffs of Pavey Ark tower dramatically above the water. The cleft of Jack's Rake rises diagonally from right to left and has long been a chal-lenge to walker/scramblers with steady nerves and heads. Occasional fatalities emphasise that this is no place for the casual and unprepared walker.

The top of Harrison Stickle is reached by turning up left. Return to the path behind the summit, turn left and descend to a wide, boggy, area, aiming for the peak of Pike of Stickle, which is nothing like as impressive when seen from behind. This peak is reached by a little gentle scrambling up to the left.

Retrace steps from the peak and bear right along a path which joins the path descending from Harrison Stickle, between the two peaks. Turn right to follow this well-used route all the way back to the New Dungeon Ghyll.

To shorten the walk, Pike of Stickle can, of course, be omitted.

3) Bowfell and the Crinkle Crags

At 902m. (2,960 feet), Bowfell just misses the great distinction of being the English equivalent of a Scottish 'Munro' – a mountain of 3,000 feet or more. Its fine shape certainly dominates the head of the valley; coupled with the jagged ridge of the Crinkle Crags, a little lower at 859m. (2,819 feet), it makes a most satisfying mountain walk of 13km. (8 miles) length. Obviously, the route can be short cut to omit one or other of the mountains. There is a fair amount of rough rock underfoot, but the only difficulty is the 'bad step', a small rock face between the fourth and fifth (counted from the north) Crinkles, which can, however, be by-passed to the west.

Park at the Old Dungeon Ghyll Hotel. Walk back to the road and turn left to take the driveway across the fields to Stool End Farm. After passing through the farm, continue uphill along the broad ridge – The Band – which leads to the summit of Bow Fell. Close to Three Tarns, keep right as tracks meet.

Langdale, New Dungeon Ghill

From the summit, descend back to Three Tarns and turn right. This path goes behind Shelter Crags as it rises to the Crinkle Crags ridge, winding among the fine rock scenery as it goes to each of the five summits in turn. The fourth is the highest.

After the fifth Crinkle, the path bends a little to the left to descend behind Great Knott towards Red Tarn. Turn left at the junction, which is to

Looking out over Little Langdale

The Langdale Pikes from High Close

Grasmere, just out of the village

The Mortal Man Inn at Troutbeck

Elterwater

the north of the tarn and follow the well-used path by Brown Howe and Oxendale back to Stool End and the Old Dungeon Ghyll.

To omit either mountain, use a footpath descending from Three Tarns close to the stream which becomes the dramatic ravine of Hell Gill, passing Whorneyside Force on the way down to Oxendale and Stool End Farm.

4) Skelwith Bridge and Elterwater

A truly gentle valley bottom ramble of 2.5km.(1.5 miles), with a waterfall and Elterwater as prime attractions. This route offers the only opportunity of being close to the lake. The views up the valley, dominated by the Langdale Pikes, are superb.

Parking at Skelwith Bridge is limited; a disused quarry on the right a little further along the Langdale road provides a good alternative. If this car park is used, cross the road to find the path to Elterwater, which is joined after Skelwith Force. A left turn is then needed to view the waterfall.

From Skelwith Bridge take the path beside the Kirkstone Galleries and through the slate dressing works behind the galleries. Sandwiched between the River Brathay and the road, the path soon reaches the famous waterfall, not high, but with impressively surging power. Keep hold of small children!

Continue along the unmistakable path, across fields and through the bog woodland by the side of the lake, all too soon reaching Elterwater village opposite the Brittania Inn. To return, retrace the route or catch the bus.

With time and energy to spare continue along the valley; for the most part the road can be avoided. From Elterwater village, use the quarry approach road to access a signposted footpath reaching the road by Wainwright's Hotel, then another road-avoiding path for a short distance, then along the road before reaching the near end of the former valley road. This road was replaced by the present road due to persistent flooding and now makes a good route for walkers as far as the New Dungeon Ghyll Hotel. From the back of the hotel a rougher but still acceptable path stays parallel with the road all the way to the Old Dungeon Ghyll Hotel, terminus of the valley bus service.

From Elterwater village to the Old Dungeon Ghyll Hotel is a very level walk of 8km. (5 miles).

Cycle Rides

1) Kirkstone Pass, Ullswater and Askham

A longer than average ride of 93km. (57 miles, including crossing the Kirkstone Pass, high and steep.

From Ambleside start up the 'Struggle', rising a a 25% gradient direct from the main street and continue climbing all the way to the top of the Kirkstone Pass at about 455m. (1,493 feet). Join the main A592 opposite the Kirkstone Inn, turning left towards Patterdale.

Descend past Brotherswater and its inn, soon reaching Patterdale and then Glenridding, both with shops, catering and public conveniences. After a minor climb the road continues along the side of Ullswater with plenty of pull-off places for idyllic lakeside views/picnics. Keep right at a junction, for Pooley Bridge.

Turn right on leaving Pooley Bridge, then left to follow B5320 for a short distance. Turn right for Askham, a lovely village with large greens and fine old cottages. Nearby is Lowther Castle. From Askham continue south via Halton, Bampton and Bampton Grange, the latter after two left turns and crossing the River Lowther. Head gradually uphill to Shap, where the A6 Kendal to Penrith road is joined.

Turn right towards Kendal. This formerly extremely busy road is now comparatively quiet and is very scenic as it crosses the high moors to the south of

Shap village, descending steadily towards Kendal. Look out for a turning on the right signposted to Burneside, and take the minor road. At Burneside turn right to Bowston, gradually angling towards the main A591 Kendal to Windermere road, joined at Plantation Bridge.

Turn right to return to Ambleside, by-passing the centre of Windermere village.

2) Coniston, Torver and Hawkshead

One modest climb and a distance of 46km (28.5 miles), encircling Coniston Water.

Leave Ambleside by the road to the west, going over the tight little bridge over the River Rothay. Pass Clappersgate, fork left at Skelwith Bridge, and climb to the summit, with fine mountain views. Descend to Coniston village and carry on to the south, soon reaching Torver.

Turn left at a junction. The road is soon close by the side of Coniston Water. A little way beyond the foot of the lake turn left at Water Yeat, then left again to take the minor road which runs along the quiet east shore of the lake, largely through woodland.

By the head of the lake fork right, then right again on joining the Coniston to Hawkshead road, B5285. Continue to Hawkshead, a lovely village, full of interest. Go through the village and head for Colthouse and Near Sawrey. At Colthouse turn left along a minor road leading to High Wray, then back

to rejoin the B5285. Turn right to head for Clappersgate, with a right turn here back to Ambleside.

3) Langdale and Little Langdale

A circuit of 26km. (16 miles), visiting two fine mountain valleys, with a short but hard climb between the two.

Leave Ambleside by the road to the west, over the tight little bridge by the Rothay Manor Hotel and continue towards Coniston, as in the previous ride. Close to the top of the climb, turn right at a road junction to descend steeply towards Elterwater and Colwith. At Colwith hamlet turn left to climb towards Little Langdale, passing the Three Shires Inn and Little Langdale Tarn.

At the next road junction the road ahead climbs towards the high Wrynose Pass. Ignore this and turn right for a lesser climb to Blea Tarn, prettily set with views of the Langdale Pikes to the north. Descend into Great Langdale, reached close to the Old Dungeon Ghyll Hotel.

Follow the valley road back towards Ambleside, passing the New Dungeon Ghyll Hotel, Chapel Stile, Elterwater and Skelwith Bridge on the way. The mountain scenery with the Langdale Pikes and at the valley head, Crinkle Crags and Bowfell, is very fine indeed.

4) Windermere/Bowness

Adapt any of the rides listed in the previous chapter with Windermere/ Bowness starting places.

Coniston

Beautifully situated between mountains and lake, the former mining and quarrying village of **Coniston** has transformed itself into a popular destination for visitors, full of bustling activity at most times of year. Shops and inns, such as the sixteenth century Black Bull, patronised by Coleridge and DeQuincey, offer plenty of choice in the compact village centre.

Best known of the shapely group of mountains overlooking Coniston is **Coniston Old Man**, most southerly of the great Lakeland peaks and a particular favourite locally.

Coniston Water is very attractive; several of the locations used by Arthur Ransome in his *Swallows and Amazons* children's story are based on actual places on and around this lake and Windermere. In the 1950s and 60s it became well known nationally and internationally when the Campbells, Sir Malcolm and Donald, father and son, made several attempts, successful and otherwise, on the world water speed record here. The attempts ended in tragedy in 1967 when *Bluebird* somersaulted at about 483km (300 miles) per hour. There is a simple memorial at the junction of Tilberthwaite Avenue and Ruskin Avenue.

Across the lake the impressive house with the fine situation overlooking both lake and mountains is **Brantwood**, home of John Ruskin, philosopher, poet, painter and social reformer, from 1872 until his death in 1900. In many ways, Ruskin was to Coniston what Wordsworth was to Grasmere and Rydal. A foot ferry service links Brantwood to Coniston during the season, with limited Sunday sailings in winter. Ruskin's grave is at the back of the churchyard in the middle of Coniston; the memorial is of local stone, carved to designs by the celebrated local historian W.G. Collingwood, for many years

Coniston

Ruskin's secretary. The designs depict Ruskin's principal interests – The Guild of St. George craft organisation, poetry, music, nature, science and some of his principal writings such as *The Stones of Venice* and *Seven Lamps of Architecture*.

The main car park, with Tourist Information Office and public conveniences is close to the centre, accessed from Tilberthwaite Avenue. A smaller car park is on the site of the former railway station, steeply uphill along Station Road. There is also car parking by the lake shore.

Events

Coniston Water Festival

Late May and late July/early August. ☎ 015394 41707.

Walks

1) Coniston Old Man

At 803m. (2,635 feet), the highest point of the Coniston group of fells, the Old Man is the obvious first choice for a mountain walk. There are several routes from the Coniston area to the top, that set out below being the most straightforward. An out and back ascent gives a total of 9km. (5.5 miles); the full recommended circuit is 13km. (8 miles). There are no difficulties involved.

Go past the Sun Inn and through Dixon Ground Farm, soon rising by the side of the turbulent Church Beck. Don't cross Miners' Bridge with its waterfall, but keep left to ascend the hillside by a well-marked path.

The route goes through extensive old quarry workings before reaching Levers Water. From here the ascent is steep, with twists and turns before reaching the fine summit. The extensive views include the Isle of Man on a clear day.

Return routes are many and varied as more of the adjacent peaks can readily be included in a day's walk. The broad ridges of this group of fells are exceptionally kind underfoot. A good circuit is as follows:

Head north from the Old Man, dropping to Levers Hause before rising again to Swirl How (801m – 2,630 feet). A right turn here gives a descent along the Prison Band ridge, with a final rise to Wetherlam (762m – 2,501 feet). From this last peak there are two footpaths to the right, both heading roughly south towards Coniston. The more westerly path drops quickly into the Red Dell valley, whilst the well-used more easterly path keeps its height for some distance along the broad south ridge of Wetherlam.

Either will complete an excellent mountain circuit.

2) Tarn Hows

One of Lakeland's finest jewels, a beautiful little lake in a partially wooded setting, with the Coniston fells providing the perfect backdrop. There is a National Trust car park adjacent to the tarn, reached from Coniston by the B5285 Hawkshead road making two left turns in the Hawkshead Hill area. (signposted). From Hawkshead, turn right at Hawkshead Hill. A limited access for wheelchair users has been created by the Trust.

Walk down from the car park and continue around the tarn in either a clockwise or anti-clockwise direction; either is delightful and needs no route guidance. 3km. (2 miles).

Hawkshead

Once a remote, off the beaten track, self-sufficient little market town, set in the gentle countryside of south Lakeland, **Hawkshead** is now readily accessible to visitors and has become a very popular place indeed. With white painted buildings, many of considerable antiquity, clustered around small squares and narrow alleyways, it is quite unlike any other Lake District town or village.

Partial pedestrianisation has been a great advantage, making Hawkshead one of the best places to wander on foot. The mixture of shops, including a National Trust shop, caters well for both residents and visitors, whilst four inns, tea and coffee shops all compete to provide varied refreshments. The associations with William Wordsworth and Beatrix Potter add considerably to visitor interest. (See p181-88)

Car parking is close to the village centre, accessed from the main by-passing road.

Events

Hawkshead Show

Hawkshead Hall Farm. Mid August.
☎ 015394 36609

Walks

Latterbarrow

Only 244m. (801 feet), but a prominent hill capped by a monument, with good views towards Ambleside and Windermere. Easy field paths but care needed with route finding. Five km. (3 miles).

Start on the east side of the Hawkshead by-pass road on a little lane which twists right then left to go round a dwelling. Go straight ahead as paths cross, turn left at Scar House Lane, then shortly right along a path which crosses fields to Loanthwaite Lane.

Turn right along the lane up to a junction with a more important road. Turn left along the road for a short distance, then right to take a path which rises to the right of Latterbarrow summit. A left turn to reach the top is obvious.

The same route may be used to return; otherwise there are many combinations of minor road and footpath which will lead back to Hawkshead without risk of losing the way.

Grizedale

A substantial area of land to the south of Hawkshead, between Coniston Water and Windermere has long been covered by the commercial forestry of Forest Enterprises.

In recent years there has been a more enlightened and visitor friendly approach to the operation of these vast woodlands than was previously the case. More regard is paid to the conservation of natural life and the environment generally; planting in this area is quite diverse in species and there are substantial clear areas.

A particular feature of this forest is that visitors are positively encouraged by the provision of a comprehensive visitor centre, the creation of numerous trails for walkers and cyclists and, by no means least, a great number of diverse and ingenious **sculptures in wood** along most of the trails, adding interest and a touch of whimsicality.

Grizedale Visitor Centre

Forestry interpretation exhibits of many kinds. Shop. Tea room, with light meals available. Art/craft gallery. Children's play area. Cycle hire. Car parks at the centre and further afield for walks/rides on the forest trails. Trail maps available at visitor centre.
☎ 01229 860010

Walks

Forest trails

Varying length as indicated by the map at the visitor centre. One of the best walks is along the designated 'Silurian Way', which has about eighty of the famous sculptures. Now includes a 'Go Ape' adventure course, on ropeways, swings and slides high above the forest floor. Advance bookings required; no children under 10 years and under 18s must be accompanied.

Hill Top

Purchased by Beatrix Potter with the earnings from her first book, *The Tale of Peter Rabbit*, and a small legacy. For some years she spent as much time as she could at Hill Top, furnishing it very much to her own taste. During this time she wrote the other children's books. After her marriage in 1913 she moved to nearby Castle Cottage, not open to the public, keeping Hill Top as a studio, study and private place of relaxation.

Near Sawrey

An attractive village along the B5285 road from Hawkshead to the Windermere ferry, close to Esthwaite Water. The prime attraction is Beatrix Potter's house, **Hill Top**, which has became a Mecca for Beatrix Potter enthusiasts from all over the world. Owned by the National Trust, it is kept almost exactly as it was in her day. Many of the scenes which provide the background to the characters in the illustrations of the famous children's books can be found in and around Near Sawrey.

Also of interest is the Tower Bank Arms, with its clock, a traditional village inn which is in National Trust ownership, a very rare situation indeed.

The National Trust car park is not very easy to find. From the Windermere approach it is about 100m. past the Tower Bank Arms, on the left.

Far Sawrey

Further along the road towards the Windermere ferry, another quite substantial village with a hotel, a general store and the parish church.

Walk

Claiffe Heights and Moss Eccles Tarn

3km. (2 miles) out and back or a circular walk of 10km (6.25 miles) including a length of Windermere shoreline.

A fine walk on well defined trails with some good viewpoints.

Leave Near Sawrey on the cul de sac road opposite the Tower Bank Arms, soon rising gently along an unmade

Coniston village, with the Black Bull Inn

roadway leading to Moss Eccles Tarn, where Beatrix Potter kept a rowing boat. The views to the Coniston group of fells are very fine.

Return either by the same route or, fork left half way back to descend to Far Sawrey. Turn right here to return to Near Sawrey along the roadside path. (4km – 2.5 miles).

For the full circular walk continue uphill after Moss Eccles Tarn, pass Wise Een Tarn, another most attractive sheet of water, and enter woodland.

There are many tracks, which can be confusing, but keep a NNE then NE general direction and descend to Belle Grange, by the Windermere shore. Turn right to follow the delightful lake side path for some distance. Opposite Belle Isle fork right to angle uphill and on to Far Sawrey. Turn right along the roadside back to Near Sawrey.

Cycle Rides

1) Grizedale forest has many of its trails approved for off-road cycling. Bikes for hire are available at the visitor centre.

2) From Coniston or the other centres in this chapter, there is ready linkage into several of the circular routes described in chapter 3.

Coniston Water

Hawkshead

Elterwater(it means Swan Lake) with the Langdale Pikes in the distance

Hawkshead Court House

Try seeing the lakes by hot air balloon. These went up near Hawkshead

The Far South

This chapter includes Newby Bridge, Lakeside, Haverthwaite and the Rusland valley. There are no towns or large villages, no mountains and no lake other than the southern tip of Windermere. Not surprisingly, this is one of the less busy parts of the district.

Having said all that, there is a great deal here for visitors and the comparatively gentle, quiet, countryside is unfailingly attractive.

The Rusland valley is a charming backwater served only by minor roads. From Grizedale head south through Satterthwaite and the tiny former industrial settlements of Force Mills and Force Forge. Even more minor is the direct road from Hawkshead, via the western shore of Esthwaite Water. From the south the road is from Haverthwaite, through Bouth. Rusland church has a commanding position in the valley with lovely views from the churchyard, which is the resting place of the renowned children's author Arthur Ransome.

Events

Lowick Show
Early September.
☎ 015394 36364

Walk

Gummers How
Only 321m (1,054 feet) in height, but a fine viewpoint at the south end of Windermere. Easily climbed from a nearby car park by a short walk of 2km. (1.3 miles) there and back. Total ascent about 110m. (361 feet).

Opposite Fell Foot Country Park leave the A592 to take a minor road rising steeply towards Bowland Bridge in the Winster valley. Near the summit of the road there is a car park on the right.

Cross the road and take the obvious footpath which heads straight to the summit of the shapely little peak. Return by the same route.

Cycle Rides

1) Grange over Sands & Cartmel
Readily accessible, using a modification of the route given from Bowness in Chapter 2. About 25km. (15 miles) minimum from Newby Bridge.

2) Ulverston to Barrow
The coastal road from Ulverston to Barrow, A5087 makes a good cycling route, visiting Ulverston, Bardsea, the stone circle on the edge of Birkrigg Common, Baycliff and Aldingham, returning to Ulverston by minor roads via Great Urswick. The disadvantage is that it is difficult to avoid using the busy A590 between Newby Bridge and Ulverston. About 45km. (28 miles) from Newby Bridge.

3) Newby Bridge
Newby Bridge, Lakeside, Stott Park Bobbin Mill, Near Sawrey, Hawkshead, Grizedale, Satterthwaite, Rusland valley, Newby Bridge is a fine circuit of 50km. (31 miles) on minor roads visiting a whole range of places described in this guide.

The Duddon Valley & Broughton in Furness

The Duddon is a long and beautiful valley which divides roughly into three recognisably different parts. The higher Duddon is wild and desolate, with the little road climbing high over the **Wrynose Pass** to Little Langdale. At the top 393m (1,290 feet) is the '**Three Shires Stone**' marking the pre – 1974 meeting place of the former counties of Cumberland, Westmorland and Lancashire (Furness). From the junction at Cockley Bridge the road to Eskdale over the **Hardknott Pass** rises even more steeply (30% gradient in several places) to its summit at the same height as the Wrynose Pass.

Below Cockley Bridge the hard landscape is much softened by trees and by farming. The trees are mostly the work of Forest Enterprise who have substantially clothed all but the higher slopes of Harter Fell, a shapely peak which dominates the west side of the middle Duddon. This part of the valley has a rich mixture of bare rock, rushing green waters and dense forest. Across the valley from Harter Fell the less spectacular side of the Coniston group of fells provides a continuous high wall along both upper and middle Duddon, unbreached by any road pass to Coniston or Torver.

The lower Duddon, below Ulpha, is softer in its landscape, but Caw and the Dunnerdale Fells to the east are still sufficiently high and rugged to permit only one steep minor road to pass over to Broughton Mills. From Ulpha a road crosses high moorland to reach Eskdale. With a final sharp little drop the valley road joins the main A595 road from Barrow in Furness to the Cumbrian coast, close to Duddon Bridge. Two kilometres (1.25 miles) further south the river broadens into the huge sandy expanse of the Duddon estuary, across which there are traditional (and possibly dangerous) rights of way on foot.

The River Duddon is highly regarded as arguably the most attractive river in Lakeland, a bold claim indeed which would be hotly disputed in Borrowdale and other places. It entranced William Wordsworth and inspired the great series of *Duddon Sonnets*. The middle section, from a little way above Birks Bridge to Ulpha, is particularly fine. Much of this part of the river can be seen only from the riverside path (see below).

There is no lake in the valley, no town and no significant village. Seathwaite, with its inn, and Ulpha come closest to the latter status. Consequently, even in high season the valley remains comparatively quiet. Both Seathwaite and Ulpha do have small, simple, churches. That at Ulpha has fragments of eighteenth century wall decorations, including the arms of Queen Anne.

Events

Millom and Broughton Show
West Park, Broughton in Furness. Late August. ☎ 01229 772556

Walks

1) Harter Fell
A steeply uphill walk to the rocky summit of this shapely peak, at 653m. (2,143 feet) the highest on the ridge

separating the Duddon valley and Eskdale. Only 9km. (5.5 miles) in length but quite demanding.

Forest Enterprise car park by roadside above Birks Bridge.

Cross the river by the bridge and turn

Broughton in Furness

A small former market town on the very edge of the National Park, 1.5km. (1 mile) east of Duddon Bridge. The main road now by-passes the town, which has lost its market and its former importance. Broughton now has more of the character of a large village but remains well provided with shops, inns and restaurant/cafes.

The Georgian Market Square is quietly attractive and has changed little in two hundred years or so. The obelisk was erected to commemorate the jubilee of King George III in 1810. Fish caught in the River Duddon were sold from the traditional slabs still *in situ* in the Market Place. Nearby are the old stocks. The former Town Hall building of 1766, now used for tourist information, at one time contained a number of small lock-up shops.

The large parish church has the predecessor Norman church as its south aisle.

To the north of the village centre the fourteenth century defensive pele tower, Broughton Tower, is now incorporated into a school, not open to the public.

left at once on a footpath, soon rising, initially in woodland, to the farmstead of Birks, standing at the top of its open area. Turn right here. Above Birks, turn left for a short distance on a forest roadway, then turn right to find the start of what becomes a steep minor path heading straight for the summit of the mountain. The true top is the middle of the three rocky tors.

To return, initially take the path towards Eskdale. When below the upper crags fork left to follow a distinct path descending to the pass linking the Duddon and Eskdale. Turn left to descend towards Grassguards Farm, forking right at a junction on the way down. By the farm, cross Grassguards Gill at a ford, then turn right immediately to continue through beech woodland down to the river. Don't cross the stepping stones but turn left again along the delightful but rough and often muddy riverside path back to the car park. The muddiest sections have been improved by the installation of boarded walkways. Apart from one section opposite Troutal the path stays close to the water.

2) Middle Duddon

Low level walk of 8km. (5 miles), with a total ascent of only about 180m. (590 feet). Rough, stony and muddy by the riverside, but with boarded walkways over the worst of the mud. Very rewarding as this section of river scenery is among the best in the whole valley.

Forest Enterprise car park, as in 1) above.

Cross the utilitarian bridge and turn left at once on to the same path as in 1) above. Join a better path, turning left to Birks Bridge, beautifully spanning a

The footpath around Tarn Hows

rocky gorge with deeply gouged pools. Follow a rudimentary path, with yellow arrow waymarks, soon going uphill to an open viewpoint.

Continue by going left, down-hill, back to the river, following a 'Seathwaite' signpost. Keep to the riverside path as far as easy stepping stones with a handrail. Cross the river and angle up to the right to join the valley road. Turn right and walk along the road as far as the bridge over Tarn Beck. Beyond the bridge turn left at a road signposted to Coniston.

Take this road, turning left at the first junction and continuing along a lane to Tongue House. Fifty metres before Tongue House turn left, cross a foot-bridge, pass Thrang Cottage and follow a rather vague track rising quite steeply to the left through woodland.

Cross the open top of Troutal Tongue before descending to a stile and reaching the valley road. Turn right, pass Troutal Farm and, as the road bends to the left, take the signposted footpath through a farm gate, straight ahead. Make for the stile in the wall ahead, go through the pine plantation, and rejoin the road close to the car park.

For a shorter version of 5.25km. (3.5 miles), after crossing the stepping stones bear left, cross the road and take a path which heads for Tarn Beck. Turn left at a junction before the beck and join the full circuit close to Thrang Cottage.

3) High level route to Coniston

9.5 km. (6 miles), with suggested return over the mountain tops – 15km. (9.25 miles) in total. No difficulty underfoot, but considerable ascent in total if done as a circuit.

From Seathwaite walk up the valley road towards the Wrynose Pass for more than 0.5km. (less than 0.5 mile). Turn right at a footpath leading to a lane which is the access road to Seathwaite Tarn (reservoir). Turn right again. Shortly leave the lane to the right to continue along the unsurfaced Walna Scar Road, which crosses the ridge at a height of just over 600m. (1,969 feet), close to the summit of Brown Pike, before descending obliquely below the slopes of Coniston Old Man to Coniston village.

For the energetic, a good return may be made by climbing Coniston Old Man, descending to Goats Hause between the Old Man and Dow Crag, and thence to Seathwaite Tarn. From the tarn start along the access roadway. After 500m. there is a choice of roadway or footpath back to Seathwaite.

Cycle Ride

Duddon and Eskdale circuit

30km. (18.5 miles). This wonderfully scenic tour of two valleys is only for those prepared to tackle long hard climbs (or pushes !) including the Hardknott Pass with its 30% gradients.

The route is easy to follow. Ride up the Duddon towards the Wrynose Pass. Turn left at Cockley Bridge to cross the Hardknott Pass, visiting the Roman fort on the way. Descend into Eskdale and follow the valley road, passing the Woolpack Inn and the terminus of the Ravenglass and Eskdale Railway at Dalegarth. Close by is the restored corn mill at Boot.

Turn left at the road junction close to an inn and keep left at the next junction. Cross Birker Fell after another climb, then descend to the Duddon at Ulpha. Turn left to return to Seathwaite.

To extend this ride to 42km. (26 miles), turn right at the second road junction in Eskdale, less than 1km. (0.6 mile) after the inn. Ride by the River Esk to the main A595. Turn left, then left again in 2km. (1.25 miles) to take the road over Corney Fell towards Duddon Bridge. As the road divides shortly after passing the top, keep left. Turn sharp left again to go by Beckstones and Loganbeck to join the Duddon valley road below Ulpha. Carry on to Seathwaite.

Places to Visit

Kendal

Lakeland Wildlife Oasis

Hale, Milnthorpe, LA7 7FE
☎ 015395 63027
www.wildlifeoasis.co.uk
Open daily except Christmas 1000–
1700 (last admission 1600).
Ⓟ(Free) ♿ ♔♔(Family Ticket) <3 Free
<15 Discount ☂

Sizergh Castle (NT)

Sizergh, nr Kendal, LA8 8AE
☎ 015395 60951
Email: sizergh@nationaltrust.org.uk
Castle open from end-Mar to end-Oct,
Sun to Thur 1300–1700.
Gardens open from end-Mar to end-
Oct, Sun to Thur 1100–1700.
Ⓟ ☂

Levens Hall

Levens, Kendal, LA8 0PD
☎ 015395 60321
Email houseopening@levenshall.
co.uk
www.levenshall.co.uk
Open Apr to early-Oct, Mon to Thur. The
Gardens, Gift Shop and Bellingham
Buttery open at 1000. The House opens
at 1200. Last entry to the House is at
1600: the house closes at 1630. The
Gardens close at 1700.
Ⓟ(Free) ♿ ♔♔(Family Ticket) <3 Free
<15 Discount ☂

Railway Station

Station Road, Kendal
The service is only by the Windermere
branch line but there are through trains
to Lancaster, Preston, Manchester and
its airport, in addition to the connection
to the main line at Oxenholme, which
gives reasonably speedy services to
London and the south, Glasgow and
the north.

Kendal Museum

Station Road, Kendal, LA9 6BT
☎ 01539 721374
Email: info@kendalmuseum.org.uk
A long established museum,
administered in conjunction with the
Abbott Hall complex. Natural history,
archaeology, and a special collection
relating to the life and work of the
celebrated local hill-walker and writer
Alfred Wainwright. Admission charge.
Open All year, Thur–Sat 12noon–5pm.
Closed for one week at Christmas.
♿ ☂

Castle Dairy

Wildman Street, Kendal
☎ 01539 730334
The oldest occupied house in Kendal.
The name may be a corruption of
'Castle Dowry' as it was believed to
have been given by Sir Thomas Parr of
Kendal Castle to his daughter Agnes as
part of her dowry when she married his
steward in about 1455. Originally a hall-
house of the fourteenth century, it was
extensively modified in the sixteenth
century but many fine traditional
structural features remain. Inside are
the arms of both the Parr and the
Strickland families. Now a restaurant,
but inside viewing is permitted from
Easter to Sept, Wed, 2pm–4pm.

Places to Visit

Lakeland Maze

Raines Hall Farm, Sedgewick

☎ 01539 561760

Maze, farm animals and other attractions primarily for children.

Open daily during summer holidays & weekends in September.

♔

Quaker Tapestry

Friends Meeting House, Stramongate, Kendal, LA9 4BH

☎ 01539 722975

www.quaker-tapestry.co.uk

An old Quaker site. Following a visit by George Fox in 1652, a first meeting house was opened here in 1688, followed by a school. The present building is of 1815–16, designed for 850 people.

The celebrated tapestry exhibition centre is open during the season, Mon–Sat, 10.00–17.00.

Ⓟ(free) ♿ ♔<16 ☂

Market Place

Small but attractively animated when the street market is held each Wednesday and Saturday. Adjacent is the Westmorland Centre, a modern shopping complex which includes a daily indoor market. Across the Market Place is the Shambles, an attractive little street, formerly the trading place of the town's butchers.

Kendal Castle

Readily accessed from Aynam Road via Parr Street and Sunnyside and a short uphill walk, or from Castle Road and a longer walk. Unrestricted access as public footpaths cross the site. Fine views over the town. Street parking.

Brewery Arts Centre

Highgate, Kendal

☎ 01539 725133

By the side of the southern part of the main street, this former brewery has been tastefully converted into a multi purpose centre, with theatrical productions, music, cinema and visiting exhibitions. Cafe.

Ⓟ (Pay & Display)

Abbot Hall

Kendal, LA9 5AL

☎ 01539 722494

Email info@abbothall.org.uk

The Abbot Hall Art Gallery, situated in a Georgian mansion by the river, and the Museum of Lakeland Life and Industry on an adjacent site, are jointly administered. This highly regarded complex has first class permanent collections, supplemented from time to time by visiting exhibitions. The Gallery is strong on Cumbrian painters, including locally born George Romney.

Open Mon to Sat 10.30–17.00 from mid-Feb to end-Dec (closing at 4pm Feb, Ma, Nov and Dec)

Admission Charge. Coffee Shop.

Ⓟ   ☂

Holy Trinity Parish Church

Mostly eighteenth century but standing on the site of an older church, this fine structure is found in Kirkland, close to the Abbott Hall. Reputed to be the largest parish church in the county, the width is particularly striking. Inside is the Parr Chapel, a memorial to Romney and the helmet and sword of 'Robert the Devil'. This character was Robert Phillipson of Belle Isle, Windermere who, during the Civil War, in pursuit of his Parliamentarian enemy Col. Briggs, rode his horse into the church during a service, creating a fair amount of mayhem. Phillipson just about escaped with his life as the Parliamentarian congregation reacted violently, but lost his helmet, since displayed for all to see.

K Village

20 Stricklandgate, Kendal, LA9 4ND
☎ 01539 732363
Email: info@kvillage.co.uk
The assortment of tasteful shops which formerly occupied the ground floor of the former K shoes factory, has partially re-located whilst the former site is being re-developed.

Kendal Leisure Centre

Burton Road, Kendal, LA9 7HX
☎ 01539 729777
Email: info@lakesleisure.org.uk
By the side of the main road from Kendal to Oxenholme, Endmoor and Burton in Kendal, this modern multi purpose sport and leisure complex offers swimming, sauna/solarium, fitness room, squash, badminton and other indoor sports. Concerts and occasional theatre are held on some evenings. Cafe/Bar.

Kendal Golf Club

The Heights, Kendal, LA9 4PQ

☎ (professional's shop) 01539 723499
Situated on high ground to the west of the town, accessed by Allhallows Lane and Beast Banks. Turn right into High Tenterfell and follow the signposts up to the left. Established golfers welcome as visitors.

Carus Green Golf Course

Burneside Road, Kendal, LA9 6EB
☎ 01539 721097
Email: info@carusgreen.co.uk
In the valley of the River Kent, almost at Burneside. Fork right from the A5284 Windermere road at the Methodist Chapel. The course is on the right in less than 2 km.

Kendal Golf Driving Range

Oxenholme Rd, Kendal, LA9 7HG
☎ 01539 733933
Close to Oxenholme station. Usual driving range facilities, including hire of clubs and tuition by appointment. Open All year except Christmas Day from 10.00–21.00 Mon, Wed, Thur, Fri. 10.00–18.00 Sat & Sun. Closed Tues.

Bowness

Royalty Cinema

Crag Brow (the main road Bowness).
☎ 015394 43364
Three screens. Up to date films.

Blackwell – the Arts and Crafts House

Bowness, LA23 3JT
☎ 015394 46139
Email info@blackwell.org.uk
www.blackwell.org.uk

Places to Visit

An important example of Arts and Crafts Architecture situated one and a half miles along the A5074, to the south of Bowness. Built as a holiday home for a Manchester brewer in 1900, the house has displays of fine arts and crafts furniture in a domestic setting. Enhanced by frequent exhibitions. Gardens, tea room, book shop.

Open daily from mid-Feb to the end of the year, 10.30–17.00 (16.00 in winter).

Old Laundry Theatre

Crag Brow, LA23 3BX

☎ 01539 488444

A conversion of a large old laundry building into:

a) a small, versatile, theatre offering occasional productions of high quality. Also some exhibitions and some musical events. Autumn festival of theatre and music features artists of international repute.

b) *The World of Beatrix Potter.* A series of animated tableaux depicting the animals created by the great children's writer, supported by audio visual displays and shop. Tea room with light meals. Open every day apart from Christmas Day and the occasional shutdown for refurbishment of the exhibits – Easter to the end of Sept 10.00 to 18.30, Oct to Easter 10.00 to 16.00.

☎ 015394 88444

St. Martin's Church

Bowness

www.stmartin.org.uk/

Built in 1483. The east window includes glass believed to have been brought from Cartmel Priory following the Dissolution in 1539. Wooden statue of St. Martin. Old font. Nineteenth century restoration has resulted in a light and bright interior. Not always open.

Public Tennis Courts and Pitch and Put Golf Course

Glebe Road. Booking at hut behind Tourist Information Centre.

Windermere Lake Cruises

(Jointly operating from Lakeside)

Bowness, LA23 3HQ

Lakeside, LA12 8AS

☎ 915395 31188

email: info@windermere-lakecruises.co.uk

www.windermere-lakecruises.co.uk

Windermere Lake Holidays

Glebe Road, behind Ship Inn

☎ 0139 443415

Email: email@lakewindermere.net

www.lakewindermere.net

Boat hire.

Lakes, Leisure, Windermere

☎ 015394 47183

On the eastern shore of the lake about 1km. (0.6 mile) north of Bowness village. Couses in dinghy sailing, canoeing, windsurfing etc. Open mid-Mar to the end-Nov, 9.00 –17.00 daily.

Windermere

Railway Station

The terminus of the branch line from Oxenholme and still an important access to the district. Much of the original station is now incorporated into the adjacent supermarket.

Lakeland Limited

Lakeland, Windermere, LA23 1BQ
☎ 01539 488200
Web: www.lakeland.co.uk
Beside the station, this trading enterprise, with its comprehensive array of kitchen and other domestic equipment has developed into a substantial visitor attraction. Cafe.
Open daily, including Sun & Bank Holidays.
ⓟ ᵚᵚᵚ(Free) ☂

Baddeley Clock

By the roadside half way to Bowness is this monument erected in 1907 in memory of M.J.B. Baddeley, author of noted guide books.

Brockhole - Lake District National Park Authority

Nr Windermere, LA23 1LJ
☎ 015394 46601
www.lake-district.gov.uk
The comprehensive visitor centre of the, 3.5km along the A591 Ambleside road. Permanent exhibition; large terraced garden; adventure playground; lake shore access; gift and book shop; audio visual presentations; frequent events, restaurant/tea room; disabled access. Free entry but charge for car parking.

Open mid-Feb to end-Oct, 10.00–17.00 every day.
ⓟ(Charge) ᕕ ᵚᵚᵚ(Free) ☂

Windermere Golf Club

Cleabarrow, Windermere, LA23 3NB
☎ (professional shop) 015394 43550
www.windermeregolfclub.net
Long established club with sporting upland course. Established golfers welcome as visitors.

Low Wood Hotel

☎ 01539 439441
By the A591 on the way to Waterhead. Water Sports Centre.

Townend (NT)

Troutbeck, Windermere, LA23 1LB
☎ 015394 32628
Open fron the mid-Mar to end-Oct, Wed to Sun, (open Bank Holiday Mon), 1300–1700 (1600 closing in Mar & Oct), last admission 30 mins before closing.
ⓟ ᕕ ᵚᵚᵚ ☂

Barrow in Furness

Dock Museum

North Road, Barrow in Furness, LA14 2PW
☎ 01229 876400
www.dockmuseum.org.uk
Open Easter to Oct, Wed to Fri, 1000–1700. Sat and Sun 1100–1700. (last admission 1615). Nov to Mar, Wed to Fri, 1030–16.00, Sat & Sun, 1200–1600. (last admission 1515).
ⓟ(Free) ᕕ ᵚᵚᵚ(Free) ☂

Places to Visit

Ambleside

Bridge House

A curious little structure which has graced a million post cards, bestriding Stock Beck by the side of the main road. Formerly the apple store to Ambleside Hall now owned by the National Trust, used as an information centre and small shop.

St. Mary's Church

At the bottom end of Compston Road. Nineteenth century with spire, very unusual in Lakeland. Colourful mural of rush bearing and also sculpture by the celebrated Josefina de Vasconcellos, formally a local resident.

Rothay Park

Behind the church. Large grassed areas, fine for picnics and children's play. Footpaths to the river.

The Armitt

Rydal Road, Ambleside
Just beyond Bridge House
☎ 015394 33949
Esteemed local history library and collection, recently expanded into an interactive exhibition of Lakeland life and times. Natural history watercolours by Beatrix Potter. Gift shop. Open all year, daily, 1000–1700.
Ⓟ ♔(Admission Charge) ☂

Bowls, Tennis, Putting

Public facilities beside the church.

Market

Very small. On car park in Kelsick Road, opposite the library. Wed.

Hayes Garden Centre

Lake Road, LA22 0DW
☎ 015394 33434
www.hayesgardenworld.co.uk

Steamer Pier, Waterhead

☎ 015394 32225

Stagshaw Gardens (NT)

Ambleside, Cumbria LA22 0HE
☎ 015394 46027
Situated along the A591 Windermere road, 500m. beyond the Waterhead traffic lights. Narrow turning to left, easily missed. Very much a spring garden, open to visitors from Apr to end-Jun, daily 10.00–18.30. No visitor facilities.
Ⓟ ♔

Galava

First century Roman fort on low lying land by the head of the lake, beyond the lakeside gardens. National Trust. Foundations only.

Rydal

Rydal Mount - Home of William Wordsworth

Rydal, Nr Ambleside, LA22 9LU
☎ 015394 33002
Email: info@rydalmount.co.uk
www.rydalmount.co.uk
Open Mar to Oct, daily, 930–1700. Nov to Feb Wed to Sun 1100 to 1600. Closed Christmas Day and Boxing day.
Ⓟ ☂

St. Mary's Church

Built by Lady LeFleming of Rydal Hall in 1823, originally as a chapel

– Wordsworth was a 'chapel warden'. His family pew is at the front on the north side. Dr. Arnold and family, who lived nearby, had the opposite pew. The church was considered to be rather cramped and was enlarged in 1884.

Dora's Field (NT)

Just behind the church, this piece of land was purchased by Wordsworth in 1826, when he was at risk of eviction from Rydal Mount. His intention was to build a house on the land. However, he stayed at Rydal Mount and later gave the land to his daughter Dora. The fine display of daffodils was not the subject of the famous poem!

Grasmere

St. Oswald's Parish Church

In the village centre. Largely thirteenth and fourteenth centuries with later extensions. The rendered exterior in unprepossessing, but the interior is full of interest, not least the curious lop-sided effect brought about by enlargement, a memorial to William Wordsworth and a *Madonna and Child* by Ophelia Gordon Bell, of the Heaton Cooper family. The Wordsworth family grave and that of Hartley Coleridge are at the rear of the churchyard.

The Wordsworth Museum & Art Gallery (Dove Cottage)

Grasmere LA22 9SH
☎ 015394 35544 (daytime)
www.wordsworth.org.uk
Open: daily, 9.30–17.00. Small car park.

Shop. Charge, but reciprocal tickets with Rydal Mount and Wordsworth House. Tea Room open daily 10.00–17.00. Restaurant open Fri, Sat and most evenings in season 18.30–21.30 (last orders).

Ⓟ(Free) ♿ ⋔(Family Ticket) <16 ☂

Old Rectory

Opposite the church. Home of the Wordsworths from 1811–1813, a very unhappy time as two of their children died during this period, and the house itself was not very satisfactory, being cold and damp. Not open to the public.

Sarah Nelson's

Church Cottage, Grasmere, LA22 9SW
☎ 015394 35428
www.grasmeregingerbread.co.uk
A tiny shop close by the church, formerly the village school room. Gingerbread made to a secret recipe has been sold here since the middle of the nineteenth century.

Heaton Cooper Studio

The Green, Grasmere, LA22 9SX
☎ 015394 35280
Fax 015394 35797
Overlooking the central village green, a prominent gallery displaying and selling the work of several members of the Heaton Cooper family. Some original works but mainly prints of favourite Lakeland scenes, of various sizes and with choices of frame available.
Open (summer) Mon to Sat, 0900–1800, Sun, 1200–1800. (winter) Mon to Sat, 0900–1700, Sun, 1200–1700.

Ⓟ ♿ ☂

Places to Visit

Allen Bank

Prominent white house on high ground to north west of village centre. Occupied by the Wordsworths from 1808 to 1811, although William had earlier expressed disapproval of its white colour and its impact on the landscape. He planted some screening trees. Not open to public.

Rowing Boats

Small boat hire premises a short distance along the road past the garden centre. Tea Room.

Langdale

Holy Trinity Church

Brathay

Italianate structure of 1836 on an open site above the River Brathay, a little way beyond Clappersgate. Fine wood carving and brass memorials inside.

Kirkstone Gallery

Skelwith Bridge

☎ 015394 34002

Extensive gallery/shop, with Lake District slate for sale, both natural and manufactured into a variety of fireplaces, ornaments etc. Good tea shop with light meals.

Holy Trinity Church

Chapel Stile.

On the site of an earlier chapel, this sturdy, no nonsense, structure is of the mid-nineteenth century. Inside there is good wood carving and a window with brightly coloured glass in the south wall. Before 1821 burials were not allowed here and the coffins had to be carried up the valley side and over the top to Grasmere.

Dungeon Ghyll

A ravine descending precipitously from the Langdale Pikes behind the New Dungeon Ghyll Hotel. There are three waterfalls in the ravine, of which the lowest may be safely visited by those prepared to climb up the path from the hotel. The two upper falls form part of a sporting route to the top of Harrison Stickle or Pike of Stickle.

New Dungeon Ghyll Hotel, Old Dungeon Ghyll Hotel

Great Langdale, Ambleside, LA22 9JX

☎ 015394 37213

Email: enquiries@dungeon-ghyll.com

www.dungeon-ghyll.com

Two old, traditional, hostelries, which have long been landmarks in Great Langdale and the starting points for important walkers' routes. Now serving a wide variety of food and drink to suit all tastes.

Judy Boyce Gallery

Elterwater

☎ 015394 35943

Gallery ☎ 015394 37514

Email: enquiries@judyboyes.co.uk

Web: www.judyboyes.co.uk

Original paintings.

Coniston

Coniston Old Hall

1.5km (1 mile) from the village centre, close to the lake shore. The oldest surviving building in the area, claimed to be based on an ancient defensive 'pele' tower. Now used for farming and as reception for a camping site. Not open to the public but a right of way passes close by.

Copper Mines Valley

1.5km. (1 mile) above Coniston. Heart of the formerly great mining industry with remains, including many entrances to dangerous tunnels and shafts, scattered over a wide area. Attempts are being made to provide limited visitor facilities, including museum and interpretation displays.

St. Andrew's Parish Church

On the site of an older chapel, the present building is of the nineteenth century, including a general renovation in 1891. Ruskin memorial in graveyard.

Coniston Launch

☎ 015394 36216

From mid Mar to early Nov, there are separate services covering the northern and southern halves of the lake, calling at several intermediate jetties, including Brantwood. Solar-electric powered launches, with links to bus services and discounted entry to Brantwood. Special interest and group cruises by arrangement. Forms a part of the Cross Lakes Shuttle.

Gondola

☎ 015394 41288

A beautiful steam launch of 1859, abandoned and derelict for many years. Restored and operated by the National Trust. Operates to a scheduled daily timetable from late March to the end of October, weather permitting. Sailings from the Coniston jetty, at the end of the cul de sac Lake Road (less than 1km. – 0.6 mile) start at 11.00, except on Sat. Calling points at Brantwood and at Monk Coniston.

Coniston Boating Centre

☎ 015394 41366

Sheltered bay with gravel beach close to the Coniston jetty (see above). Operated by the National Park Authority. Electric launches, rowing boats, sailing dinghies and Canadian canoes for hire. Firm slipway, picnic area and cafe.
Ⓟ

Brantwood

Coniston, LA21 8AD
☎ 015394 41396
Email: enquiries@brantwood.org.uk
www.brantwood.org.uk

In Jan and Feb the Coach House Gallery is open at weekends only. Elegant eighteenth century house purchased, extended and renovated by John Ruskin in 1872, and his home until his death in 1900. Became one of the greatest literary and artistic centres in Europe. Displays of Ruskin's drawings and watercolours; video programme; bookshop; special exhibitions; tea room with light meals; nature trails; lake shore and woodland gardens.

Open daily from mid-Mar to mid-Nov, 1100–1730. Winter season, Wed to Sun. 1100–1630. Closed Christmas Day and Boxing Day.

Ⓟ (free) ♿ (Partial) ♟ (Family Ticket)
<5 free <15 discount ☔

Places to Visit

Ruskin Museum

Yewdale Road, Coniston, LA21 8DU

☎ 015394 41164

Specialises in Ruskin memorabilia, Donald Campbell and *Swallows and Amazons*. Open: daily Easter to mid-Nov, 10.00–17.30, winter, Wed to Sun inclusive, 10.30–15.30.

Ⓟ(Nearby) ♿ ♔(Family Ticket) <5 free <16 discount ☞

Summitreks Ltd

14 Yewdale Road, Coniston, LA21 8DU

☎ 015394 41212

☎ Shop Sales 015394 41822

Email info@summitreks.co.uk

www.summitreks.co.uk

Adventure activities on lake and mountains. Equipment for hire.

Hawkshead

Hawkshead Grammar School

Hawkshead, LA22 0NT

☎ 01539 436735

Across the village street from the car park. Founded in 1585 by locally born Edward Sandys who became Archbishop of York. The present building dates from 1675. The school continued in use until 1909. Wordsworth was a pupil here from 1779-87. A desk on which he carved his initials can still be seen. Upstairs is a famous old bible and initials carved on a window sill by Wordsworth's brother John. Open from Apr to Sept, Mon to Sat, 10.00–17.00. Closed 12.30–13.30. Sun 13.00–17.00. Closes 16.30 in Oct.

♔ <16 Free ☞

St Michaels & All Angels Church

Part of the structure, including the tower, is more than seven hundred years old, side aisles being added in about 1500. Wordsworth's 'snow white church upon her hill'. The white painted rough cast was removed in 1875/76. Sandys family private chapel. Primitive dug out chest about four hundred years old. Season of 'summer evening' concerts.

Ann Tyson's Cottage

Wordsworth Street, Hawkshead, LA22 0PA

☎ 015394 36405

Email: stay@anntysons.co.uk

www.anntysons.co.uk

Accessed by a narrow passage by the Methodist church. Boys from the Grammar School, including William Wordsworth, lodged here with Ann Tyson for some years. Not open to the public.

Red Lion Inn

Main Street, Hawkshead, LA22 0NS

☎ 015394 36213

Email: reservations@redlionhawkshead.co.uk

www.redlionhawkshead.co.uk

Claimed to be a fifteenth century coaching Inn. Two interesting carved figures high on the front wall, one depicting a farmer taking his pig to market and the other of a man holding the whistle which was blown at market opening time.

Beatrix Potter Gallery (NT)

Main Street, Hawkshead, LA22 0NS

☎ 015394 36355

The former office of Beatrix's husband, William Heelis, now a gallery displaying a selection of the 500+ water colours and drawings which provided the wonderful illustrations for the famous books. The display is changed each year; enthusiasts will be able to recognise some of the buildings of Hawkshead and district which provide the background to the characters in the books. Open from end-Mar to end-Oct, Sun to Thur, 1030–1630 (last admission 1600).

Ⓟ(Nearby) ♔ ♿ (Ground Floor Only) ☂

Old Courthouse

Two thirds of a km. (more than 1/4 mile) along the B5286 towards Ambleside, is the gatehouse which is the only surviving portion of the former Hawkshead Hall, used by the monks of Furness Abbey as an outpost from which they administered the estates in this area. Later used as a courthouse, hence the name. Nothing to see inside but key is available from either the National Trust shop or the Beatrix Potter Gallery in Hawkshead.

Trout Fishing

Esthwaite Water
☎ 015394 36541
The Boathouse, on the west side of the lake. Brown and rainbow trout may be fished from hire boats and from the shoreline. Rods available for hire. Fly fishing tuition can be given on two days minimum notice.

The Home of Beatrix Potter (NT)

Hill Top, nr Sawrey, LA22 0LF

☎ 015394 36269
Open from end-Mar to end-Oct, Sat to Wed and Good Fri, 1100–1700 (last admissions 1630). Shop is open every day from 1000–1700, during the house opening season.

Ⓟ(Nearby) ♔ ☂

Far South

Gleaston Watermill

Gleaston, Nr Ulverston, LA12 0QH
☎ 01229 869244
www.watermill.co.uk
Open Easter to end of Oct, Tue to Sun 1030–1700. Closed Mon except Bank Holidays.

Ⓟ(Free) ♿ (Except top floor) ♔(Family Ticket) <16 ☂

Laurel and Hardy Museum

King Street, Ulverston
☎ 01229 582292
Open daily from 1000 to 1630 (1600 in winter) all year except Jan.

Fell Foot Country Park (NT)

Newby Bridge, Ulverston, LA12 8NN
☎ 015395 31273
Seven hectares (17 acres) of gardens and park at the foot of Windermere, accessed from the A 592 Newby Bridge to Bowness road. Formerly the garden of a demolished grand house, Fell Foot now offers car parks, formal garden, children's adventure playground, picnic areas, informal lake swimming- with care!, rowing boat hire, slipway, toilets, shop and tea room. There is a passenger ferry across the lake to

Places to Visit

Lakeside (see below). Occasional theatre productions. Charge per car. Open: all year, daily (park and garden) 9.00–19.00 (or dusk if earlier). Shop and tea room – late-Mar to end-Oct 11.00–17.00.

Newby Bridge

A large, impressive, stone arched structure across the River Leven a short distance below the outfall from Windermere. A small settlement has grown around this important river crossing, including two sizeable hotels. Downstream of the bridge is the weir which regulates the water level in Windermere.

Lakeside

At the foot of Windermere, on the west side. The southern terminus of the scheduled 'steamer' service on the lake and the northern terminus of the Lakeside and Haverthwaite railway line. Interchange facility and combined tickets available. Café.

Lakes Aquarium

Lakeside, Newby Bridge, LA12 8AS
☎ 015395 30153
Fax: 015395 30152
Email: info@lakesaquarium.co.
www. lakesaquarium.co.uk
At Lakeside. Opened in 1997, this major attraction displays the water, animal, bird and plant life of a typical Lakeland river from mountain top to the final outfall into Morecambe Bay. Multi-media presentation. Water laboratory. 'Under water' walk. Shop. Restaurant/cafe. Wheelchair access to all areas. Charge. Open daily from 9.00 throughout year except Christmas Day.
Ⓟ ♿ ⋔(Family Ticket) <15 ☎

Lakeside and Haverthwaite Railway

☎ 015395 31594
A branch line of the former Furness Railway, leaving the main line near Ulverston and terminating at Lakeside. Closed by British Railways in 1967. The length from Haverthwaite to Lakeside has been subsequently taken over by a preservation group and re-opened as a visitor attraction, using steam locomotives for haulage. Depot with static railway exhibits and visitor facilities including car parking, shop, cafe, toilets, at Haverthwaite, 4km. (2.5 miles) south-west of Newby Bridge on the A590 main road. Operating from the beginning of Apr to the end-Oct. Combined boat and train tickets with Windermere Lake Cruises. Events including 'Santa Specials' and 'Ghost Train' for children.

Stott Park Bobbin Mill

North of Lakeside on western shore of Windermere
☎ 015395 31087
One kilometre (0.6 mile) north of Lakeside on the road to Hawkshead. Built 1835, this was one of a large number of similar mills which combined the coppiced woodland and abundant water power of south Lakeland to produce wooden bobbins for the Lancashire cotton industry. The mill also used its lathes to make a variety of other wooden articles. The introduction of plastic bobbins and the shrinkage of the

cotton trade rapidly killed off the bobbin mills. Stott Park was one of the last to close, in 1971. The machinery was originally powered by a water wheel, later a combination of water turbine and steam engine, and latterly by electricity. Minimal restoration has been carried out by English Heritage and the mill is now a wonderful working museum with nineteenth century machinery, powered by the steam engine on Tues, Wed and Thur and electrically on other days. Charge. Open late-Mar to end-Oct, daily 1000–1800 (last tour 17.00).

Ⓟ ♿ (Ground Floor Only) 👪 ☂

Holker Hall

Cark in Cartmel, Nr Grange-over-Sands, LA11 7PL
☎ 015395 58328
Email: info@holker.co.uk
www.holker.co.uk
House open end-Mar to end-Oct, Sun to Fri, 1100–1600. Gardens open mid-Mar to End-Oct, Sun to Fri, 1030–1730 (1600 closing out of season). Food Hall & Restaurant open early-Jan to end-Dec, daily 1030–1730 (1600 closing out of season). Gift shop open early-Feb to end-Dec, daily 1030–1730 (1600 closing out of season).

Ⓟ ☂

Duddon

Duddon Furnace (NT)

Situated in woodland along the minor road which leaves the A595 immediately to the west of Duddon Bridge, Duddon Furnace was at the forefront of modern technology when constructed in 1736, close to the abundant supplies of iron ore, charcoal and water power required at the time for the production of iron. This is one of the best preserved furnaces in Britain. Ore store, charcoal barn and remains of the water system which powered the bellows are all evident.

Swinside Stone Circle

From Duddon Bridge, 3km. (2 miles) along the A595 towards Hallthwaites take a right turn into a minor road to Broadgate. Continue uphill for just over 2km. (1.3 miles), forking left before Cragg Hall. The circle is at the end of a long track. After Castlerigg, near Keswick, this is the finest stone circle in the Lake District.

Eskdale is a long and very attractive valley. Its upper reaches are ringed by Scafell, Scafell Pikes – at 978m (3,210 feet) the highest mountain in England - Esk Pike, Bowfell and the Crinkle Crags, whilst the foot of the valley reaches the sea at Ravenglass. The wild upper part of the valley is accessible only on foot, a great boggy waste quite devoid of farm or other human habitation.

Eskdale

From the point where the little road over the **Hardknott Pass** (with 30% gradients) drops precipitously into Eskdale, the landscape is quite different.

Close to the foot of the pass are the two highest farmsteads in the valley, Brotherikeld and Taw House. Below these farms, the River Esk meanders a

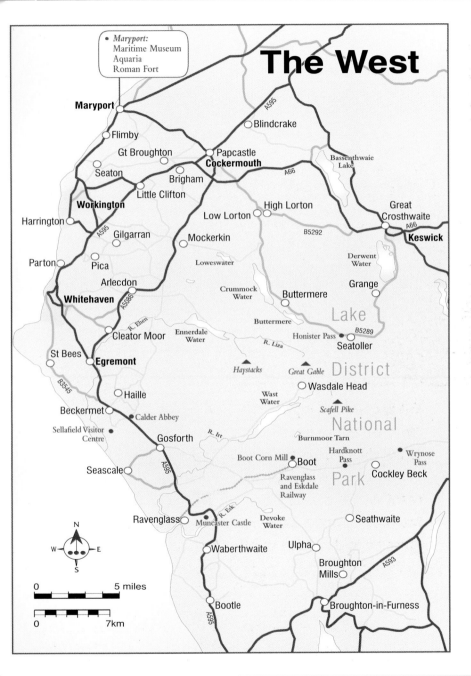

The West

Maryport:
Maritime Museum
Aquaria
Roman Fort

Maryport

Flimby

Blindcrake

Gt Broughton

Papcastle

Cockermouth

Bassenthwaie Lake

Seaton

Brigham

Little Clifton

Workington

High Lorton

Low Lorton

Great Crosthwaite

Harrington

Gilgarran

Mockerkin

B5292

Keswick

Parton

Pica

Loweswater

Derwent Water

Arlecdon

Crummock Water

Buttermere

Grange

Whitehaven

Lake

Cleator Moor

R. Ehen

Ennerdale Water

Buttermere

Honister Pass

B5289

St Bees

Egremont

R. Liza

Seatoller

Haystacks

Great Gable

District

Haille

Wast Water

Wasdale Head

Beckermet

Calder Abbey

Scafell Pike

National

Sellafield Visitor Centre

Gosforth

R. Irt

Burnmoor Tarn

Seascale

Boot Corn Mill

Boot

Hardknott Pass

Wrynose Pass

Cockley Beck

Park

Ravenglass and Eskdale Railway

Ravenglass

R. Esk

Muncaster Castle

Devoke Water

Seathwaite

Waberthwaite

Ulpha

Broughton Mills

A593

0   5 miles

0   7km

Bootle

A595

Broughton-in-Furness

little as the valley floor levels out and, although the valley is never wide, there are fields providing reasonable grazing for farm animals.

Like the nearby Duddon, Eskdale is without lake, town or significant village. Tiny *Boot* is the highest hamlet. It does have a restored corn mill, the parish church of St. Catherine, an inn and the terminus of the **Ravenglass and Eskdale Railway** close by at Dalegarth. The church structure is largely of 1881, when extensive restoration/rebuilding was carried out. Inside, the font and the stained glass windows are of interest. In the churchyard are memorials to two legendary Lakeland huntsmen. One of these, Tommy Dobson, rivalled John Peel in his local fame. His tomb carries a portrait and appropriate carvings. A little further down the valley, by the George IV inn, the road towards the coast separates and the countryside becomes altogether more gently pas-toral, although the long, narrow, bulk of Muncaster Fell (231m)(758 feet) is between the two routes. From close to this junction, a road goes over to Ulpha in the Duddon valley, to the south. The River Esk runs to the south of Muncas-ter Fell, together with the more minor of the two roads.

To the north of the Fell, **Eskdale Green** is a rather scattered community, but with inns, shops and two stations on the little railway.

On the desolate high ground above Boot, between Eskdale and Miterdale, there is a noted Bronze Age occupation area, with extensive small stone circles and cairns as evidence, accessible only on foot.

As the River Esk reaches the sea, it is joined by the River Irt and the River Mite to form the great sandy estuary at Ravenglass, part of which is a Nature Reserve, although the southern section has Ministry of Defence danger areas. The Barrow in Furness to Carlisle railway line, with a station at Ravenglass, hugs this part of the coast.

Events

Eskdale Show

Late September.
☎ 015394 44444

Walks

1) Eskdale Middle

An easy, almost level walk of 6 km (3.75 miles) around the middle section of the valley.

Cars may be parked at the foot of the steep descent of the Hardknott Pass.

Start down the road, soon turning right along a track to Brotherikeld Farm Bear left past the farm, cross a small stream on a sleeper bridge and follow a sign pointing to, inter alia, Taw House. At Taw House Farm turn left to follow the farm access roadway as far as the public road.

Turn right to walk along the road, passing the Woolpack Inn and the youth hostel. Two hundred metres after the Woolpack turn left towards Penny Hill Farm Cross the River Esk by Doctor Bridge, a fine picnic spot. Fork left to Penny Hill Farm After the farm, bend right into a walled lane.

A good path returns along the valley side. Keep left at a waymarked post and follow further waymarks. Cross a stream and reach a signpost by a wall. Go straight on to take a route signposted 'footpath, Hardknott'. Rise a little through bracken before a left fork and a plank bridge over Dodknott Gill and a gate in the wall ahead.

Traverse woodland, then open hillside, go through a kissing gate and join a wider path.

After two more kissing gates descend to cross Hardknott gill by the tiny Jubilee Bridge. Climb the far side to return to the parking area.

2) Scafell

A circuit over the summit of one of the great Lakeland peaks, 964m (3,162 feet) high. Hard ascent, rough in places. 15km (9.25 miles).

The car parking at the foot of the Hardknott Pass is closest to Scafell.

As in 1) above, go past Brotherikeld to Taw House, but turn right here, cross Scale Bridge, then turn sharp left for a climb to the Eskdale upper basin. In about 5km (3 miles), turn left at a junction of paths. The rough, stony, Cam Spout path now heads steeply uphill for Mickledore, the col linking Scafell and Scafell Pikes at a high level.

Before reaching Mickledore, turn left to take a path leading below East Buttress to Foxes Tarn, a small pool below the summit. From the tarn climb a long scree slope to the saddle above. The top is a further 250m of easy going.

To return, set off in a southerly direction along a broad ridge, going over Slight Side. The way is straightforward in clear weather, after Slight Side descending steeply for some distance, still generally to the south. This is the Terrace Route, much of it an attractive path, which goes all the way down to join the Eskdale valley road opposite Wha House Farm.

Turn left to walk along the valley road back to the car park.

If so desired, the walk can be adapted to climb Scafell Pikes – 978m (3,207 feet) instead of Scafell. Continue up Cam Spout to Mickledore, then turn right to cross the boulder-strewn waste to the highest of the three Scafell Pike summits. Continue along the top for a further 0.5km (0.3 miles), then turn right to return to Eskdale down Little Narrowcove. Turn right at the junction at the bottom or go straight across. Either path leads back to the parking area.

Cycle Rides

1) West of Eskdale

Coast and mountain circuit of 57km (35 miles). Hard climbing but wonderful views.

From any base in Eskdale ride down towards the coast, forking left by the George IV Inn and then right a little further on, to keep Muncaster Fell on the right. Turn left at the main A595 for 3km (2 miles). At Waberthwaite the Woodall family have produced Cumberland sausage and traditional dry-cured bacon for several generations. The Royal Warrant is held in respect of the sausage. Turn right at Lane End to head for Newbiggin.

The road goes under the railway before bending left to follow the coast, passing the M.O.D. 'danger area'. Cross the railway again at Bootle Station and carry on to join the main road at Bootle. Turn right and stay with the main road for 13km (8 miles).

Turn left to take a minor road close

Above: The Buttermere Valley from the top of Warnscale Beck

Right: The Ravenglass and Eskdale Railway at Ravenglass

Left: Black Sail Hut Youth Hostel in Ennerdale

Above: Walking to Little Langdale from Tarn Hows

Buttermere

House in the remote village, Ennerdale Water

to Broadgate and climb back over Thwaites Fell, passing close to the fine **Swinside stone circle**. The top of the road reaches a height of 400m (1,313 feet), from which point there is a long downhill to re-join the main road at Broad Oak, north of Waberthwaite, and return to the start.

The above return route is best for Ravenglass and the lower part of Eskdale.

To return to a base further up the valley than the George IV Inn, stay with the main A595 road as far as Duddon Bridge, turn left up the Duddon valley as far as Ulpha, then turn left again to return to Eskdale over Birker Fell.

2) *Circumnavigation of Muncaster Fell*

A shorter, altogether easier, ride of 22km (14 miles). From a start above The George IV Inn, fork right by the inn and continue through Eskdale Green to the main A595 road. Turn left, passing by Muncaster Mill on the way to Ravenglass (for the railway and Muncaster Castle).

Leave Ravenglass by the same road but turn right along the A595. After crossing the River Esk, turn left at a minor road which stays with the river until it joins the road which goes over Birker Fell. Turn left to return to the George IV Inn.

From a start at Ravenglass the same circuit is completed, turning left by the George IV Inn unless, of course, exploration higher up Eskdale is desired.

Wasdale & Ennerdale

With the grandest valley head in the whole country and the uniformly steep slopes of The Screes plunging fjord-like below the surface of **Wastwater**, deepest lake in England, **Wasdale** is a valley of great character, with a severe beauty all of its own.

The ring of mountains which contributes so much to this character includes Yewbarrow, Kirkfell, Great Gable, Scafell Pikes and Scafell. Despite the general severity of the landscape, the precious flat land between the head of the lake and the mountains has been painstakingly farmed since at least Viking times. The immensely thick field walls and the great piles of stones bear evidence to the efforts of generations of farmers in clearing their meagre fields.

Ancient yew trees all but hide one of **England's smallest churches**, dwarfed in this mighty landscape. The

tiny building, dedicated to St. Olaf, is of uncertain age, but the roof timbers are believed to have come from Viking ships. The church was largely restored in 1892. The south window has a stained glass depiction of Napes Needle, a climbers' pinnacle on nearby Great Gable, as a memorial to members of the Fell and Rock Climbing Club killed in World War I. The churchyard has the gravestones of climbers who have perished over the years in following their sport in the Wasdale area. The nearby Wasdale Head Hotel is widely regarded as the birthplace of rock climbing in Britain.

Behind the hotel the lovely packhorse bridge is a reminder that important trade routes used the **Styhead** and **Black Sail** passes.

Below the lake, the broad valley drained by the River Irt and its principal tributary the River Bleng is gently pastoral, with farms and hamlets such as Nether Wasdale and Santon Bridge connected by delightful little lanes. The major village is **Gosforth**, just off the A595, an attractive place with shops and refreshments. Here, pride of place goes to St. Mary's church and its churchyard. This very early Christian site probably had a pre-Norman church, then a Norman building in about 1100, in turn replaced by the present Early English church. Ancient relics include pieces of Norse (Viking) crosses. Inside the church are 'hogback' tombstones of the tenth century, which were originally erected over the graves of Viking chieftains, with a roof to represent a house for each man. Of more recent times are a Chinese bell captured in a nineteenth century skirmish on the

Canton River, and cannon balls from the Crimean War.

Finally, and greatest of all, is the **Gosforth Cross**, at 14.5 feet high the tallest ancient cross in England, a remarkable survival from the late tenth or early eleventh centuries. Carved by Viking craftsmen, the cross shows acceptance of the Christian religion by a people who still to some extent embraced traditional Scandinavian mythology. The carving is explained in a leaflet available in the church.

Ennerdale

In common with the western dales generally, **Ennerdale** is remote of access and is probably the quietest of all the major Lakeland valleys. There are fine mountains at the head of the valley, notably the dominant **Pillar**, with its famous climbers' Pillar Rock standing out below the summit. The northern side bounded by the less spectacular side of the high ridge comprising of Red Pike, High Stile and High Crag. The latter is separated by the Scarth Gap Pass (footpath only) from the lower Haystacks, beloved of the late Alfred Wainwright and resting place of his ashes.

Ennerdale Water is a large, attractive lake, fed by the River Liza, but the valley is probably best known for its forestry plantations, originally dating from the 1930s, when the regular outlines and limited variety of conifer species were severely criticised. In more recent years the Forestry Commission, now Forest Enterprises, has greatly improved the appearance of the commercial forestry and has also become much more visitor friendly, with waymarked forest trails and information boards.

Within the National Park, the only settlement is the small village of **Ennerdale Bridge**, with an inn. Below Ennerdale Bridge the River Ehen wends its short course to the sea at Sellafield, passing through much of the former mining and general industrial area of West Cumberland.

Close to the main A595, about 1km (0.6 mile) along a minor road to the east from Calder Bridge is Calder Abbey. Founded more than 800 years ago, the abbey had a chequered early history, including pillaging by the Scots and a subsequent period of disuse. Later reoccupied, a new church was constructed by 1180, in turn superseded by the construction of a more comprehensive abbey, including a new church, in the 13th century. Most of the substantial ruins seen today are of this structure. The site is privately owned and public access is possible only on an occasional basis, although a right of way footpath starting near the church at Calder Bridge does pass quite close to the ruins. Prior enquiry at a tourist information office is recommended.

Tourist Information Office
(Egremont) ☎ 01946 820693
(Whitehaven) ☎ 01946 695678

Events

Ennerdale Show

Late August. ☎ Tourist Information Centre, as above.

Walks

1) Around Wasdale Head

An easy, level, walk of 5km (3 miles),

Wasdale Hall

close to the great mountains.

Car park close to the head of the lake, a right turn from the valley road, then past the National Trust camping site.

Set off along the lane. Turn left before the bridge over Lingmell Gill. Turn left at a gate into the camp site and follow the camp roadway to a gate/stile at the far end.

The path crosses a stony floodwater bed and is then easily followed to the valley road.

Head for the inn, but fork right by a car parking area towards the church. Continue past the church to Burn-thwaite Farm Turn sharp left at the farm to follow a path which crosses and re-crosses a small beck.

Join the major track which descends from the Black Sail Pass and turn left to reach the packhorse bridge behind the Wasdale Head Hotel. The route continues along a path on the far side of the bridge, keeping close to Mosedale Beck. Join the road at a kissing gate by Down in the Dale Bridge. Turn right to return to the car park.

2) Great Gable

The shortest ascent of this most shapely mountain of 899m (2,950 feet) is from Wasdale. There are several possible routes; the following keeps to well-used paths. There is no difficulty but, inevitably, there is a fair amount of steep, hard, ascent. The full circuit is 9.25km (5.75 miles).

Great Gable summit

Walk to Burnthwaite Farm, as in 1) above, but keep right here to commence the great walkers' highway to Styhead. The path forks in 1km (0.6 mile). Either route leads to Styhead. At the top of the pass many paths come together.

Turn left to take the well-cairned route which goes directly to the top. Close by the summit cairn is the bronze war memorial tablet dedicated to members of the Fell and Rock Climb-

ing Club; remembrance services are held here and this has long been a very special place for generations of climbers and fell walkers.

The most direct return to Wasdale Head is by the path over Gavel Neese ('Gable Nose'); but with very steep uncomfortable sections. A better circuit is made by descending north-east to Wind Gap, between Great Gable and Green Gable. Turn left, to descend, then left again to head due west to Beck Head Tarn. Turn left here to follow the Moses Trod path back to Wasdale.

Wastwater with Yewbarrow, Kirk Fell, Gt. Gable & Lingmell (l. to r.) beyond

3) Scafell/Scafell Pikes

The previous chapter (Eskdale) includes a route for the ascent of England's highest mountain and its close companion. Wasdale offers the shortest routes to both these superb mountains, with circuits of 9km (5.5 miles) in either case.

From Wasdale Head set off down the valley road. Where the road bends to the right, turn left to take a path which soon crosses Lingmell Beck on a footbridge, before angling up the hillside. *From the car park suggested in route 1) above, a connecting path follows close to Lingmell Gill, rising steeply to meet the path from Wasdale Head.* After crossing Lingmell Gill, the path continues by Brown Tongue and a right fork to head for Mickledore, the high col connecting the two mountains.

Before reaching Mickledore, cross the scree to the right to reach the foot of Lord's Rake, a wide gully which is a classic route of ascent for Scafell. The Rake is steep and a bit awkward, but not sensational or dangerous. The surrounding rock scenery is magnificent. From the top of the Rake, the path to the nearby summit is obvious.

For a straightforward descent, return along the same path but ignore the right turn into Lord's Rake. Carry on down over Green How to join the Eskdale to Wasdale track close to Groove Gill. Turn right to return to Wasdale, reaching the valley bottom near the camping site. See route 1) above for the best route to Wasdale Head.

For **Scafell Pikes**, start as above, but continue all the way to Mickledore. Turn left to cross the stony waste to the main Scafell Pikes summit. After savouring the experience of being on the highest ground in England, turn left along a path a little west of north, descending over rough ground. Keep left at a junction of paths and bear round to the left again to descend over Hollow Stones and rejoin the outward route.

Strong walkers may well wish to combine these two summits, which seems from the map to be straightforward and quite obvious. But, the straight route is out of bounds to walkers, the step over Broad Stand being for rock climbers only. A detour via Lord's Rake or, alternatively, Foxes Tarn is required. In either case there is a considerable loss of height and commensurate extra effort. Allow about one hour from peak to peak.

4) Circuit of Ennerdale Water

A ramble of 13km (8 miles) for the most part very level, but with one short section including a few short, sharp rises and falls and two mini scrambles, entirely without danger.

The car park which is easiest to access is 1.5km (1 mile) from Ennerdale Bridge, on a cul de sac road passing through part of a forested area. It is close to Bleach Green Cottage.

Leave the car park through a high kissing gate and walk down to the lake outfall, with weir. Turn left to cross the River Ehen on a footbridge. The path along the shore is easy to follow, passing through National Trust land and the occasional muddy section. White painted Beckfoot Farm is in view ahead before a right turn is made to descend a stony lane leading back to the lake shore. The track now heads for Bowness Farm.

Just before the farm there is a choice of route – left to reach a Forest Enterprise car park, with picnic area and toilets (closed in winter) or right to stay close to the lake shore and by-pass the car park.

The tracks rejoin as a roadway, part surfaced, along the lower edge of the extensive Bowness Plantations. The view ahead includes a good profile of Pillar and its rock. As the wetland at the head of the lake is approached, a gravel path on the right provides an alternative to the roadway.

Turn right at a wide junction and cross the River Liza on a rather utilitarian bridge. Cross the valley bottom and turn right over a ladder stile, signposted 'lakeside path', and follow the grassy path back towards the lake. Continue along the lake shore path, now largely stony underfoot and to some extent artificially improved. Towards the end of the walk, the side of Anglers' Crag, falling steeply into the lake, is crossed; a little more exciting but not in any way dangerous.

After the Crag, the path goes obviously to the weir and back to the car park.

5) Forest trail

Drive to the Forest Enterprises car park mentioned above and select a forest trail from the map on the information board. The various trails are waymarked. Best known is the 'Nine Becks Walk'.

6) Ascent of Pillar

At 892m (2,928 feet) one of the Lakeland giants and very much Ennerdale's mountain. No particular difficulty with the route set out below, but the usual amount of hard climbing to reach this elevation. Thirteen kilometres (8 miles)

from Gillerthwaite.

Pillar is remote from public roads and the nearest car park is the Forest Enterprise car park already mentioned.

From the access roadway 1km (0.6 mile) below Gillerthwaite head across the valley bottom, crossing various waterways. Enter the forest, turning left then right at junctions to rise steadily. Leave the woodland on a path rising straight towards the summit of Tewit How.

Continue beyond the summit in the same direction until a cross-paths is reached, close to Haycock. Turn left here to walk over Scoat Fell and Little Scoat Fell to Pillar, in almost 3km (2 miles), ignoring all diversionary paths along the way.

From Pillar take the path descending to the north-west, over White Pike. As Ennerdale Forest is reached the path continues. Bear right at a junction, still downhill, to reach the valley bottom.

Turn left here to return to the crossing place and retrace the outward route.

Cycle Rides

1) Gosforth, Seascale and Lower Wasdale countryside

An easy ride of 28km (17.5 miles).

From the foot of Wastwater, where there is a youth hostel at Wasdale Hall, set off towards the coast, shortly turning right to pass through Nether Wasdale. This minor road leads directly to Gosforth (see above for features of this interesting village).

Cross the main road to head for Seascale along the B5344. Victorian Seascale had ambitions as an off the

Loweswater

beaten track seaside resort, particularly after the construction of the railway in the 1850s. Never really succeeding, Seascale is now a quiet backwater with a few shops and the occasional hotel and inn.

From Seascale follow the **Cumbria**

View of Fleetwith Pike from the road to Buttermere

Cycleway south-east to Drigg and Holmrook. Turn right at the main road, then shortly left to head for Santon Bridge. Go left then right here for a return to Wasdale Hall, passing Nether Wasdale on the way.

2) Cumberland coast and Sellafield

A more strenuous ride of 38km (23.5miles). From Ennerdale Bridge follow the minor road along the south side of the River Ehen to **Egremont**. Go through the town to take the road to the north-west to **St. Bees**. Turn left to climb the hill and then fork right along the minor road closest to the sea, leading to Nethertown, despite the name just a village, with inn.

Continue to the attractive village of Braystones, bearing left to Beckermet. Turn right here to take the Cumbria Cycleway direct to the Sellafield Visitor Centre.

Return to Ennerdale by leaving the centre by heading to the main road at

Calder Bridge. Turn left into the minor road by the church, turning left then right just before the ruins of Calder Abbey. A very minor hill road now goes via Cold Fell and Blakeley Moss all the way back to Ennerdale Bridge.

From a Wasdale base a ride to the **Sellafield Visitor Centre** means initially heading for Gosforth, turning right at the main road, then left at Calder Bridge. A return via Egremont, Haile and Calder Abbey to Calder Bridge keeps use of the main road to a minimum.

Sellafield Visitor Centre
☎ 01946 727027

Small rural church in Buttermere

3) The Whitehaven to Ennerdale Cyclepath

16km (10 miles) Whitehaven to Ennerdale Cyclepath uses the trackbed of a long disused mineral railway line to create a link from Ennerdale to the sea. (for Whitehaven visitor facilities see motor tours). Sculpture trail and other features along the way. This is the first leg of a sea to sea route from Whitehaven to Sunderland. Futher information from Tourist Information Centre (Whitehaven). ☎ 01946 695678

The Western shore of Buttermere with a grazing goat in the foreground and High stile in the distance

Buttermere, Crummock Water, Loweswater & Borrowdale

Generously endowed with no less than three lakes, the fine valley containing Buttermere, Crummock Water and Loweswater has long been a great favourite among the western dales, not least because of its comparative accessibilty by road. Although for visitor purposes it is convenient to call this area the 'Buttermere' valley, in strict geographical terms there is one very large valley, the **Vale of Lorton**, drained by the River Cocker, and a small tributary valley containing Loweswater. The outfall from Loweswater flows east to join Crummock Water. The low head to the tributary valley can give a quite misleading impression.

At the main valley head Fleetwith Pike, in height a comparatively modest, mountain, is seen at its best, with the formidable Honister Crag guarding the high 356m (1,168 feet) pass of the same name over into **Borrowdale**. The mountains on the south-west side are the isolated Melbreak, by Crummock Water, then the more spectacular side of the continuous ridge of Red Pike, High Stile and High Crag. After the dip through which the Scarth Gap Pass (foot only) climbs over to Ennerdale, Haystacks makes the most of its small stature.

The north-east side of the valley has Whiteside, then the huge bulk of Grasmoor. After the interuption of the valley of Sail Beck, which allows the little road to pass on its steep route to the Vale of Newlands, the relatively bland sides of Robinson, Hindscarth and Dale Head

form a long wall above Buttermere and the Honister Pass.

Forested areas are by no means dominant, the most substantial being Burtness Wood by Buttermere, Lanthwaite Wood at the foot of Crummock Water and Holme Wood by Loweswater. All add to, rather than detract from, the overall beauty of the valley.

Buttermere village is situated in magnificent surroundings between Buttermere and Crummock Water, where the flat land is the alluvial accumulation now dividing what was formerly one lake. The village is a popular little place, with two hotels, cafe, car park and toilets. The small church of St. James must rank highly in any contest for the most beautifully situated church in Lakeland.

The easiest road access to the valley is from **Cockermouth**, along the lower part of the Vale of Lorton, comparatively rich agriculturally, with small villages/hamlets such as High and Low Lorton and Loweswater. High Lorton and Loweswater have inns and churches. St Cuthbert's at High Lorton and St. Bartholomew's at Loweswater are both early nineteenth century, although the fomer does occupy an old religious site.

From the Keswick area the **Whinlatter Pass**, B5292, (see p156 for Whinlatter visitor centre) provides a lower and easier route to Buttermere than either the Honister or Newlands Passes and may be combined with one or other as a circular drive. The final easy way to reach Buttermere is from the coastal plain via Mockerkin and the road along the side of Loweswater.

Events

Loweswater Show

Mid September. ☎ Tourist Information Centre, Cockermouth.

Walks

1) Buttermere – circuit of the lake

A great favourite for walkers/ramblers of all ages. An easy 6.5km (4 miles) without significant gradient.

From the public car park in Buttermere village, start along the road towards the Honister Pass. Take the public bridleway through Syke and Willinsyke Farms and follow the broad track which descends gently towards the lake shore.

The path traverses through light woodland and a tunnel where a steep rocky slope leaves no space at the edge of the water. At any junction keep as close to the lake shore as possible. On reaching the Honister road, turn right and continue to Gatesgarth Farm, with the fine ridge of Fleetwith Pike ahead. The prominent white cross is a memorial to Fanny Mercer, accidentally killed in 1887.

Turn right and carefully follow the signed bridleway through the farm, heading for the lake shore. Turn right at the far corner of the lake to follow the bridleway back towards the village, largely through the National Trust owned Burtness Wood. For one section there is a choice between lake shore path and a broad track a little way further up the hillside.

At the foot of the lake cross Sour Milk Ghyll on a small bridge, then Buttermere Dubs on a longer bridge. The route back is now entirely straightforward.

2) Circuit of Crummock Water

In character quite similar to the previous walk, but at 13km (8 miles) about twice the length.

In addition to the public car park in Buttermere village, there are small car parks by the roadside which can be used as start/finish for this walk.

From the village walk along the road towards Cockermouth. In 2/3km (0.5 mile) a track on the right may be used to avoid one length of road. Re-join the road. As it reaches the edge of the lake, a path rises diagonally to the right. At the expense of a modest ascent this path avoids more of the road and gives enhanced views both up and down the valley.

Back on the road continue past Rannerdale Farm and Cinderdale Common. Turn left to leave the road at a kissing gate 120m beyond the second of the car parks on the Common, signposted 'Fletcher Fields', turn right. All apparent paths lead eventually to a well defined route by the lake shore, with abundant picnic spots and a shingle beach.

Woodland is entered, firstly High Wood, followed by Lanthwaite Wood. Fork left at a junction to descend towards the lake. Bear left to cross the footbridges at the outfall, where the waterworks structures, including a double fish ladder, are reasonably discreet.

Bear left again to keep to the lake shore. Cross another footbridge to pass the octagonal pump house with its

Hardknott Roman Fort

'Workington Corporation' plaque of 1903. Go over the stile on the right and turn left to keep close to the shore, soon reaching a bay with shingle beach. The continuation along the shore is without complication.

After the inviting little promontory of Low Ling Crag, a diversion by a path on the right leads to Scales Force, highest waterfall in Lakeland. An ascent of about 90m (295 feet) is required.

Before the head of the lake is reached, there are pretty little islands. By this time the path has left the shoreline and has been joined by the major track linking Buttermere village and Scale Force. Turn left to cross Scale Bridge over Buttermere Dubs and return to the village.

3) Red Pike and Scale Force

Red Pike is the mountain directly facing Buttermere village across the valley, the name resulting from the pinkish colour of much of the rock, geologically a granitic intrusion into the predominant Borrowdale series

volcanics of this area. Its height of 755m (2,478 feet), reached in a comparatively short horizontal distance, ensures a steep ascent, with little respite. The recommended return is by Scale Force, highest waterfall in Lakeland, giving a distance of 9km (5.5 miles). *For a longer walk of 11km (6.75 miles), turn left at the summit and follow the broad ridge over High Stile and High Crag. After the latter turn left along an indistinct path to join the Scarth Gap Pass track, turning left again to descend to the valley. Return to the village may be along either side of Buttermere. (see 1 above)*

From the village head across the flat land towards the foot of Sourmilk Gill, a fine sight after rain as it tumbles down the steep hillside. Cross the footbridges and commence the ascent, initially through woodland on a track which has been extensively engineered to combat erosion.

This track first goes left across the hillside, then turns back right to join Sourmilk Gill below its outfall from

Bleaberry Tarn, sitting prettily in its fine text book corrie. From the tarn the path is steep and scrambly up to the Saddle, on the right, separating Dodd from the Red Pike summit. Turn left at the Saddle for the final ascent to the top.

Turn right to follow the broad descending ridge into the valley containing Scale Force, ignoring a path which goes left to Little Dodd and Starling Dodd. From the waterfall a very well-used path heads back to the village.

4) Fleetwith Pike & Haystacks

From the valley floor Fleetwith Pike is a fine mountain, its dominance belying its modest height of 648m (2,127 feet). Another lesser height at 597m (1959 feet), Haystacks is noted for the interest and beauty of its summit and as a viewpoint. Most of all, it is a special place for the legions of admirers of the late Alfred Wainwright, legendary walker and writer, whose ashes were scattered here a few years ago. From a start/finish at the privately-owned car park (charge made) by Gatesgarth Farm, the distance is approximately 8km (5 miles).

Walk a little way up the road and take the footpath on the right which heads unmistakably for the well-defined ridge climbing steeply up to the summit of Fleetwith Pike. As height is gained, the views back down the valley are superb.

From the summit the way is basically to the right to join a path which runs from the top of the Honister Pass to Warnscale Bottom or Haystacks. However, there is no continuous path across the rough intervening ground and many walkers might prefer to follow the good path from Fleetwith summit towards the Honister Pass, turning right on meeting the first mentioned path. The extra distance is about 1km (0.66 mile).

By whichever route, Warnscale Beck is crossed and the path rises to cross broken ground towards Blackbeck Tarn before bearing right to the top of Haystacks. Avoid any track which descends, right, towards Warnscale Bottom. Innominate Tarn is passed before the summit.

Footpath on the east side of Wastwater

From Haystacks there are two paths descending to the top of the Scarth Gap Pass. Use either, then turn right to follow the well-worn route down to Gatesgarth.

Alternatively walkers can overnight at Black Sail Youth Hostel which is situated below Haystacks in the upper reaches of Ennerdale. This former bothy has not a lot in the way of comfort, but is tremendously popular. It serves meals and has a shower, so allowing a stay high in the mountains, especially on warm summer evenings!

Cycle Rides

1) Buttermere, Newlands, Whinlatter

Circuit of 50km (31 miles). Includes strenuous climbs.

Leave Buttermere along the minor road past the church, soon climbing steadily to the 333m (1,093 feet) summit at Newlands Hause. Apart from the views, the reward is a long downhill through the beautiful Newlands Valley, virtually all the way to Braithwaite.

Turn left in Braithwaite, well before reaching the main A66 road, to start the ascent of the Whinlatter Pass, B5292, largely in woodland. Well before the 253m (830 feet) summit of the Pass is the Forest Enterprises Whinlatter Visitor Centre, well worth a visit.

The road descends to join B5289, Buttermere to Cockermouth road, but a left turn to High Lorton provides a short cut to B5289, which provides a straightforward return to Buttermere village. *From close to High Lorton a minor road via Hopebeck provides an alternative to B5289 for part of the distance along* *Lorton Vale.*

2) Lorton Vale, Cockermouth and Mockerkin

A fairly level ride of 39km (24 miles)

From Buttermere ride down the Vale of Lorton along B5289 to Cockermouth.

Return by leaving Cockermouth on the road connecting to the bypass. This starts as Station Road in the town centre. Go straight across at the large roundabout, towards Egremont on the A5086. If this road is busy, which is unusual, there are minor roads between villages to right and left. In 7km (4.25 miles) turn left for Mockerkin and climb a little before descending to the shore of Loweswater. Continue to the junction with B5289. Turn right to return to Buttermere.

For a more adventurous return leave A5086 on a left turn 2km (1.3 miles) from Cockermouth. Turn right in 1km (0.66 mile) to follow a very minor road through farming hamlets and over Mosser Fell, rejoining the basic route by the Loweswater shore.

To extend this short ride to 65km (40 miles), cross the River Derwent in Cockermouth, soon turning left to go through Papcastle, site of a Roman fort. Continue through Great Broughton and Broughton Moor to Maryport.

Leave Maryport by the A596 towards Carlisle. Turn right at Moor Park, cross the River Ellen, and go through Dearham bearing left towards Gilcrux. Well before Gilcrux turn right to Tallentire. After Tallentire fork left to Bridekirk and continue to the main A595 road. Turn right to return to Cockermouth and then back to Buttermere as above.

3) Keswick

Only 37km (23 miles) in length, but a tough circuit using two high passes.

Set off along the B5289 on the northern side of Buttermere, pass Gatesgarth, and climb to the top of the Honister Pass. at 332m (1,090 feet). Descend carefully into Borrowdale, reached at Seatoller (refreshments and tourist information).

Continue along the delightful valley road through Rosthwaite, by-passing Grange in Borrowdale before reaching Derwentwater and Keswick.

Should the Borrowdale road be busy, a good diversion would be to turn left through Grange on the little road which goes attractively above the lake and on through Portinscale to the A66, turning right then right again to Keswick.

From Keswick take the main A66 to Braithwaite. Turn right at the bridge over the Coledale Beck and start the long but generally gradual ascent to Newlands Hause at 333m (1,093 feet), followed by the shorter, steeper, descent to Buttermere. For a longer but lower return the Whinlatter Pass (see above) may be used instead of Newlands Hause.

Car Tours

Tours from bases in the western section of the Lake District must, of necessity, heavily involve the coastal towns and villages, with visitor attractions such as the Sellafield nuclear establishment adding variety. Because the mountains are close to the sea, these tours are generally short in distance.

Although each tour has a notional starting place based on one or other of the valleys, obviously the various places of interest can be reached from any of the western valleys, generally by using the A595 as a link. For a longer drive, one or more of the routes may be linked together and many places listed for tours in the south and north sections of the book can also readily be reached.

1) Eskdale-Haverigg-Millom-Ulpha-Eskdale

From Eskdale drive down the valley to Ravenglass and Muncaster Castle. Continue along the A595 through Bootle, with the great bulk of Black Combe above to the left. Keep right to follow A5093 to **Millom** as the A595 turns left. A small diversion right to **Silecroft** reaches a sand and shingle beach in 1.5km (1 mile). Formerly a hive of industry as a bustling nineteenth century iron town, Millom has had to come to terms with being a quiet backwater. The site of the former iron ore mining at **Hodbarrow** is now a major Royal Society for the Protection of Birds nature reserve. At nearby **Haverigg** there are children's adventure play features and safe beaches, with a water ski centre at an artificial lake. In Millom itself there is still a fair range of shops and a park with bowling green, putting green, tennis courts and children's facilities.

The **Folk Museum** has a reconstruction of a drift mine and a permanent exhibition of the life and work of the late Norman Nicholson, the celebrated twentieth century local writer and poet. ☎ 01229 774819. There is still a railway service on the Barrow to Whitehaven (and Carlisle) coastal line. To return to Eskdale, head north along the A5093. Just out of Millom, close to the road,

113

Buttermere, with Haystacks beyond and Scarth Gap to its right

are the remains of Millom Castle and a twelfth century church with a 'fish' window. Join the A595 and continue to Duddon Bridge and take either left turn to Ulpha. The second turning is the more direct route. Turn left again at Ulpha to return to Eskdale over Birker Fell. Distance – 85km (53 miles) from Eskdale Green.

2) Wasdale-Seascale-Sellafield

From Wasdale drive via Nether Wasdale to Gosforth. Go across the A595 and take the B5344 to **Seascale**, a minor Victorian seaside resort, now very quiet with just a few shops and the odd inn. Go back to the A595, turn left, then left again at Calder Bridge to visit **Sellafield**, the major centre of British Nuclear Fuels Ltd. The comprehensive visitor centre has 'hands on' interactive scientific experiments, shows and a welter of technology designed to inform and entertain the whole family. Admission is free. Open every day except Christmas Day, April to October 10.00 to 18.00, November to March 10.00 to 16.00. ☎ 019467 27027. Fax. 019467 27021.

From Sellafield return to the A595

at Calder Bridge. Turn right, then left by the church into a minor road which passes close to the ruins of **Calder Abbey**, which are occasionally open to the public. Back again to the A595 and a left turn to return to Gosforth and Wasdale. Distance – 36km (22.5 miles) from Wasdale Hall.

3) Ennerdale

From Ennerdale the most interesting drive is through part of the former Cumberland iron ore mining area to Whitehaven, returning via St. Bees and Egremont, a distance of only about 35km (22 miles) from Ennerdale Bridge, but packed with features.

From Ennerdale Bridge take the minor road to **Cleator Moor**, a former iron ore mining town. Before the town centre is **St. Mary's Roman Catholic church**, designed by Pugin. The church has a grotto similar to that at Lourdes, built by local people during the depression of the 1930s. Each September there are pilgrimages to the grotto. There is a street market in the square at Cleator Moor every Friday.

Continue along B5295 to **Whitehaven**, a largely Georgian town with the town centre streets set out on a regular rectangular pattern. During the eighteenth century Whitehaven ranked, after London and Bristol, as the third largest port in England. The main export was coal from the highly productive local mines, matched by imports of tobacco and rum from America and the West Indies. George Washington's grandmother was a local resident; she is buried in **St. Nicholas Gardens** and a memorial plaque can be seen in **St. Nicholas Chapel**.

The notorious American sea captain

and privateer, John Paul Jones, raided the town in 1778 during the American War of Independence. The raid was of little consequence but a spiked cannon can still be seen near the old fort. This was the last occasion on which England was 'invaded' from the sea. Today the port activity is much reduced, but the fine **west pier**, built by the great engineer Sir John Rennie can still be admired. The entire harbour has been declared a conservation area and the **Beacon Centre** has been opened as a modern museum telling the story of Whitehaven's social, industrial and maritime heritage. Beyond the harbour a notable landmark is the **'candlestick' chimney**, actually a ventilation shaft for one of the mines. Nearby are other mining relics: the last mine closed as recently as 1986.

As would be expected in a substantial town, there are parks and recreation facilities to suit most tastes. In Roper Street, **Michael Moon's bookshop** has long been a Mecca for book collectors and browsers; there is also a small gallery. Street markets are held on Thursdays and Saturdays. **Tourist Information Centre** – the Old Market Hall, tel. 01946825939. Of the various churches, the most unusual is **St James**, in High Street opposite the top end of Queen Street. This eighteenth century Georgian

Wasdale Head packhorse bridge

structure has a beautiful altar piece by a pupil of Coreggio, a decorated ceiling and interesting windows. Railway service north to Carlisle and south to Barrow in Furness.

From Whitehaven head south along the B5345 **St. Bees** road (Newtown, then Preston Street in the town centre). Most of the village of St. Bees rises along one street, with shops, inns and the odd restaurant. There is, however, a sizeable detached area right by the sea, with some visitor facilities including a cafe. **The priory church of St. Bega** has a fine twelfth century Norman doorway and a wealth of stone relics from the tenth century onwards. St Bega was the daughter of a minor Irish chieftain. In the seventh century she was believed to have crossed the Irish Sea, landed here, become a nun and, after a period at Whitby, founded her own small convent by the shore of Bassenthwaite, on the site of the present St. Bega's church. Railway station.

Immediately to the north of the village a path climbs to the top of **St. Bees Head**, site of an R.S.P.B. nature reserve. Wainwright's 'Coast to Coast' long distance footpath to Robin Hood's Bay starts (or finishes) at St. Bees.

From part way up the main street in St. Bees there is a left turn direct to **Egremont**, a small but historic market town with a ruined **Norman castle** on a hill overlooking the River Ehen. **Lowes Court Gallery** on Main street combines the functions of a gallery, local craft shop and **tourist information centre,** tel. 01946 820693. Opposite are two attractive sculptures commemorating the former iron ore mining of the area. On the third Saturday in September each year the 'Crab Fair' is celebrated. First held in 1267, the fair is based on the giving away to the public of crab apples, originally by the Lord of Egremont. The apples are still given away but the fair now includes a variety of events. Most unusual is the **World Gurning Championship**, in which contestants pull ugly faces through a horse collar. Street market each Friday.

Of the mining industry which, not so long ago, covered this area there is just one working mine remaining. This is the **Florence Mine**, found on a minor road to the east at the south end of the A595 Egremont by-pass.

From Egremont a minor road leaves the by-pass near its northern end, crosses the River Ehen, joins another road just east of Cleator Moor and stays southeast of the river all the way back to Ennerdale Bridge.

4) Buttermere-Cockermouth-Maryport

From Buttermere a drive via Cockermouth to Maryport is recommended; a suitable circuit gives a distance of about 65km (40 miles).

Drive by the side of Crummock Water, then the Vale of Lorton, on the B5289 to **Cockermouth**. Leave Cockermouth by the A594, cross the River Derwent and rise to a large roundabout. Go straight across to drive to **Maryport,** a small town which has grown from mid eighteenth century origins. The development was started by Humphrey Senhouse II, Lord of the Manor at the time. The town which he built was named after his wife, Mary. Once a busy little port, Maryport has shared in the general industrial decline of the area. However, successful efforts

are being made in re-developing parts of the harbour for leisure and tourism. The **Maritime Museum**, at the foot of Senhouse Street, has objects, models and paintings illustrating Maryport's proud maritime tradition.

Back in the town, a short walk to **Fleming Square** will reveal a well restored former market square bounded by Georgian and Victorian houses. Continuing uphill, at the top is a substantial building known as the Battery, once a Royal Naval Reserve Station and now housing the **Senhouse Roman Museum**, noted for its collection of Roman sculpture. Charge.

Adjacent to the Battery is the site of the **Roman fort of Alauna**, an important link in the coastal defensive system which complimented the better-known Hadrian's Wall.

On South Quay, not far from the Maritime Museum, is Maryport Aquaria with more than thirty creative displays revealing the underwater sea life of the Cumbrian coast. The town has a railway service on the line from Whitehaven to Carlisle.

From Maryport a different return to Cockermouth may be made by taking the minor road through Broughton Moor, Great Broughton and Papcastle, joining the A594 on the edge of Cockermouth.

From the centre of Cockermouth take Station Road and continue up to the big roundabout on the by-pass. Go straight across towards Egremont, A5086. In 7km (4.5 miles) turn left to Mockerkin and continue by the side of **Loweswater** to Loweswater hamlet. The B5289 is soon joined; turn sharp right to return to Buttermere.

Places to Visit

Eskdale

Hardknott Fort

Perched high above the valley by the side of the pass of the same name, the remains of this remarkable Roman fort are well worth a visit, not least for the spectacular views down the valley. Its commanding position secured the safety of the road which crossed the mountains at this point, leading from the port of Ravenglass to Galava fort at Waterhead, Ambleside.

Eskdale Mill

Boot, Eskdale, CA19 1TG
☎ 019467 23335
www.eskdalemill.co.uk
Small restored water-powered mill, with small shop, exhibition and picnic area. The Lake District's last working cornmill. Pre 1578 (one of the oldest water powered corn mills in England).
Open daily from 1130–1730. Apr to Sept (Maybe closed Mon & Sat).
♿ ♔♔(Family Ticket) <18 ☂

Ravenglass end Eskdale Railway

Ravenglass, Cumbria, CA18 1SW
☎ 01228 717171
www.ravenglass-railway.co.uk
This much-loved narrow gauge (15 inch) railway was originally opened in 1875, to a broader gauge (3 feet), primarily to carry iron ore down to the sea at Ravenglass. Passenger services were added and there was also traffic in stone from Eskdale quarries. However, a few years later the line was struggling financially, closing in 1913. Conversion to the narrower gauge and re-opening as a tourist attraction in 1914 has, in recent years, proved to be one of Lakeland's most popular features. The line runs for nearly 11km (7 miles) from its base at Ravenglass, where it connects with the coastal railway service, to Dalegarth, close to Boot. There are intermediate stations at Muncaster Mill, Irton Road, The Green and Beckfoot. The full journey lasts for 40 minutes. Although there are diesel locomotives, it is predominantly a steam railway, with a collection of beautifully turned out little engines.

There are services for all but a few winter weeks, although those in winter are minimal and likely to be diesel-hauled other than at weekends. Museum, Ratty Arms Inn and other facilities at Ravenglass. Café and shop at Dalegarth.
Open daily, Mar to Nov, 0900–1700. Weekends, Christmas holidays and Feb Half Term 1000–1600.
● ♿ (Mostly) ♔♔(Family Ticket) <5 Free ☂

Muncaster Castle

Ravenglass, CA18 1RQ
☎ 01229 717614
Email: info@muncaster.co.uk
www.muncaster.co.uk
Castle open from mid-Mar to end-Oct, daily except Sat, 12.30–1600

Places to Visit

(last entry).

Gardens and owl centre are open daily throughout the year, 1100–1700.

Standing on land granted to the Pennington family in 1208, the castle is founded on an ancient defensive pele tower. Still the home of the same family, the castle has a fine site, surrounded by formal and woodland gardens. A replica of the 'Luck of Muncaster', a glass drinking bowl given to the family in 1464 by King Henry VI in gratitude for shelter and hospitality after defeat in battle, is on display. The King declared that as long as the bowl remained intact the Penningtons would live and thrive at Muncaster. The church of St. Michael, with twelfth century nave and fragments of Saxon crosses, is within the castle grounds. Audio tour of castle. Paintings by Gainsborough and Sir Joshua Reynolds. Fine furniture. Children's play area. Plant centre. Nature trail. Cafe/restaurant. Owl Centre ('meet the birds' daily at 14.30 mid-Mar to end of Oct). Gift shops. Programme of special events each season. Charges. Please call to check opening dates and times as may vary.

Ravenglass

An interesting village with hotel, tea shop and many former fishermen's cottages, straggling along one street to the shore of the estuary.

The Ravenglass and Eskdale Railway

Former Roman port. Home of the Ravenglass and Eskdale Railway ('La'al Ratty' in local dialect). 'Walls Castle', the bath-house of a former Roman fort, is less than 1km (0.5 mile) along a track to the south of the village. The surviving stonework is claimed to be the highest genuinely above ground Roman building in England. The railway along the coast was opened by the Whitehaven and Furness Junction Railway in 1849, later becoming part of the Furness Railway. There are still passenger services south to Barrow and north to Whitehaven, Workington and Carlisle.

Wasdale

Sellafield Centre

Seascale, CA20 1PG
☎ 019467 27027
www.sellafieldsites.com
Mon–Fri, 1000–1530. Closed 24 Dec–09 Jan, Bank Holidays and some week days for special events.
ⓟ(Free) ぉ ♔♔(Free) <16 ☂

Ennerdale

In common with the western dales generally, Ennerdale is remote of access and is probably the quietest of all the major Lakeland valleys. There are fine mountains at the head of the valley, notably the dominant Pillar, with its famous climbers' Pillar Rock standing out below the summit. The northern side is bounded by the less spectacular side of the high ridge comprising Red Pike, High Stile and High Crag. The latter is separated by the Scarth Gap Pass (footpath only) from the lower Haystacks, beloved of the late A. Wainwright and resting place of his ashes.

Ennerdale Water

Is a large, attractive, lake, fed by the River Liza, but the valley is probably best known for its forestry plantations, originally dating from the 1930s, when the regular outlines and limited variety of conifer species were severely criticised. In more recent years the Forestry Commission, now Forest Enterprises, has greatly improved the appearance of the commercial forestry and has also become much more visitor friendly, with waymarked forest trails and information boards.

Gosforth Pottery

Hardingill House, Gosforth, CA20 1AH
☎ 019467 25296
www.gosforth-pottery.co.uk
The Gosforth Pottery and shop offers instruction in pot throwing. Open, summer, 10.00–17.30 every day. Winter from 10.00–17.00, Sun, 12.30–17.00, closed Mon. Jan and Feb, closed Mon, Tues and Wed.

Florence Mine Heritage Centre

Egremont, CA22 2RD
☎ 01946 820683

Places to Visit

Email: info@wcmrg.org.uk

www.florencemine.co.uk

Heritage centre at the mine, with facilities for the disabled, souvenir shop, coffee shop.

Open daily from Apr to end-Sept, 1000–1600. Underground tours at 1030–1330 each Sat, Sun and Bank Holiday.

Within the National Park, the only settlement is the small village of Ennerdale Bridge, with inn. Below Ennerdale Bridge the River Ehen wends its short course to the sea at Sellafield, passing through much of the former mining/general industrial area of West Cumberland.

Calder Abbey

Close to the main A595, about 1km (0.6 mile) along a minor road to the east from Calder Bridge. Founded more than 800 years ago, the abbey had a chequered early history, including pillaging by the Scots and a subsequent period of disuse. Later re-occupied, a new church was constructed by 1180, in turn superceded by the construction of a more comprehensive abbey, including a new church, in the thirteenth century. Most of the substantial ruins seen today are of this structure. The site is privately owned and public access is possible only on an occasional basis, although a right of way footpath starting near the church at Calder Bridge does pass quite close to the ruins. Prior enquiry at a tourist information office is recommended.

The Beacon

West Strand, Whitehaven, CA28 7LY

☎ 01946 592302

www.thebeacon-whitehaven.co.uk

Five floors of exhibitions and events. Charge. Shop and Café.

Open daily except Mon (open Bank Holidays) 1000–1630 (last admissions 45 minutes before closing). Closed for 24–26 Dec.

Ⓟ ♿ ⋔ <16 Free ☂

Buttermere, Crummock Water & Loweswater

St. James' Church, Buttermere

Constructed in 1846, this small building is entirely appropriate for its surroundings and purpose. Of particular interest are the wrought iron gate depicting shepherd and sheep and, inside, a tablet by the south window. This tablet is a memorial to the late Alfred Wainwright, Lakeland walker and writer supreme. Through the window the resting place of his ashes, the summit of Haystacks, is visible.

Lake District Coast Aquarium

South Quay, Maryport, CA15 8AB

☎ 01900 817760

www.lakedistrict-coastaquarium.
co.uk
Email: info@ld-coastaquarium.
co.uk
Gift shop. Cafe. Charge.
Open daily, except Christmas Day
and Boxing Day, 1000–1700.
Ⓟ (Pay and Display) ♿ 👪 (Family Ticket)
<4 Free <16 Discount ☂

Senhouse Roman Museum

The Battery, Maryport, CA15 6JO
☎ 01900 816168
www.senhousemuseum.co.uk
Open daily, July to Oct 1000–1700.
Nov to Mar, Fri to Sun, 1030–1600.
Ⓟ (Free) ♿ 👪 (Family Ticket) <18 ☂

Maryport Maritime Museum

1, Senhouse Street, Maryport,
CA15 5AB
Open all year, Mon to Sat, 10–
1600. Free admission. May be of
little interest to children.
☂

Fish Hotel

Buttermere, Cockermouth,
CA13 9XA
☎ 017687 70253
www.fish-hotel.co.uk
Formerly the Fish Inn and home
of Mary Robinson, a celebrated
local beauty later immortalised as
the 'Maid of Buttermere'. Mary was
deceived, seduced and 'married'
in 1802 by Joseph Hatfield, a
remarkable swindler and bigamist
posing as the 'Hon. Alexander
Augustus Hope'. Following his
return from the honeymoon, Hatfield
was apprehended and hanged at
Carlisle in 1803 for forgery. The
romantic story caught the mood
of the nation at the time; even
Wordsworth and DeQuincy were
intrigued and became involved.
Melvyn Bragg's novel The Maid of
Buttermere is firmly based on the
story. Happily, Mary was apparently
none the worse for this experience,
later marrying a farmer and bringing
up a family in Caldbeck, where
her grave may be seen in the
churchyard.

Helena Thompson Museum

Park End Road, Workington, CA14
4DE
☎ 01900 64040 (am only)
☎ 01900 606155
Open daily except Mon, 1330–
1630. May be of little interest to
younger children.
Ⓟ (Free) ♿ (Ground Floor Only) 👪 (Free)
☂

Cockermouth

Cockermouth is a historic market town, with a charter of 1221. The focal point of the medieval town was, inevitably, the castle, originally mid twelfth century, sited close to the meeting point of the **Derwent** and **Cocker** rivers. Most of today's ruins, not open to the public, date from 1360 to 1370. Even earlier in history is the site of a Roman fort, **Derventio**, at **Papcastle** to the north-west of the present town.

The Main Street is wide, tree-lined and quite handsome and, together with Station Street (there is no longer a railway), is well provided with shops, inns and other refreshment places. The street market is held on Mondays.

At one end of Main Street is Wordsworth House, a well-proportioned Georgian house of 1745, with some eighteenth century furnishings, now in the ownership of the National Trust. William Wordsworth was born here in 1770, leaving on the death of his mother in 1778. Across the road is a bust of William.

The impressive statue in the middle of Main Street is the Earl of Mayo, local Member of Parliament in the mid nineteenth century, then Viceroy of India until his unfortunate assassination in the Andaman Islands in 1872.

All Saints church was rebuilt in 1852-54 following a disastrous fire. Wordsworth attended the previous church and his father, John, is buried in the churchyard. There is a memorial window to the great poet. Close to the church is a former grammar school; among its pupils was, inevitably, Wordsworth and also Fletcher Christian, of *Mutiny on the Bounty* fame.

At no. 7, Market Place, in a niche in the wall, is the 'butter bell' which for many years was rung to signal the start of the weekly market. Behind the market area is the site of the former Fletcher Old Hall, now used for car parking. Here, on 17th May, 1568, the wealthy local merchant Henry Fletcher received Mary Queen of Scots and a handful of followers as they fled from defeat in Scotland. According to legend, Fletcher provided Mary with material to replace her tattered clothing. There is a plaque on the site.

Kirkgate is a narrow turning to the right from St. Helen's Street, close to the Market Place. The narrow street soon opens out into a surprisingly attractive area of small but gracious houses with horse chestnut trees and a cobbled forecourt. The Bitter End Inn claims to be Cumbria's smallest brewery

A little way from the town centre, to the left of Station Road as it climbs towards the by-pass, is Harris Park. Here a little statue commemorates the childhood of William and Dorothy Wordsworth.

Events

Cockermouth Show

Early August. Small local agricultural show. ☎ 01900 822634

Bassenthwaite

Not the most spectacular in Lakeland but nevertheless a fine large sheet of water with the distinction of being the only true 'lake' in the district actually called Lake (all the others use the word 'water' or 'mere'. Despite the rather intrusive presence of the main A66, Penrith, Keswick, Cockermouth and west coast road along the western shore, Bassenthwaite is maintained as one of the more quiet lakes, with emphasis on wildlife, particularly waterfowl. It is best appreciated from the quieter eastern side, where the Keswick to Carlisle road, A591 keeps well away from the lake and the tiny but historic and evocative church of St. Bega stands lonely by the shore.

Walks

1) Mirehouse and St. Bega's Church

A fairly level walk on good tracks, including both woodland and more open country close to Bassenthwaite Lake. 5.25km. (3.25 miles).

Start at the Forest Enterprises car park by the Old Sawmill cafe, across the road from the Mirehouse entrance.

Walk past the cafe, bearing right to a footbridge over Skill Beck. Turn sharp left after the bridge following blue and yellow waymarks for a short distance, then go uphill to join a surfaced roadway.

Turn right then, in a few metres, turn left to take a forest track which rises steadily, with Ullock Pike above. There are occasional glimpses of the lake as height is gained.

Join another track and bear left.

The way here is level but it soon rises again.

After narrowing and beginning to descend, Sandbeds Gill is crossed. Continue downhill on a broad track; keep left at a fork and head for the Ravenstone Hotel, in view ahead. Join the road and turn right, pass the hotel and Ravenstone Lodge, and turn left immediately after the Lodge at a 'public footpath' signpost in the hedge.

Go through a gate/stile and cross a meadow on a lightly worn path to a kissing gate.

Cross the next field towards a group of trees and bear left to a tiny stream and a stile over a fence. The path is now obvious among oak trees, going through more kissing gates to reach an electricity sub station.

Cross a minor road to a gate/stile and follow the 'St. Bega's Church' sign along a farm track. A gentle descent along the edge of Highfield Wood leads directly to the church and the modern cross. Continue from the church by returning for 50 metres, then turning right immediately before a stream to follow the line of the stream and an avenue of great oaks towards Mirehouse.

Go through metal gates and keep to the designated footpath through the grounds. Turn right by some outbuildings to take a gravelled driveway, reaching the public road by a gate to the right of a roadside house. Turn left for 40 metres and cross the road to return to the car park.

2) Barf

A middling height mountain of 513m. (1,536ft.) which rises steeply above the shore of Bassenthwaite Lake on its western side, providing a wonderful viewpoint over the lake to mighty Skiddaw. Apart from one short rocky section, the path is good but the ascent is unremittingly steep. Three kilometres (2 miles) up and down. The ascent of Barf may be extended by continuing over **Lord's Seat**, 552m. (1,811ft.) and returning through the Whinlatter forested area, a circuit of 12km. (7.5 miles).

Close to the route is the '**Bishop of Barf**', a white painted large rock which marks the spot at which an Irish bishop is said to have died. The bishop, possibly for a wager and possibly after drinking unwisely, was attempting to ride his horse directly up the mountainside. Not surprisingly, the animal fell, killing itself and rider. Re-painting of the rock is traditionally carried out by the landlord of the nearby inn.

From the car park at Powter How, on the minor road less than one mile north of Thornthwaite, cross the road and turn left. Very shortly fork right, then right again to follow an obvious path, soon rising by the side of Beckstones Gill.

The path climbs steeply throughout and there is one rocky section to be negotiated. Most of the ascent is in woodland. Near the top of the valley bear right across open land to reach the summit of Barf and enjoy the reward for all the hard work.

If a longer walk is required, continue along the path which heads to Lord's Seat 552m. (1,811ft.) in approximately one kilometre. Stay with the path after Lord's Seat; route finding becomes more complicated as the forestry land is entered and there are many forest trails. Additionally, felling and re-planting of trees quickly outdates the Ordnance Survey maps. A plan of the forest, available at the Whinlatter Visitor Centre, is very helpful. The route is broadly to the west, bending south west after

Looking out over Derwentwater towards Cat Bells (left), with Grisedale Pike beyond

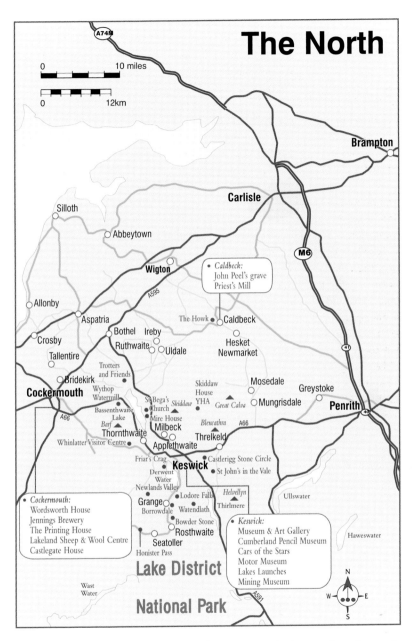

one kilometre. Darling How farm is passed, well to the left hand, before the road is reached, close to the top of the Whinlatter Pass.

Turn right, along the road. In about 1.5km (1 mile), by an informal car park, fork right to use a forest track parallel to the road for almost 2km (1.25 mile). As this track bends away to the right, turn left to descend by a minor footpath to rejoin the road. Turn right to walk to the visitor centre.

Leave the centre on a forest trail descending gently towards Thornthwaite. Look out carefully for a bridleway descending to cross Comb Gill. Join another forest trail which follows round the contours to pass above Thornthwaite village. This trail becomes a minor roadway, staying roughly parallel with the public road and rejoining the outward route close to the car park

Cycle Rides

1) Circular ride to Maryport

From bases in Cockermouth and the Bassenthwaite area destinations on the west coast can easily be reached. A good example is the following 32km. (20 mile) circular ride to **Maryport**, also visiting several of the more interesting villages.

From Cockermouth head west along **Brigham** Road through a residential area, to the main A66, crossing almost directly into a minor road to Brigham or head straight up to the main road and turn right for one kilometre to reach the Brigham road on the left. Turn right in Brigham to head for the main road. Turn left, then right in a short distance, cross the River Derwent, and reach the large village of **Great Broughton**. Proceed through Broughton Moor to Maryport.

Leave Maryport on the A596, Carlisle, road, forking left on the B5300 in 1.5km. This road is part of the Cumbria Cycle Way. Turn right in 3km. to **Crosscanonby** where the church is Norman, with Roman stones built into the walls. There are also pre-Norman memorial

stones, including a hogback gravestone. Rejoin the main road at Crosby, turning left At Crosby Villa leave the main road by turning right, to **Greengill, Tallentire and Bridekirk,** where the ruined chancel of a Norman church stands close to its replacement. The new church has two Norman doorways from its predecessor, a fragment of a Roman altar and a very finely carved font, probably of the twelfth century.

From Bridekirk head south to the A595 and turn right to reach to the large roundabout just outside Cockermouth. Turn left here to return to the town.

From a start at Bassenthwaite, add a few kilometres to the overall distance of the ride; use minor roads either to the north or the south of the A66, as appropriate.

2) A circuit visiting Loweswater

Extendable to Crummock and Buttermere if desired. Basic route 30km. (19 miles).

Leave Cockermouth by the B5292, Lorton Road, passing under the bypass, and continue along the beautiful **Vale of Lorton**. At Low Lorton turn right to take the very minor road through Thackthwaite hamlet, heading for Loweswater hamlet, with inn and church.

Bear right to cycle along the edge of Loweswater, prettily set beneath Holme Wood.

Unless a steep climbing road over Mosser Fell, on the right, appeals, go on to Mockerkin. Turn right for Pardshaw and Pardshaw Hall. Keep right then left to Brandlingill. Fork left here to reach a 'T' junction. A left turn now reaches the main A 5086, with a right turn back to Cockermouth or a right turn, then a left turn, crosses the R. Cocker and rejoins the outward route, with a left turn back to base.

From a start in Bassenthwaite use the minor road through Wythop Mill, to the south of the A66 to reach Lorton Vale, or, from the southern and of the lake, ride over the **Whinlatter Pass** to High Lorton and Low Lorton, joining the main route at the latter.

Extension of the ride to Crummock and Buttermere is achieved by keeping to the B5289 along the Vale of Lorton.

3) Caldbeck

A ride through some lesser known but still beautiful Lakeland countryside to the northern outpost of **Caldbeck** Approx. 40km. (25 miles).

Take the minor road which leaves Cockermouth to the east, St. Helen's Street/St. Helen's Road, keeping left at a fork just out of town, then climbing past Setmurthy Common before descending to Higham Hall. Keep left to Ouse Bridge, where the R. Derwent leaves Bassenthwaite Lake and continue to the road junction by the Castle Inn.

Go almost straight across and climb below the mound of Binsey before descending to **Uldale**. After an initial climb from the village, the road becomes unfenced, crossing Aughertree Fell on its way to join the B5299 and reach Caldbeck. **Hesket Newmarket** is another good village just over 2km (1.25 miles). further along the road.

The return can be varied in several ways. A right fork from the B5299, followed by a left turn, leads to **Ireby,** a former small town which is now nothing more than a large village. From Ireby head south through **Ruthwaite**, home of the huntsman John Peel, immortalised in the famous song, then keep right at a junction to reach the A591 at Bewaldeth.

Go straight across to take the road to **Iselgate**. St. Michael's church, Norman and with many interesting features, is nearby. Turn left to cross the R. Derwent, then right to pass Hewthwaite Hall and return to Cockermouth.

4) Modified circuits

Circuits recommended in West Section, chapter two, can be modified to start from Cockermouth.

Keswick

The focal point of this chapter is **Keswick**, 'Queen of the Lakes', a very popular small market town beautifully situated between the foot of Derwentwater and the soaring height of Skiddaw.

The oldest part of the town, at **Great Crosthwaite**, is now off-centre. Here, the splendid church is dedicated to St. Kentigern (or Mungo) who was active in Cumbria in the sixth century, when there could well have been a first church on this site. His symbols – tree, bell, fish and bird – are displayed in the churchyard entrance gate. Today's structure is mostly fifteenth century, with just a little Norman work remaining from a church of 1181. Large scale restoration in 1844 has fortunately left a dignified and spacious church.

Inside is a well-carved fourteenth century font and a striking white marble memorial to the great poet **Robert Southey**, a native of Keswick for many years. The epitaph was written by William Wordsworth, his successor as Poet Laureate. The legendary **Canon Rawnsley,** one of the three founders of the National Trust, is buried in the churchyard.

As the centre of a great sheep farming area, Keswick became a notable wool town for several centuries, part of the widespread domains of Fountains Abbey.

From the sixteenth century industry also came to Keswick. Queen Elizabeth I founded the Company of Mines Royal and experienced German miners opened up the Goldscope Mine in the Vale of Newlands, with rich deposits of copper. Other mines followed and furnaces were built at Keswick. Later, graphite was discovered near Seathwaite, in Borrowdale. This valuable mineral had a variety of uses, eventually becoming the foundation of the world's first pencil industry. Mining activity ebbed and flowed until early in the twentieth century.

In the second half of the eighteenth century Keswick became the Lake District's first tourist destination, visited by most of the early travellers of the 'Romantic' period, such as John Dalton, John Brown and Thomas Gray

Grange in Borrowdale

(of *Elegy* fame). Fortunately, several of these travellers set down their impressions of the district, which now make fascinating reading.

Not far behind in discovering the beauty of the Keswick area were the first '**Lakeland Poets**', Coleridge, Southey, Shelley; Wordsworth was a frequent visitor from Grasmere.

The great and the famous were followed by lesser mortals in considerable numbers after the branch line from the main railway line at Penrith was opened to Keswick in 1865. The town's role as a holiday destination had begun in earnest. Sadly, the railway closed in 1972 but Keswick's popularity has in no way diminished.

The present town centre is mainly of nineteenth century buildings, not particularly distinguished, but with a pleasant bustle around the Market Place, where the prominent Moot Hall of 1813 now houses the tourist information office. Plentiful hotels, inns, shops and restaurants all contribute to the holiday atmosphere. **Derwentwater** is Keswick's own lake, truly beautiful, and normally so tranquil that nearby mountains such as Cat Bells are mirrored in the water.

The road into the Borrowdale valley skirts the eastern shore, with parking and picnic areas, whilst the Grange in Borrowdale to Portinscale road on the west side provides gallery-like viewpoints over lake and town. At the Keswick end of the lake are extensive boat landings, beyond a huge car park and the Theatre by the Lake. A little way further along this shore is **Friar's Crag**, a viewpoint beloved of John Ruskin, from which the mountains

Watendlath

Ashness Fell from Ashness Bridge

along the sides and at the head of Borrowdale, seen across the water, are truly picturesque. Close to Friar's Crag are a memorial tablet to Canon Rawnsley and a John Ruskin memorial stone.

The lake has four islands, all owned by the National Trust. Of these, the seven acre **Derwent Island** is inhabited. In the sixteenth century it was the home of some of the German miners employed locally. They cleared the dense tree growth and constructed a range of domestic buildings. After their departure the island changed hands several times. One notable late eighteenth century owner was Joseph Pocklington, who built a large house and a miscellany of other structures including a mock church, a boathouse in the style of a Gothic chapel, a pseudo Druid circle and a small fort. The porter's lodge was also fortified and was used in

A jetty on Derwentwater

the 'naval battle' annual regattas which Pocklington organised from 1787. Understandably, Wordsworth ridiculed Pocklington's excesses. The island was later purchased by the Marshall family, Leeds based industrialists, who acquired several estates in Lakeland. The house was much altered and, with diversified tree planting, the effect is now much more tasteful. The family gave the island to the National Trust in 1951; it is now tenanted. In recent years, with the tenant's co-operation, the Trust has organised a limited number of visits to the island, including entry to parts of the house.

St. Herbert's Island is believed to have been the home of a religious hermit, possibly as early as the sixth century.

Borrowdale

From Keswick and Derwentwater the Borrowdale valley penetrates to the very heart of Lakeland, with dramatic mountain scenery all the way contrasting with the woodland, water and green fields, to give Borrowdale its high scenic attraction and its popularity among the favourite valleys of Lakeland.

In travelling from Keswick, the first village reached is **Grange in Borrowdale**, with its fine double bridge over the R. Derwent. A little further are the **Lodore Falls**, close to the Lodore Hotel, where the Watendlath Beck tumbles abruptly down the precipitous valley side.

Three kilometres (two miles) above the head of the lake, the valley sides squeeze the road and the river tightly together for some distance in the '**Jaws**

of Borrowdale', a very scenic part of the valley, with Castle Crag trying to make up for its lack of real height 299m. (980 feet) with its aggressively steep upthrust. Fairly close to the roadside, the '**Bowder Stone**', a huge detached boulder 9m. (30ft.) high and weighing 1,900 tons, has been an object of awe and wonderment since the arrival of the first travellers. In those far off days sensitive souls were known to have drawn tight the curtains of their carriage windows when passing through this savage and frightening scenery. There is now a ladder to the top of the stone.

After the 'jaws', the valley opens out to an area with a few riverside fields, which have been subject to serious flooding from time to time. Here, centuries ago, the 'Kings of Borrowdale' reigned supreme over their tiny domain. **Rosthwaite**, with inn and post/office stores is the largest settlement, with other hamlets at **Stonethwaite**, just off the main road, **Longthwaite**, with the youth hostel, and **Seatoller**, with tourist information and restaurant, the terminus of the valley bus service. The farmstead of **Seathwaite** provides the end of the road car parking for those heading on foot to Styhead Tarn, Great Gable, and/or Scafell. Seathwaite is also the proud possessor of the gauge which consistently records the maximum rainfall in England – about 365cm. (144 inches) per annum.

As the valley head is approached, it seems to be impossible for the road to be anything but a cul de sac, petering out at the foot of uncompromisingly steep and high mountains. But this is not so; a turn to the right, through

Seatoller, exposes a gap between Honister Crag and Dale Head which allows a vehicular escape over the **Honister Pass** 356m (1,176 feet) in height to Buttermere. Despite 25 per cent gradients this is not a difficult pass to drive. At the top of the pass part of the formerly extensive quarrying area has been opened as a visitor attraction – The **Honiter Slate Mine**, open all year apart from Christmas and early January, offering underground tours (reservation only) at 10.30, 12.30 and 15.30. ☎ 017687 77230.

Situated at the end of a cul de sac road in a side valley is **Watendlath**, a tiny farming hamlet prettily set beside its tarn among the mountains. There is a strong literary association with Hugh Walpole's *Rogue Herries* novels, which have a firm base in Borrowdale; his heroine Judith Paris lived in Watendlath. The little road climbs steeply from the side of Derwentwater, passing a famous 'surprise view' and traversing Ashness Bridge, probably the most photographed in Lakeland.

Threlkeld

A pleasant but rather workaday large village a few kilometres to the east of Keswick, along the main A66, Penrith, road, superbly situated at the foot of Blencathra (Saddleback). The village has inns (one of the seventeenth century), and a post office/store.

St. John's in the Vale

An attractive farming valley with a minor road (B5322) leaving the A66 near to Threlkeld and connecting with the A591 Windermere to Keswick road at Legburthwaite hamlet, which

has a small chapel. To the east of the valley, Clough Head and Great Dodd are heights at the northern end of the long Helvellyn ridge. Castle Crag, near Legburthwaite, has long been esteemed as a 'romantic' scenic feature. The much lower hills of High Rigg and Low Rigg form the western boundary of the valley, with a very minor cul de sac road climbing between them to the church of St. John's in the Vale, an 1845 rebuild of a much earlier church, strong on scenic location but weak on likely congregation.

Further south, near Sosgill Farm, St John's Beck is crossed by Sosgill Bridge, an old packhorse bridge.

Thirlmere

For more than 100 years Thirlmere has been a major supplier of water to Manchester. The former Manchester Corporation dammed the lake at its northern end, raising the level by about 15m. (50 feet) and constructed a pipeline all the way to Manchester. Part of a hamlet at Wythburn, including an inn patronised by Wordsworth, was demolished and submerged. At the same time, for water quality reasons, vast numbers of regimented coniferous trees were planted and the public was excluded from as much of the catchment area as could be contrived. In short, Thirlmere and its valley for many years constituted a sad hole in the heart of the district; a place to travel through along the main Windermere to Keswick road rather than to linger and enjoy.

Fortunately, more enlightened attitudes now prevail and the successor water authority and company have diversified some of the tree planting,

Derwentwater, Nichols End

opened up footpaths along the valley sides and provided access points to the lake, with car parking. At the south end, the simple little church at Wythburn survived the raising of the water level and can readily be visited; there is a car park behind.

Scenically, the valley is dominated by Helvellyn, third highest of the Lakeland mountains.

Vale of Newlands

Despite its proximity to Keswick, Newlands is one of Lakeland's quieter valleys, much less visited than its neighbour, Borrowdale. This comparative neglect has nothing to do with the quality of the scenery. Cat Bells and its ridge, Dale Head, Hindscarth and Robinson, and the grouping of Causey Pike, Sail and Grizedale Pike form a superb mountain arena, whilst the valley itself has bright green meadows spread around centuries old farming hamlets of weathered stone. The lack of a lake or other particular focal point is probably most significant.

There is only one road of significance in the valley, climbing high on the

Castlerigg ancient stone circle near Keswick

Keswick

western flank to Newlands Hause 333m (1,093ft.) before descending steeply to Buttermere

Newlands church is tiny, charming and well-kept. At one end of the building was the former school room.

Events

Keswick Jazz Festival

Mid May.

Lorton Sheep Dog Trials and Hound Show

Late July.

Walks

The Keswick and Borrowdale area has a tremendous variety of walks, both mountain and lowland, including some of the best in Lakeland. The following suggestion are just a small sample of what is available.

1) Skiddaw

At 931m. (3,053ft.) England's fourth highest mountain, Skiddaw soars above Keswick, its triangular shape being distinctive from most angles. From Keswick area it is the obvious challenge for those who want to climb a high mountain which is near at hand. The standard route is not difficult or exciting, just a long steady plod but with the compensation of the magnificent views over Derwentwater and along Borrowdale. 17.5km. (11 miles). By using the car park at the end of Gale Road, above Applethwaite, the ascent is considerably reduced and the out and back distance is only 10km. (6.2 miles).

Leave Keswick by the Cumbria Way footpath, with its bridge over the bypass road. Skirt around the flanks of Latrigg, partly in woodland, rising to the car park at the top of the cul de sac road. From here the 'Jenkin Hill' route, broad and well-used, wends its way, climbing behind the summit of Little Man to reach the top of the mountain.

Return can be made by the same way but there are options. The designated 'Allerdale Ramble' descends over Carl

135

Side, a subsidiary summit. Half a kilometre after Carl Side this path forks; left is direct to **Millbeck** hamlet, whilst right heads for the forest before a sharp left turn reaches the minor road just west of Millbeck.

In either case, from Millbeck take the footpath parallel to the minor road, on its south side, to Applethwaite, then turn right to follow the 'Allerdale Ramble' back to Keswick. To return to the high car park, rejoin the road at **Applethwaite** and fork left by the hotel to walk up the lane for about 1.5km. (1 mile).

2) Cat Bells

Another great Keswick favourite. The shapely peak rises above Derwentwater to a height of 451m. (1,490ft.).
Quite steep in places, but easy underfoot, with well-used footpaths. Beautiful circuit of almost 6km. (3.75 miles).

From the small car park by the side of the Portinscale to Grange in Borrowdale road, a well-marked path starts the ascent of the long northern ridge of Catbells. No route finding is necessary; just follow the path up the ridge for nearly 2km. (a little more than one mile).

From the summit continue along the ridge to a depression and a meeting place of paths. Turn left here, downhill. Most of the way down, at a major junction turn sharp left, towards Keswick. A lovely path, with gallery-like views over Derwentwater and Keswick to Skiddaw, goes straight back to the car park.

3) Derwentwater Shore

The timetabled service provides several opportunities for lake shore walks with a return to Keswick or other starting place by the use of the launch, a most enjoyable combination. The following walk starts at the major car park close to the boat landings area in Keswick. Virtually level and easy underfoot apart from one section of stony ground along the lake shore. 3.5km. (2.25 miles).

From the car park, turn left along the road to the boat landings. Continue along the shore, passing the memorial tablet to Canon Rawnsley. The island close on the right is **Derwent Isle**. The celebrated **Friar's Crag** viewpoint is soon reached; close by is the John Ruskin memorial stone. From Friar's Crag back track a short distance and bear right down a flight of steps to follow the lake shore around Strandshag Bay. Continue along the edge of marshy woodland, over a footbridge and through a gate at the far end of the wood. Turn right.

Lord's Island is now close as the track heads for Calf Close Bay, with Rampsholme as the next island. The path is squeezed between the lake and the Borrowdale road, with some up and down which can be avoided by walking over the stones of the lake shore. Ashness Gate jetty follows this section. The anti-clockwise launch provides a short sail back to Keswick.

To extend this all too short walk, continue along the shore of Barrow Bay to the Kettlewell car park. Cross the road and take the broad track opposite, through Strutta Wood, avoiding nearly 1km. of road walking. On re-joining the road, cross over to a roadway leading directly to the Lodore jetty. Alternatively catch the bus back to Keswick. This extension adds just over 1.5km.

(1 mile) to the distance.

For a longer walk still, the lake shore path can be followed round the head of the lake, to High Brandlehow landing stage, or beyond.

4) Borrowdale

There are many lovely walks by the side of the R. Derwent. The bus service facilitates a linear walk which is appropriate to a long, narrow, valley.

The following suggestion is almost level and is generally good underfoot. 4km. (2.5 miles).

There is a small amount of parking space at **Grange in Borrowdale**, close by the river, with a superb picnic spot to hand. Walk into the village and turn left at a signposted bridleway to Rosthwaite. There is another small car parking area along this bridleway. Shortly after passing the National Trust Hollows Farm sign, turn left to follow a gently rising stony track. Keep left, towards the river, after passing a camping site.

At a 'footpath to Rosthwaite' sign keep left. A stony section of path climbs before reaching a gap in a wall. Turn left again and continue through woodland to yet another left turn just over the crest of the rise, heading downhill to a cairn. At a quarry spoil heap on the right, a short diversion uphill leads to a rock face with interesting mineral colouration and a large rock arch.

Cross the R. Derwent on a stone bridge or, if the water level is not too high, continue for a further 300m. and cross by stepping stones, more fun than the bridge. In either case, a lane leads directly to **Rosthwaite**. The return bus service is not very frequent.

5) Blencathra (Saddleback)

A fine and very distinctive mountain when viewed from anywhere to the south, east or west, rising steeply above **Threlkeld** village to its height of 868m. (2,849ft.). There are many routes of ascent, including the celebrated Sharp Edge; the following is recommended for those who enjoy a little, safe, scrambling.

Park in the village car park, Blease Road, Threlkeld.

Go uphill from the car park, forking right at once to take a good track by the side of a stream. In about one third of a kilometre turn right and walk across to Gategill. Turn left and commence the climb of the Hall's Fell ridge on an obvious track. Gate Gill, below to the left, has a waterfall and the remains of lead mining. No route finding is necessary; the higher part of the ridge has some steep rock but there is no danger for the average walker.

The ridge has the great advantage of heading straight for the highest point of the great plateau which is the summit of Blencathra.

Turn left and walk along the edge of the plateau towards the Blease Fell end of the mountain. The well-used path slants downhill towards the Blencathra Centre but, to return to Threlkeld, look out for a left turn, more than half way down, aiming towards Blease Farm and the top of the stream-side path along which the walk started. Turn right to return to the car park along this path.

Cycle Rides

1) Circuit of Derwentwater

A very easy ride of only 16km.(10

Boat jetty leading into Derwentwater

miles), with possible extension along the delightful Borrowdale Valley (see above). Wonderful views and lakeside picnic spots.

From Keswick head south along the B5289, Borrowdale, road. After passing the far end of Derwentwater, turn right over the double bridge into **Grange in Borrowdale**, where refreshments are available. Bear right to follow the minor road towards Portinscale, with elevated views over lake and town to Skiddaw and Blencathra.

Weave through **Portinscale** to the main A66 road and turn right to return to Keswick.

2) Circumnavigating Skiddaw and Blencathra

A longer and more demanding ride of 48km. (30 miles).

Leave Keswick by the A591 Carlisle road, passing **Mirehouse**. At High Side fork right to take a very minor road which rises and falls around the edge of Skiddaw, passes Orthwaite, and joins a more important road on Aughertree

Fell Turn right, join the B5299, and continue to **Caldbeck**.

Keep right to ride to **Hesket Newmarket**. Head south on a minor road, keeping as close to the mountains (High Pike and Carrock Fell) as possible. This is another hilly road, largely unfenced, heading for **Mosedale**, followed by **Mungrisedale**. The latter village has an inn.

Turn right in less than 1km. to head for **Scales** along the base of Souther Fell. At the main A66 road turn right to return to Keswick.

Caldbeck

The area north of the Skiddaw and Blencathra mountain groups is without doubt the most quiet and remote part of the Lake District, although it is just within the boundary of the national park.

Autumn Colours by Thirlmere

As the mountains diminish progressively towards the Solway Plain, sheep farming dominates and there are only two settlements which are of general interest to visitors. Even these villages attract only a small fraction of the attention which is given to, say, Grasmere or Elterwater.

Caldbeck is the main centre of this spacious area, sitting attractively in a shallow valley, with village green and duckpond. From the thirteenth century the nearby hills have yielded a variety of minerals in commercial quantities; wolfram and barytes were mined until the early 1960s. In Elizabethan times the imported German miners re-opened several mines which were already old.

Closer to the village, woollen, paper, corn and bobbin mills all made use of the water power available from the Cald Beck and its tributaries.

Today, Caldbeck is best known as the resting place of John Peel, the relentless huntsman who ran a pack of hounds for more than 50 years. Peel became famous because the words strung together by a close friend and applied to a local tune or 'rant' were later set to a better tune by the conductor of the Carlisle Choral Society. Despite the dubious literary and musical merit, this refrain has ensured immortality for a man whose sole achievement in life was to pursue foxes a little harder and, presumably, more successfully than most of his fellow huntsmen.

The story of Mary, Maid of Buttermere is set out on p133. After the heady excitement and fame of her youth Mary, apparently none the worse for her experience with 'Hon. Augustus Hope', spent the remainder of her life in Caldbeck as a farmer's wife and a mother. She is buried quite close to John Peel.

From a total of six at the time of peak activity, one inn remains, together with a post office/store/petrol station.

Hesket Newmarket

Now just a peaceful, unspoilt, village, with inn, shop, market cross and bull ring, Hesket Newmarket did have ambitions 200 years ago. A market charter was granted in the mid eighteenth century and for about 100 years a market was held. Although a fair amount of trade was generated, this extended role was never entirely successful and Hesket reverted to its previous status as a quiet village.

Events

Hesket Newmarket show
Traditional local agricultural show. Late August. ☎ 017687 72803

Walk

1) The Howk
Very short and easy. A gentle stroll of only 2km. (1.25 miles) to a celebrated glen-like wooded gorge which was Caldbeck's concentrated water mill area. Some parts of the track can be muddy and there are steps which need care.

From the village centre car park head for the green. Turn left, then left again. In a short distance turn right at a sign 'The Howk' to pass between farm buildings.

The way ahead is now straightforward, with the beck cut deep into the limestone, rushing over falls and rapids

Places to Visit

Cockermouth

Wythop Water Mill and Woodworking Museum

Wythop, Embleton, nr Cockermouth
☎ 017687 76394
Open from Good Fri to end-Oct, daily except Mon, 1030–1730.

Wordsworth House (NT)

Main Street, Cockermouth, CA13 9RX
☎ 01900 820 884 (Infoline)
☎ 07900 824 805 (Office)
www.wordsworthhouse.org.uk
Childhood home of William and Dorothy. Eighteenth century furnishings. Garden and terrace. Restaurant. Discounted combined tickets with Dove Cottage and Rydal Mount are available.
Open from late Mar to end-Oct, Mon to Sat, 1100–1700.
Ⓟ(Nearby)　🚻　☂

Jennings Brewery

Castle Brewery, Cockermouth, CA13 9NE
☎ 0845 1297 190
Long established brewery at foot of castle mound.
Open Mon to Fri, 0900–1700, Sat 10.00–16.00, Sun 1000–1600 (Jul & Aug only). Gift shop. Admission charge. Group bookings are invited. May not be suitable for younger children.
Ⓟ(Disabled Only)　♿(Ground Floor Only)
🚻<12　☂

Castlegate House

Cockermouth, CA13 9HA
☎ 01900 822149
www.castlegatehouse.co.uk
Opposite the entrance to the castle. Listed Georgian house and garden of 1739. Original paintings, ceramics, sculpture and glass. Private home, with public access. Programme available on request.

Lakeland Sheep and Wool Centre

Cockermouth, CA13 0QX
☎ 01900 822673
www.sheep-woolcentre.co.uk

---

past the remains of a bobbin mill, where a huge water wheel once powered the machinery.

Go a little further up the valley, cross the beck on a bridge, and turn left to pass through woodland and across fields to the B5299 road. Turn left to return to Caldbeck.

Cycle Rides

1) Skiddaw & Blencathra

Use the route set out in north section, chapter 2, but start from **Caldbeck**.

2) Carlisle

An easy ride, fairly level apart from the beginning and end, of a little more than 40km. (25 miles) largely across the Solway Plain, visiting Cumbria's historic border city. Carlisle's many features are listed in north section motor tours.

Leave Caldbeck to the north by the B5299. Go straight on at a cross-roads as the main road turns right. In less than

By the roundabout on the A66 on the edge of town. Exhibition based on live sheep of many different breeds, including shearing and sheepdog displays four times each day. Restaurant. Gift shop. Disabled access. Admission charge. The centre includes overnight accomodation.
Open daily 0930–1730. Shows Sun–Thur.
ⓟ & ᵐ <16 ☂

Cockermouth Golf Club

Embleton, Cockermouth, CA13 9SG
☎ 017687 76223
www.cockermouthgolf.co.uk

Cockermouth Sports Centre and Swimming Pool

☎ 01900 823596

Percy House Gallery

38-42 Market Place, Cockermouth
☎ 01900 829667
www.percyhouse.co.uk
Open all year.

Keswick

Cumberland Pencil Museum

Southey Works, Greta Bridge, Keswick
☎ 017687 73626
www.pencils.co.uk
'Home of the world's first pencils'. Easy to find by the side of Main Street, close to the bank of the River Greta. Historical displays. Video shows and audio tours. Children's activities. Gift shop. Admission charge.
Open daily except Christmas Day, Boxing Day and New Year's Day, 0930–1600 (last admission).

Keswick Museum & Art Gallery

Station Road, Keswick
☎ 017687 73263
Fascinating local history and curio collection, including a scale model of the Lake District, made in 1834. Original manuscripts and memorabilia from the Lakes Poets in 'poets corner'. Admission charge.
Open daily from Good Fri to end of

1km. turn right

Go right then left to cross the B5305 and head for Thursby, turning right at a 'T' junction 2km. before reaching the village. Join the A595 and turn right along this former Roman road to Carlisle.

Leave Carlisle by the same main road, but fork left on the B5299 to Dalston. With a few twists and turns and a climb over Warnell Fell the same road continues all the way to Caldbeck.

3) Maryport and vicinity

70km. (43 miles) approx. Ride via Uldale to Cockermouth and link in to route described in north section. A return direct to Caldbeck can be made by way of Crosby Villa, Gilcrux, Bothel, Torpenhow (St. Michael's church, in a lovely situation, is almost entirely Norman in character, with a decorated Jacobean ceiling) and Ireby.

4) Penrith and Greystoke

Reverse the route set out in east section, to start at Caldbeck.

Places to Visit

Oct, 1000–1600.

Keswick Cars of the Stars Motor Museum

Standish Street, Keswick, CA12 5LS
☎ 017687 73757
www.carsofthestars.com
Celebrity television and film vehicles.
Admission charge.
Open daily from pre-Easter to end-Nov, including Feb half term holiday and at weekends in Dec, 1000–1700.
Ⓟ(Nearby Pay & Display) ♿ ♨ <16 ☂

Puzzling Place

Museum Square, Keswick, CA12 5DZ
☎ 017687 75102
Email: info@puzzlingplace.co.uk
www.puzzlingplace.co.uk
Optical illusions.
Open daily, 10am–6pm.

Hope Park

Lake Road
Attractive gardens, pitch and putt, putting and obstacle golf. Games open from late-Mar to early-Nov.

Fitz Park

Station Road
Spacious recreation area. Bowls, tennis and putting. Children's playground. Games open from May to Sept.

Keswick Golf Club

Threlkeld Hall, Threlkeld, CA12 4SX
☎ 017687 79010
www.keswickgolfclub.com
Visitors welcome.

Keswick Leisure Pool

Station Road, CA12 4NF
☎ 017687 72760
Pool with wave machine and water slide. Cafe, sunbed and beach area. Disabled facilities. Open daily (closed Mon and Tues afternoons in winter).

Theatre by the Lake

Lakeside, Keswick, CA12 5DJ
☎ 017687 74411
www.theatrebythelake.co.uk
Beautifully sited modern theatre, with main auditorium and smaller studio. Usually three plays each, in repertory throughout the season plus many extra productions and musical events. Special children'sevents at Christmas. Café and bar. Adjacent to huge car park.

Alhambra Cinema

St. John's Street
☎ 017687 72195
www.keswick-alhambra.co.uk
Traditional cinema open from Feb to Nov.

Keswick on Derwentwater Launch Co. Ltd

Manor Park, Keswick, Cumbria, CA12 5AB
☎ 017687 72263
Email: info@keswick-launch.co.uk
www.keswick-launch.co.uk
Timetabled service of launches calling at total of seven landing stages around the lake, alternately clockwise and anti-clockwise. Daily summer (half hourly from 10.00–15.30 and up to 18.00 in high season) and winter (hourly from 10.30–15.30) timetables. Special evening cruises in summer and Father

Christmas sailings for children. Boats for hire.

Nichol End Marine

Portinscale, Keswick, CA12 5TY
☎ 017687 73082
Email: nicholend@aol.com
www.nicholendmarine.co.uk
Windsurfing, boats for hire, Canoeing and café. Open daily, all year round

Castlerigg Stone Circle

Two and a half kilometres (one and a half miles) east of Keswick, reached by the A5271, the A591 (Penrith) road for a very short distance, then a signposted right fork direct to the stone circle. Finest of all Lakeland pre-historic stone circles, with unrivalled mountain backdrops in all directions.

Armathwaite Hall Equestrian Centre

Coalbeck Farm, Bassenthwaite Lake, Keswick
☎ 017687 76949
Variety of horse riding on offer, including tuition.

Keswick Mining Museum

Otley Road, Keswick, CA12 5LE
☎ 017687 80055
www.keswickminingmuseum.co.uk
Geology, rocks, minerals and gold panning. Open: Daily 1000–1700, Bank Holidays except Christmas and New Year (winter opening times may vary).
Ⓟ(Opposite) ♿ ⅲ<6 Free <16 Discount ☂

Newlands Adventure Centre

Stair, Keswick, Ca12 5uf

Castlerigg Stone Circle

☎ 017687 78463
www.activity-centre.com
Various outdoor pursuits, including climbing, high ropes, mountain bikes and canoes.

Bassenthwaite

Bassenthwaite village

With inn and village green, has a peaceful situation a little to the north of the A591 road, reached only by minor roads.

Whinlatter Pass

The Whinlatter Pass leaves the A66 at Braithwaite, to the west of Keswick and climbs relatively gently over to the Vale of Lorton, for Crummock and Buttermere. Much of the Whinlatter area is covered by commercial woodland owned and managed by Forest Enterprises (the former Forestry Commission), with a visitor centre a little way short of the road summit.

Whinlatter Visitor Centre

☎ 017687 78469
Well equipped forest centre and park, with adventure palyground, 'rabbit run' and 'fox trot' for children, displays,

shop, refreshments and information. Open all year, summer 10.00–17.00, winter 10.00–16.00.

Thornthwaite

A small village with a well known craft gallery situated on a minor road parallel with the A66.

St. Bega's Church

By the shore of Bassenthwaite Lake, accessed only on foot from the Mirehouse area. Much rebuilt but partially pre-Norman structure on a legendary site. The circular churchyard is a strong clue to an Anglo-Saxon church here. Associated with St. Bega, daughter of an Irish chieftain, who landed at St. Bees in the seventh century and who may have ministered from an abbey on this site. Melvyn Bragg's *Credo* is based on the St. Bega legends. Outside the church is a modern cross; open air services are occasionally held at this point.

Mirehouse

Nr Keswick
☎ 017687 72287 (house)
☎ 017687 74317 (tea room)
A small stately home situated between mountains and lake a few miles north west of Keswick by the A591 Carlisle road. Since 1688 the house, with its gardens and grounds, has passed by inheritance. Still occupied by the Spedding family, it has a wealth of literary and artistic connections. Tennyson stayed here when working on his 'Morte d'Arthur', gaining inspiration from the Bassenthwaite lake side and St. Bega's church. Woodland adventure playgrounds. Varied gardens. Walks over private grounds to lake shore. Tearoom in former sawmill nearby. Admission charge.
Open Apr to Oct, 1000–1730 (gardens and tearoom). House: Sun and Wed (also Fri in Aug), 1400 to 16.30 (last entries).

Wythop Watermill Woodworking Museum

☎ 017687 76394
In the hamlet of Wythop Mill, at the entrance of Wythop Valley, half a mile from the A66 and one and a half miles from the Pheasant Inn. Signposted from the main road. Vintage woodworking tools and machinery powered by an overshot waterwheel. Victorian kitchen, wheelwright and blacksmith displays. Local history exhibition. Admission charge.
Open daily except Mon from Good Fri to the end-Oct, 1030–1730.

Trotters World of Animals

Coalbeck Farm, Bassenthwaite
☎ 017687 76239
www.trottersworld.com
By the foot of the lake, close to Armathwaite Hall and the Castle Inn. Collection of farm and other animals, including rare breeds. Play areas. Tea Shop. Picnic area. Gift shop. Admission charge.
Open daily from late Mar to end-Oct, 1000–1730 (last admission 1700).
Nov to late-Mar, Sat and Sun, 1100–1630 (last admission 1600) and daily during Christmas holidays.

Borrowdale

Honister Slate Mine

☎ 017687 77230
www.honister-slate-mine.co.uk
Open all year apart from Christmas
and early Jan, offering underground
tours (reservation only) at 10.30, 12.30
and 15.30.

Threlkeld

Rookin House Farm

Troutbeck, Penrith, CA11 0SS
☎ 017684 83561
www.rookinhouse.co.uk
Equestrian and activity centre. Go-
karts, archery, JCB driving, off-road
vehicles. Cafe. Open all year.

Caldbeck

Caldbeck parish church

Like the church at Crosthwaite,
Keswick, this church is dedicated to
St. Kentigern (or Mungo), exiled Bishop
of Glasgow, who promoted Christianity
in the northern part of Cumbria in
the sixth century. It is likely that there
was an early church on this site, but
the present building is largely of the
sixteenth century, with a Norman porch
doorway, Victorian windows and other
features spread over the centuries.

Churchyard

Contains the graves of John Peel and
Mary Harrison (nee Robinson), Maid of
Buttermere. Both are close to the west
wall of the churchyard.

St. Kentigern's Well

By the packhorse bridge over Cald
Beck, close to the church. St. Kentigern
is reputed to have preached and
baptised here.

Priest's Mill

Last used as a mill in the 1930's, now
restored and used as a craft workshop,
bookshop and restaurant.

Old Smithy

Behind the Oddfellows Inn, now a craft
and tea shop.

Carlisle

Tullie House Museum &
Art Gallery

Castle Street, Carlisle, CA3 8TP
☎ 01228 34781
Open daily except Christmas Day
and Boxing Day, 1000 to 1700.
Sun, and New Year's Day opening
at 1200.
℗ ♿ ⛄ <18 Free ☂

Hadrian's Wall

Birdoswald Fort

Hadrian's Wall, Gilsland, CA6 7DD
☎ 016977 47602
Five miles east of Brampton.
Open daily from late-Mar to end-
Sept, 1000–1730 (last admission
5pm). Oct 1000–1600.
℗ (Free)

4. The East

Penrith & Around Ullswater

Penrith

Strategically placed between the Lake District and the Eden Valley, yet really belonging to neither, is the ancient market town of Penrith, very much the centre of the area covered by this chapter of the book. Easy access from north and south brought the Romans and, nearly a thousand years later, several centuries of sporadic raiding by the Scots, not finally checked until 1603. The original defensive pele tower of 1397 – 9 grew into a sizeable castle, which is now a meagre ruin, its stones taken as ready to hand building material by sixteenth century vandals. A visit by Bonnie Prince Charlie at the head of his army in the 1745 rebellion, the A6

trunk road, the west coast main railway line and, latterly, the M6 motorway have all resulted from the same geographic considerations.

William and Dorothy Wordsworth lived in Penrith as young children, attending a little 'dame' school close to the church, also attended by William's future wife, Mary Hutchinson.

Despite its historic and strategic importance, Penrith has never grown into a big town; it remains compact and friendly, a good mixture of old and new, with winding streets and yards and some of the best of its sandstone buildings clustered around the parish church. Old signs distinguish several shops in which the same business has been carried on for up to 200 years. These old

Ullswater and Birk Fell

shops are supplemented by an attractive small modern pedestrianised shopping area at Angel Lane behind the Market Place, and by the Devonshire Arcade

Ullswater

Favourite lake of many residents and visitors, this large and beautiful sheet of water has just about everything in its favour, not least the fine ring of mountains around its head, including St. Sunday Crag, Fairfield and mighty Helvellyn. To sail on the lake 'steamer' or to walk along the lake side path from Howtown to Patterdale is to experience Ullswater at its best.

At the foot of the lake is **Pooley Bridge**, a pleasant village with inns, shops and cafe, right at the foot of Dunmallard Hill, a concentric little mound with the site of an iron age fort on top. Half way along the east shore of the lake, **Howtown** is a tiny hamlet, important only as the sole intermediate calling place of the scheduled boat service.

At the head of the lake **Glenridding** and **Patterdale** are both popular visitor centres, not only for lake-related activities. The former was for centuries a busy mining village; the Greenside Mine, up the valley behind Glenridding, closed as recently as the 1960s. The best routes to climb Helvellyn start at Patterdale, as does the walkers' route to Grasmere by way of Grisedale. The name Patterdale is derived from St. Patrick who is said to have preached in the dale. By the roadside, almost opposite the refreshment hut, is St. Patrick's Well.

From Patterdale the A591 climbs long and hard to the summit of the **Kirkstone Pass**, at 454m. (1,489ft.)

one of the highest in Lakeland. Close to the start of the climb, the charming hamlet of **Hartsop** has a range of old traditional Lake District houses, including the odd 'spinning gallery', which allowed home spinning of yarn to continue in good light, but under protective cover, during bad weather.

Greystoke

Just outside the National Park and a little off the beaten track, Greystoke is a fine village, with charming houses round the green and an ancient market cross. **Greystoke Castle** is comparatively modern, its predecessors having twice been burned down. As it is surrounded by a large expanse of park land without public right of way, it can hardly be seen. Of much more interest to visitors is **St. Andrew's church**, approached along Church Road, where an ancient 'sanctuary stone' has been preserved. Passing this stone on the way to the church was sufficient to claim sanctuary from pursuers. St. Andrew's is a spacious former collegiate church, the college being closed at the time of the Reformation. A modern experiment to reinstate the church as a pre-theological college lasted only from 1958 to 1979, owing to the shortage of suitable candidates. The village has inn, shop and swimming pool.

Dacre

A fourteenth century defensive pele tower, Dacre Castle, now used as a farmhouse, is the outstanding feature of this quiet and attractive village. Even older is the church of St. Andrew.

According to Bede there was an Anglo-Saxon monastery here, but the present structure is of the twelfth to fourteenth centuries, with nineteenth century restoration including rebuilding the tower. Inside, the tower archway into the nave is original Norman. In the chancel window there is a fragment of a carved Anglian stone cross shaft and, on the floor, a tenth century Viking period stone, also carved. There are monuments to the Hasell family, owners of nearby Dalemain for more than three centuries. Sir Edward Hasell was steward to Lady Anne Clifford; the south door has a large lock and key dated 1671 and inscribed 'A.P.' (Anne, Countess of Pembroke). The churchyard houses the four famous 'Dacre Bears', carved stone creatures, one by each corner of the church. There is also a small, cat-like animal present in two of the carvings. Starting at the south-west corner and moving anti-clockwise, there might be a simple story sequence.

Dalemain

To the East of **Darce**. A basically Elizabethan building with a Georgian facade, Dalemain has evolved piecemeal over the years. Home of the Hasell family since 1665. Fine furniture and portraits. Westmorland and Cumberland Yeomanry Museum. Gardens with many rare plants and collection of more than 100 old fashioned roses.

Around Shap & Haweswater

This area, much of it poised along the eastern boundary of the district, is the part of Lakeland generally least known to visitors. There is good hill country, leading to the rugged east slopes of High Street, there are attractive villages such as Askham. The main reasons for the comparative neglect must be the lack of a focal point town, village or lake and the remote access by road, well away from the rest of the district.

Shap

Stretching for some distance along the main A6 road, Shap is the biggest village but it has no pretensions to tourism, although several inns remain from the days when the village was a noted staging post on the route to Scotland, the highest point on the road which climbed laboriously over the bleak moorland. In the mid 19th century the railway builders also had problems in constructing what is now known as the West Coast main line, and in the days of steam power, **Shap Summit,** a little way to the south of the village was reached only after a long, hard struggle up the steep gradient, particularly from the south. The depot at Tebay housed several locomotives specifically for the purpose of 'banking' – pushing from behind – particularly heavy trains.

There is a good deal of prehistory of the Late Neolithic and Early Bronze Ages in the Shap area, largely disturbed by the construction of the railway line and by local farmers. Most notable was an avenue of standing stones, now represented by a few isolated specimens such as the **Goggleby Stone.**

Large operational granite quarries dominate the approach to Shap from the south.

West of the village is **Shap Abbey,** reached along a sign-posted lane from the road to Bampton. Dedicated to St

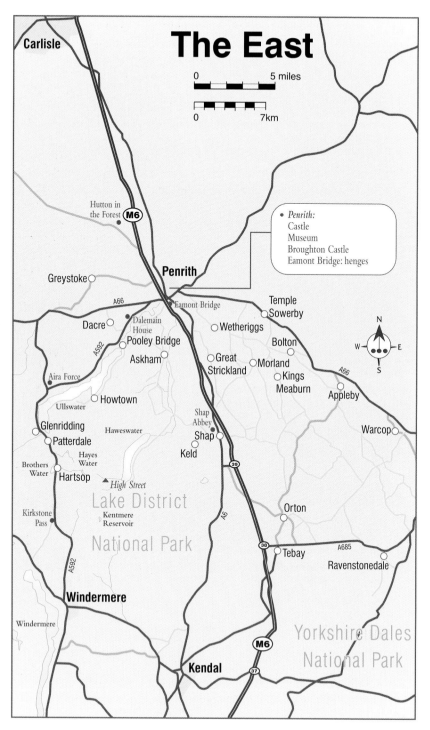

The East

0 —— 5 miles

0 —— 7km

Carlisle

Hutton in the Forest **M6**

• *Penrith:*
Castle
Museum
Broughton Castle
Eamont Bridge: henges

Penrith

Greystoke

A66 Eamont Bridge

Dacre
Dalemain House
Pooley Bridge
Askham

A592

Aira Force

Howtown

Ullswater

Glenridding
Patterdale

Haweswater

Brothers Water
Hartsop

Hayes Water

Kirkstone Pass

Kentmere Reservoir

▲ *High Street*

Lake District

National Park

A592

Windermere

Windermere

Temple Sowerby

Wetheriggs

Bolton

Great Strickland
Morland
Kings Meaburn

Appleby

Warcop

N
W — E
S

A66

Shap Abbey
Shap
Keld

39

A6

Orton

38
Tebay

A685

Ravenstonedale

M6

Kendal
37

Yorkshire Dales
National Park

Heading for Howtown from Patterdale along Ullswater

Mary, this abbey was founded early in the 13th century by the Premonstratensian or the order of White Canons. It was home to about a dozen of these brethren, who ministered in surrounding parishes in addition to their monastic duties. The only substantial surviving part is the 15th-century tower, but there are plentiful ruins revealing various phases of construction. Although Shap was never an enormously wealthy foundation, the monastic land holdings, both locally and throughout Westmorland, were considerable. Dissolution came quietly in 1540, followed by centuries of steady decay. The abbey is now in the care of English Heritage and is open to the public without charge.

Keld Chapel is about 1.5km (1 mile) from Shap village, to the south-west and reached by Keld Road. Prob-ably of the 15th century, this is a most interesting example of an unrestored pre-Reformation chapel, with many original features, including four of the five windows. The east window is similar to a window in the tower of Shap Abbey. In more recent years the building

was used as a cottage, hence the fireplace, chimney breast and chimney. The roof had to be renewed following the collapse of the original some years ago. The simply furnished chapel has for some years been in the care of the National Trust and is open to visitors without charge. The key is kept at the house across the road, usually hanging in the porch. The chapel remains consecrated, a service being held in August each year.

North-west of Shap is **Askham** a charming village with more of the character of the Yorkshire Dales than of the Lake District. Spacious greens are

Patterdale Church

fringed by trees and by houses of the 17th and 18th centuries, with two inns and a post office-stores. **Askham Hall** is a privately owned former defensive pele tower of the 14th century, converted into an Elizabethan mansion in the 16th century. The parish **church of St Peter**, close to the River Lowther at the bottom end of the village was constructed in 1832 to the design of the architect of nearby Lowther Castle.

The latter is not a real castle, but a mansion in a castellated style, built between 1806 and 1811. By the 1930s it was becoming too expensive to maintain and was abandoned. The great façade remains as a spectacular sham but there is no public access.

St Michael's Church stands on a a very early Christian site, opposite Lowther Castle, an early 13th century, with many later additions, principally of the 17th century. Evidence of earlier worship here is provided by Norse hoghack gravestones of about 950 AD and a cross of the 11th – 12th centuries outside. There are good Victorian windows on the east and a modern carving depicting the Last Supper. Close to the church is a sizeable mausoleum, built in 1857 for the Lowther family. Although the site is now isolated, until the 17th century Lowther village was adjacent to the church. It was then moved to a new site 1.5km (1 mile) away.

Haweswater

The only large sheet of water in this part of the district, Haweswater is about 6km (4 miles) in length and a little less than 1km (0.6 mile) in width. Until 1940 Haweswater was a much smaller lake, with the village of Mardale, including church and inn, at its head. Manchester Corporation then constructed a large dam, raising the water level by 29m (nearly 100ft), dramatically increasing the size of the lake and drowning the village. In extreme drought some of the remains become exposed, although all the buildings were demolished (and the bodies from the graveyard were re-interred at Shap) prior to flooding. Haweswater is not a particularly pretty lake, but the scarred eastern slopes of High Street and adjacent heights do provide an impressive valley head.

Events

Patterdale Sheepdog Trials

Late August. Tourist Information Centre ☎ 017684 82414

Penrith Show

Broughton Hall Farm. Local agricultural show. Late July. ☎ Tourist Information Centre.

Appleby New Fair

Early June.

Lowther Horse Riding Trails and Game Fair

Lowther Park. Major three day event, usually held on the first or second weekend in August.
☎ 01931 712378

Walks

1) Helvellyn

At 950m. (3,118ft.), third highest mountain in England and probably the most visited of them all. Fairly bland on its western (Thirlmere) side, but wonderfully ice scraped into dramatic cliff scenery on the east, hence the preference for ascents from Patterdale and Glenridding. The route below includes Striding Edge, in good weather not quite as spine-chilling as some might believe, but not a place for the faint hearted or for unsupervised young children. A good deal of rock scrambling. Full circuit 13km. (8 miles).

Car parking for the ascent of Helvellyn may be found along one side of the lane from Grisedale Bridge; there are also a few spaces by the George Starkey Hut, a little further towards Patterdale. Start by walking along the lane at Grisedale Bridge (not far from the church), pass the entrance to Patterdale Hall, and turn right, uphill, at a junction. At the next junction turn right to cross the river and ascend steeply up the opposite hillside.

Turn left at the top and then bear right to follow the path which climbs diagonally across the steep side of Grisedale. At the top of this section is the 'hole in the wall'. The near end of Striding Edge is soon reached. In high season the edge is likely to be congested. Cross the edge on foot or whatever other part of the anatomy seems to be appropriate; at the far end there is an awkward 'step', a mini rock face to be descended before scrambling up the shoulder of Helvellyn proper. The summit is a broad, flattish expanse with a rough shelter.

Turn right and, in about 200m., look carefully for the start of the track which descends steeply towards the shapely outlying peak of Catstye Cam. Cross Swirral Edge, less sharp than Striding Edge. Before the track rises to Catstye Cam, bear right to continue the descent, towards the outlet of Red Tarn in its hanging valley below.

Cross below Red Tarn to head towards the 'hole in the wall'. The outward route can be rejoined here or, for a varied return, keep left along a path with a wall on the right. Stay with the wall as it bends to the right, now descending quite steeply. Keep left at a junction to follow Mires Beck on its way down to Glenridding, ignoring cross paths to right and left.

Turn right at a junction just before Glenridding Beck and follow the beck into the village. Turn right along the side of the road. There is a roadside path for most of the way back to the parking place.

For a longer but easier return, turn left at the summit and follow the broad track which passes by Nethermost Pike and Dollywagon Pike before descending to Grisedale Tarn. Turn left to go all the way down Grisedale back to Patterdale.

If Striding Edge does not appeal as part of the ascent, go right at the 'hole in the wall', pass by the outlet of Red Tarn and ascend the less spectacular Swirral Edge. (the reverse of part of the return route above).

2) Glenridding to Howtown

With a return by 'steamer'. One of the best loved walks in Lakeland. Eleven kilometres (7 miles) of delightful footpath, never far from the shore of Ullswater, but rising and falling, into and out of woodland, with many picnic opportunities. The return sail on the lake faces the great ring of mountains at the head of the lake.

From the car park by the steamer

St Patricks boating harbour, Glenridding

pier walk across the adjacent field to reach the road by the refreshment hut. Turn left and use the roadside footpath for rather more than 1km. (0.75 mile) towards Patterdale. By the 'George Starkey Hut', a substantial stone build-

ing, turn left into a lane to cross the valley to Side Farm.

Turn left. The well-used path is now continuous and easy to follow. After passing a camping field there is a fork; keep left here to avoid unnecessary

Boats for hire on Ullswater

ascent. On reaching a surfaced road just short of Hallin Fell, turn left and then right to follow a 'footpath to Howtown' sign. Cross Sandwick Beck on a bridge and continue by the lake shore.

As Howtown is approached, turn left down a flight of steps and follow the signs to the pier, where there is usually a timetable inside the shelter building.

3) Pooley Bridge and Ullswater

There are several pleasant walks from Pooley Bridge. This gentle little ramble of about 3.5km. (2.25 miles) includes a length of the shore of this lovely lake. Entirely easy underfoot.

Ullswater Steamer

Ullswater

Use either of the public car parks in Pooley Bridge. From the car park on the village side of the river, go through a small gate opening on to a lane and turn left. In a short distance keep left along a surfaced driveway, soon reaching the outbuildings of the large eighteenth century house 'Euse-mere', frequently visited by William and Dorothy Wordsworth, who were friends of the first owners, Thomas Clarkson and his wife.

As the drive bends right, turn left through a gate with a 'public bridle-way' sign and cross a meadow, angling towards a gate obvious on the far side. Go through a kissing gate and turn right to follow the Pooley Bridge to Howtown road, usually quiet and pleasant to walk.

Waterside Farm, on the right, is reached in a little more than 1km. (0.75 mile). Turn right here, at a public footpath sign, between farm buildings, to reach the lake shore. The way along the shore of the lake is now entirely obvious, passing the slipway where the old 'steamers' are sometimes pulled from the water for overhauling.

4) Hartsop

A well varied circuit visiting the hamlet of Hartsop and the beautiful Brothers Water with its adjacent woodland. No significant ascent and no problems underfoot. Seven kilometres (4.5 miles).

Use the signposted car park at the point where the Windermere to Patterdale road bends right and crosses the Goldrill Beck at Cow Bridge, opposite Hartsop hamlet. From the car park, cross the beck and, by the National Trust information board, go through a kissing gate. Turn very sharp right to follow a permissive footpath towards Patterdale, keeping generally close to the road.

Rejoin the road at a gate and cross over to take another permissive footpath signposted 'Patterdale via Beck-stones'. Cross the valley bottom, then the beck on a farm bridge, and rise to join a bridleway. Turn sharp right towards Hartsop. The route is now straightforward, nicely elevated to give enhanced views across to Fairfield and its neighbours. Pass Angle Tarn Beck with its leaping falls and rapids and continue to the road which leads to Hartsop. Turn left to ascend the street through the hamlet.

At the car park at the far end, go through the gate and turn right to follow the 'Pasture Beck' signpost. Cross a bridge and turn right to return along the side of the stream. Bear left into an unsurfaced lane which continues to join the main road. Go straight across to a gate with a National Trust 'Brothers Water' sign and bear left along a narrow, winding, lakeside path. At the far end rise steeply to rejoin the road. At Sykeside by the Brothers Water Inn, turn right and follow the driveway through the camping site, crossing the valley bottom to Hartsop Hall, one of the oldest farmsteads in Lakeland.

Go round the back of the Hall and return to the car park along a lovely lakeside track.

Cycle Rides

1) Hutton in the Forest, Greystoke, Dacre & Dalemain

An easy ride of 32km. (20 miles) in

pleasant countryside.

Leave Penrith to the north, forking right from A6 at the edge of the town on to a minor road which runs parallel with A6 as far as a large roundabout. Go left here, on B5305, cross over the M6 and continue to **Hutton in the Forest,** a stately home which is open to the public. From Hutton turn left to ride via Blencow to Greystoke (ref. above). Leave Greystoke to the south, along B5288, but fork left in less than 1km. (1/2 mile) into a very minor road. Go straight across the main A66. After Hutton John and Sparket Mill turn left at a cross roads to go direct to Dacre.

Head south from Dacre to join A592, Glenridding to Penrith road. turning left to reach Dalemain. From Dalemain the return to Penrith is by A592/A66.

2) Shap Abbey, Haweswater, Askham and Lowther

Fifty kilometres (31 miles) of varied countryside, quite up and down but without serious hills, visiting an abbey ruin, a much admired village and the large Haweswater reservoir.

Take to A6 main road as far as Eamont Bridge. Turn right by the great henge monuments to Yanwath, cross the railway, then turn left to ride to Askham. Continue along the road to the south, bearing right at Bampton to visit Haweswater. At Burnbanks some of the original 'temporary' housing constructed in the 1930s for the reservoir construction workers is still in use, somewhat modified.

Return to Bampton Grange, cross the River Lowther, and head towards Shap. Turn right to take the signposted lane down to the Abbey ruins.

Return to the road, turn right, then very shortly right again to go to Keld, where the primitive chapel is well worth a visit.

From Keld ride to the A6 main road at Shap village, turning left to head towards Penrith. With the parallel M6 close at hand, this main road is quite reasonable for cycling. At Hackthorpe fork left for Lowther.

Return to Penrith either by rejoining the outward route at Askham, which is just a little way down the road from Lowther, or by using A6.

3) Wetheriggs, Morland, Appleby and Acorn Bank

A ride of 50km. (31 miles) to the fine old town of Appleby, also giving the opportunity to visit established attractions along the way.

Leave Penrith by heading south along A6 as in 2) above. One kilometre (0.75 mile) after Eamont Bridge fork left towards Clifton Dykes and Wetheriggs. At the latter, Wetheriggs Country Potterys, a nineteenth century industrial monument, with working pottery, rare breed pigs, natural wildlife habitats, children's' play areas, 'country shopping', events, fun days and tea room.

After the pottery turn right on to a minor road, then left before the railway line to reach Great Strickland. Turn left here for Morland, where the Anglo-Saxon church tower is claimed to be the oldest in Cumbria.

Head south from Morland, soon turning left to King's Meaburn. Turn right here, then left along a very minor road to Colby and Appleby. Once a more important centre and, for more than 100 years, county town of the former Westmorland, Appleby is now a relative backwater, a very attractive

little market town in the broad valley of the River Eden. The elegant, wide, Boroughgate is the spine of the town, rising from church to castle, with the historic Moot Hall of 1596 at the lower end and St. Anne's Hospital, an almshouse complex of 12 cottages and a chapel built by Lady Anne Clifford in 1653, higher on the left. The fine sandstone parish church has an entrance through 'cloisters' which formerly housed the butter market. Inside, look for the historic organ, the corporation pews and the Clifford monument. The Courtyard Gallery occupies a 300 year old building in Boroughgate. Appleby Castle has a twelfth century keep, but is not open to the public. Appleby explodes into life in early June each year for the Appleby New Fair, when gypsies and other travellers from all over the country gather in and around the town. The main line of the former Midland Railway, the 'Settle and Carlisle', with

A farm track passing through farmland at the bottom of the kirkstone Pass

Ullswater

a station at Appleby, still has a rather limited passenger service.

From Appleby return to Colby, carry on to Bolton and turn right in about 3km. (2 miles) to reach the main A66 road near Temple Sowerby. Go through Temple Sowerby to Acorn Bank, a National Trust garden with the largest collection of herbs and medicinal plants in the north of England, orchards, mixed borders and roses. A watermill is under restoration. Tea room. Open late Mar to Oct, Wed to Sunday and Bank Holiday Mondays, 10.00 – 16.30. The obvious

Haweswater and Mardale from Harter Fell

return to Penrith is along A66; to avoid this busy road means a considerable detour along minor roads.

Car Tours

1) Penrith, Alston, Penrith

A climb over a high Pennine road to an outpost of Cumbria beautifully situated in the valley of the South Tyne. A former market town, **Alston** has a wealth of interest for visitors and a good choice of hotels, restaurants and inns. The cobbled main street has a distinctive market cross. Features include: Gossipgate Gallery, Pennine Pottery and other craft centres, 'Derwentwater clock' inside the parish church of St. Augustine. **The South Tynedale Railway**, a narrow gauge line using some of the trackbed of the former British Rail branch, is claimed to be the highest narrow gauge railway in England. Trains operate between Alston and Kirkhaugh generally from Easter throughout the season, with some services in December. The line is in process of extension towards Slaggyford. 'Talking timetable ☎ 01434 382828. General enquiries ☎ 01434 381696. Opposite the station, the Hub is a small transport and heritage museum, generally open at weekends and during school holidays. Enquiries to the Tourist Information Centre, ☎ 01434 382244.

Alston is at the heart of an area which was for centuries extensively mined for lead. A few kilometres to the south east of Alston, at **Nenthead**, the heritage centre has an exhibition featuring this rich industrial history. The centre is open daily from Easter to the end of October. ☎ 01434 382726

Leave Penrith by the A686, crossing the River Eden close to Langwathby before climbing to **Hartside Cross,** at 580m. (1,904ft.) one of the highest passes in England, with its lonely inn claiming a similar distinction. Continue downhill to Alston. Leave Alston to the south east along the A689, soon reaching Nenthead.

From Nenthead a minor road climbs over Nunnery Hill, even higher than Hartside Cross, before descending towards Garrigill. Turn left then right to cross the river, then right again to continue along a minor road to Leadgate. Turn left here to angle up to the main A686, turning left towards Penrith.

For a varied return, turn right into a minor road 2km. (1.3 miles) after Hartside Cross, soon reaching Renwick. Turn left to **Kirkoswald**, a charming village with cobbled former market square, close to the River Eden. Although the remains of the former castle are scant, there is a great deal of historic interest in and around Kirkoswald. The ancient church of St. Oswald has its bell tower some distance away from the main structure. The most interesting house is The College, instituted as a college of priests in 1523 and home of the Fetherstonhaugh family for 400 years.

Leave Kirkoswald on a minor road heading east of south to Glassonby. Carry on through the village to a cross roads in 1km. Turn right here to visit the stone circle, '**Long Meg and her Daughters**'. Continue through Little Salkeld and Langwathby where Ostrich World, with tea room and other attractions, is open daily except on Thursdays.

☎ 01768 881771. Join the main A686, turning right to return to Penrith. Full circuit 87km. (54 miles).

2) Appleby, Acorn Bank, Warcop, Brough & Kirkby Stephen

(see details under cyle rides). Kirkby Stephen is an fine small town. An excursion of 85km. (53miles) full of interesting places from which a selection will obviously have to be made.

Take the main A66 from Penrith towards **Appleby**. The first possible diversion is at Temple Sowerby, for **Acorn Bank**. Continue along the A66 to Appleby. The main road carries on towards **Brough**. **Warcop** is a short diversion to the right, a charming village close to the River Eden, with a good bridge, said to the oldest in the former county of Westmorland and a church with thirteenth century and later work on Norman foundations. Just a few kilometres further, Brough is divided into two separate settlements, Market Brough and Church Brough. The development of Brough is firmly linked to the major crossing of the Pennines via Stainmore, a route in use at least since Roman times when it linked York and Carlisle. Church Brough has the remains of the castle, a Norman structure erected on the earthworks of the previous Roman fort. It was restored by Lady Anne Clifford in the seventeenth century, and is now in the care of English Heritage. Small admission charge. A medieval village grew up around the castle and St. Michael's church, originally of the mid twelfth century but with much fourteenth and sixteenth century work. From the early fourteenth century, Market Brough became the dominant settlement when the market traders set up a trading site by the new crossing of the Swindale Beck. Inns and shops flourished, particularly in the eighteenth and nineteenth centuries, when the village was a stopping place for many cross country coaches. Old Hall, on Market Street, dating from the early seventeenth century, is the oldest remaining house in Brough.

From Brough head south on A685 to **Kirkby Stephen**. Continue along A685, fork right for **Orton**, go under the M6 motorway and join the A6 a little way to the south of Shap. Turn right to return to Penrith.

From Orton, an alternative return route goes north along the B6260, over Orton Scar, forks left to Crosby Ravensworth, Maulds Meaburn and Morland). Turn left at Cliburn, soon reaching **Wetheriggs Pottery** *(see details under Cycle rides). The same road continues, joining the A6 just to the south of Eamont Bridge.*

3) Modified shorter ride

For a shorter drive, follow any of the cycle routes set out in East Section.

A view of the Northern end of Ullswater from Beda Fell

A view of Martindale Chapel

Places to Visit

Penrith

Nenthead Mines

Nenthead, Alston, CA9 3PD
Five miles east of Alston on the A689
☎ 01434 382037
www.nentheadmines.co.uk
Open from Easter to end-Oct, daily, 1030 to 1700.

℗(Free) Ġ ⋔(Family Ticket) <16

Little Salkeld Water Mill

Langwathby, nr Penrith, CA10 1NN
Off A686 Penrith to Alston road
☎ 01768 881523
www.organicmill.co.uk
Open daily, 1030 to 1700 (or dusk).
Closed Christmas to Mid-Jan.

℗(Free) Ġ(Partial) ⋔(Family Ticket) <5 ⌣

Street Market

Held each Tuesday in the wide space of Great Dockray. Original charter granted in 1223.

Cornmarket

A covered market cross by one end of Great Dockray.

George Hotel

Market Square
Provided lodgings for Bonnie Prince Charlie in 1745.

St. Andrew's Church

The thirteenth/fourteenth century tower is the oldest surviving part of the building. The nave was rebuilt between 1719 and 1722 after fire damage. The architect is believed to have been Nicholas Hawksmoor, pupil and colleague of Sir Christopher Wren. The Georgian style, with wide balconies, is similar to that of several of Hawksmoor's City of London churches. There is an interesting exposed clock mechanism near the west door. The churchyard has a very fine and unusual monument – the 'Giant's Grave' This is made up of the remains of two stone crosses and four Viking 'hogback' tombstones. A Tudor house dated 1663, by the churchyard, was the former school attended by William and Dorothy Wordsworth and Mary Hutchinson.

Penrith Castle

Sitting on a mound in Castle Park, facing the railway station. Ruins only, with deep ditch. Free public access.

Castle Park

Tennis, putting, crazy golf and bowls.

Wetheriggs Country Pottery and Craft Centre

Clifton Dykes, Penrith, CA10 2DH
☎ 01786 895617
A 19th Century industial monument with working pottery. Open Easter to end-Oct, 1000–1730. Nov to Easter, 1000–1630. Closed Christmas, Boxing Day and New Years Day.

℗(Free) Ġ ⋔(Free) ⌣

Swimming Pool

☎ 01768 863450
Southend Road, at southern end of town. Indoor, with indoor climbing wall.

Penrith Golf Centre and Driving Range

Redhills, Penrith, CA11 0DR
☎ 01768 892167
www.penrithgolf.co.uk

Places to Visit

ⓟ Parking Available
  ᵭ Disabled Facilities
  ᴟ Family Attraction
  ᐸ№ Concession for under certain age
  ☂ Suitable in Wet Weather

On fringe of town at Redhills, near M6 intersection.

Penrith Golf Club

Salkeld Road, Penrith, CA11 8SG
☎ 01768 862217
Email: secretary@penrithgolfclub.co.uk
www.penrithgolfclub.co.uk
On northern fringe of town.

Penrith Museum

Middlegate, Penrith
☎ 01768 212228
Housed in the former Robinson's school, an Elizabethan building altered in 1670, used as a school until the early 1970's. Open daily except Sun, Jun to Sept, 0930–1800. Oct to May, 1000–1700.

Eamont Bridge

One and a half kilometres (one mile) south of Penrith on the A6 road, at the crossing of the River Eamont which was formerly a county boundary. Many inns used by drovers and travellers are now converted into houses. Two great Neolithic henge monuments – Mayburgh Henge and King Arthur's Round Table.

Brougham

Two kilometres (1.25 miles) south-east of Penrith. Site of Roman fort of Brocavum. Adjacent are the ruins of Brougham Castle, one of the northern strongholds of the remarkable Lady Anne Clifford in the seventeenth century. Close to Brougham Hall is St. Wilfrid's, a chapel of ease rebuilt by Lady Anne in the seventeenth century when she inherited the Brougham Estate. The chapel is a simple low sandstone building, with exceptionally good medieval carved woodwork. In the care of English Heritage, open daily, Apr – Sept, 10.00 – 18.00, Oct, 10.00 – 17.00.

Noah's Ark Soft Play Centre

Burrowgate, Penrith, CA11 7TA
☎ 01768 890640
For (accompanied) children aged 8 years and under. Open Mon to Fri 1000–1545pm, Sat 1000–1645, Sun 10.30–1545, closed Wed.

The Highgate Farm & Animal Trail

☎ 01931 714347
Range of Animal based activities. Snack and burger bar, souvenir shop, disabled facilities. Admission charge. Open daily from late Mar to end-Sept, from 1030. Oct, 1100–1500.

Dalemain

Dalemain Historic House & Gardens

Nr Pooley Bridge, Dalemain, Penrith, CA11 0HB
☎ 017684 86450
www.dalemain.com
Attractions for children. Licensed restaurant. Gift shop. Facilities for the disabled. Annual craft fair. Admission charge. Open late-Mar to late-Oct, Sun to Thur, 10.30–1700. House guided tours open at 11.15. Open house ater midday. Winter opening: Sun to Thur, 1100–1600. May be of little interest to

younger children.

℗(Free) ♿(Limited to garden & ground floor) 👫<16 Free ☂

Ullswater

Ullswater Motor Yachts

The Pier House, Glenridding, CA11 0US

☎ 017684 82229

www.ullswater-steamers.co.uk

The motor yachts *Lady of the Lake* and *Raven* have more than earned their keep plying between Glenridding and Pooley Bridge for well over 100 years. The former was built in 1877 and the latter in 1889. Originally steam powered, both were converted to diesel in the 1930s. In recent years supplemented by two further craft, there is a complex timetable providing an all the year round service. There are 'pirate weekends' and 'Santa Specials' for children.

Aira Force Waterfall (NT)

One of Lakeland's finest and most accessible falls, close to the main road along the west shore of Ullswater. Cafe and large National Trust car park.

Howtown Outdoor Centre

Hackthorpe Penrith, CA10 2HX

☎ 01768 486508

Water based activities during the summer.

Glenridding Sailing Centre

The Spit, Glenridding, Ullswater, CA11 0PE

☎ 01768 82541

www.glenriddingsailingcentre.co.uk

Close to the steamer pier at Glenridding.

Ullswater Information Centre

Glenridding

☎ 017684 82414

Rheged

Redhills, Penrith, CA11 0DQ

☎ 01768 868000

www.rheged.com

Claimed to be The Lakes' biggest tourist attraction. A large all-weather complex which includes films, exhibitions, crafts, cafes, shops, childrens' play area and tourist information. Free entry. Open daily from 10.00–17.30.

Beckstones Art Gallery

Greystoke Ghyll, Nr Penrith, CA11 0UQ

☎ 01768 483601

www.beckstonesartgallery.co.uk

Signposted off A66, three miles west of M6 junction 40. Over 300 carefully chosen paintings of high quality. Open daily, Mar to Oct, 1000–1730, Nov, 1000–1700. Dec–Feb, Fri, Sat, Sun, 1030–1630.

Upfront Gallery

Nr Hutton-in-the-Forest, Unthank Penrith, CA11 9TG

☎ 017684 84538

www.up-front.com

6 miles north of Penrith. Exhibitions, shops, café, marionette theatre at Easter, Aug and Dec.

Hutton in the Forest

Nr Penrith, CA11 9TH

☎ 017684 84449

www.hutton-in-the-forest.co.uk

Open Easter to Oct (House & Gardens) Wed, Thur & Sun, 1230–1600. Gardens Sun to Fri 1100–1700. May be of little interest to younger children.

℗(Free) 👫(Family Ticket) <16 ☂

The Lake District has long had a reputation for inspiring great poetry. Prose of comparable stature to Wordsworth, despite the enormous success of both **Beatrix Potter** and **Arthur Ransome** in their very different writing for children, is less in evidence.

Literature

A general guide can do little more than survey the field and point those wishing to extend acquaintance with particular writers in the right direction. Included below is a selection of those writers whose poetry or prose has been significantly influenced by the special qualities of the district.

First must come the pioneers of Lakeland travel, the first 'tourists', who 'discovered' the picturesque and the sublime (awesome and/or horrid) features, analysing and writing in great detail. Notable among these intrepid travellers were **Daniel Defoe** (1724-7) who found the district to be 'barren and wild, of no use or advantage to man or beast'. To Defoe the hills were filled with 'inhospitable terror', and **Thomas Gray** (1769) who exclaimed on the mixture of horror and beauty, being particularly overwhelmed by the scenery in the Jaws of Borrowdale. **William Gilpin**, was brought up in

Brantwood, the home of John Ruskin

the district and was very concerned to analyse and to lay down ground rules for the translation of landscape features into good pictures. The first guide book was **Thomas West's** *Guide to the Lakes* of 1778. The recommendation of 'viewing stations', from which the discerning tourist might obtain the best views of any particular scene, was a notable feature of this popular guide.

The firm establishment of the Lake District as the most picturesque part of the country set the scene for the arrival of the 'Lakes Poets'. Now a term applied with some acclaim, it was originally coined in 1801 by a critical newspaper editor who was by no means enamoured of the work of Wordsworth, Southey and Coleridge, the three originals.

Samuel Taylor Coleridge *(Rime of the Ancient Mariner)* was born in Devon in 1772 and shared a tour of the district in 1799 with Wordsworth, the men being great friends for many years. Coleridge was enchanted with the scenery. From 1800 to 1803 he lived at Greta Hall, Keswick with his family then, from 1808 to 1810, he shared the occupation of Allan Bank, Grasmere with the Wordsworths. After leaving the district he wandered extensively until his death in London in 1834. Unfortunately Coleridge became an addict of opium. Coleridge's son **Hartley**, born in 1796, was a child prodigy doomed to lead an unfulfilled life largely due to the effects of alcohol and opium. He died at Nab Cottage, Rydal, in 1849 and is buried at Grasmere, beside Wordsworth.

Robert Southey was born in Bristol in 1774. He married Coleridge's sister-in-law and joined Coleridge at Greta Hall in 1803, spending the rest of his life in the Lake District, exchanging visits with the Wordsworths. Southey became Poet Laureate in 1813. He died in 1843 and is buried at Great Crosthwaite, Keswick.

Thomas DeQuincey was born in Manchester in 1785. He took over the tenancy of Dove Cottage from Wordsworth in 1808, staying until 1830. For some years he was the editor of the *Westmorland Gazette*. Unfortunately he was yet another opium addict, his best known work being *Confessions of an Opium Eater* of 1821. Another well known work is his *Recollections of the Lake Poets*. De Quincey died in Edinburgh in 1859.

Among prose writers, pride of place probably goes to **Sir Hugh Walpole**, once immensely popular but now rather out of fashion. Walpole settled in the Lake District in 1924, producing the four *Herries* novels, including *Rogue Herries* and *Judith Paris*, with settings in the Borrowdale area. Walpole died in 1941 and is buried at St. John's, Keswick.

Alfred, Lord Tennyson hardly qualifies as a Lakeland resident, but his *Idylls of the King*, including the death of Arthur, was largely conceived by the Bassenthwaite lake shore whilst he stayed with his friends at Mirehouse. **John Ruskin** was much more than a writer. The interests of this extraordinary man also embraced philosophy, social reform, the establishment of craft guilds, botany and painting. From 1871 until his death in 1900 he lived at Brantwood, Coniston and is buried at Coniston church. **Harriet Martineau**

lived at Ambleside from 1844 to 1876. Best known of her work is the *Complete Guide to the Lakes* of 1855.

Quite different from anything published before or since are **A. (Alfred) Wainright's** *Pictorial Guides to the Lakeland Fells* produced in seven volumes between 1955 and 1963. An eighth volume covering the outlying fells was added in 1974. These books, arguably the most significant contribution to Lakeland literature this century, are a fascinating blend of the painstaking research of every route on every mountain, with hand drawn maps, sketches and hand-written homespun comment, much of it of a philosophical nature. Although now in some respects outdated as route guides, the books remain in print and are still revered, at least by the older generation, as minor works of art. Many other books followed, including sketch books and lavishly illustrated coffee table volumes. More significant than the latter are the Pennine Way guide and the 'Coast to Coast' walk. Wainright came to the Lake District from his home town, Blackburn, in 1941 on gaining an appointment in the Borough Treasurer's office in Kendal. He was promoted to Borough Treasurer in 1948, staying in Kendal until his death in 1991, when his ashes were scattered on the top of Haystacks, a favourite place selected by the author many years previously. A recent biography has revealed important facets of Wainwright's character which had not featured in the publicly perceived personality which he had established by his own writing.

Arthur Ransome has a secure place in children's literature. Born in Leeds in 1884, he had an adventurous early career as a journalist, travelling all over the world, often in areas of conflict. He moved to the Lake District in 1925 for the first of four residential spells, changing house each time. The work by which he is best remembered is the series of twelve children's novels beginning with *Swallows and Amazons* in 1930. His enthusiasm for boating and his fine sense of place combined to give these novels a lasting authenticity. Ransome died in 1967 and is buried at Rusland church.

Among other twentieth century writers the most significant are the poet **Norman Nicholson,** born in Millom in 1914, novelist and broadcaster **Melvyn Bragg,** born at Wigton in 1939, (*Maid of Buttermere; Credo*) and **Hunter Davies** (*A Walk around the Lakes*), journalist and biographer of A. Wainright.

Beatrix Potter & The National Trust

Peter Rabbit is undoubtedly one of the most famous characters in children's literature, along with favourites such as Jemima Puddleduck, Squirrel Nutkin and Mrs Tiggy-Winkle. Beatrix Potter, the creator of these delightful animals, wrote and illustrated the numerous small volumes which have been enjoyed all over the world throughout this century.

Contrary to popular belief, Beatrix Potter was not born in the Lake District but in London, in 1866. Typical of the Victorian era, she was educated at home, in Kensington, by a series of nannies and governesses. She and her young brother kept all kinds of small animals from caterpillars to rabbits and mice, which she drew and painted. She also did botanical studies, and often found inspiration for drawings in the nearby **Natural History Museum**.

She was 16 when she first visited the Lake District; her parents had rented Wray Castle near Ambleside for their annual holiday.

Some years passed before the Potter parents took over Larkfield (now Eeswyke Country House Hotel) for another of their long sojourns. Beatrix loved this house with its fine views of Esthwaite Water. She described Sawrey 'as near perfect a little place as I have ever lived in'.

It was then, at the age of 30, that she decided that somehow, sometime, a small part of this area would belong to her.

In 1893, she illustrated a letter to the son of one of her governesses with pictures of a little rabbit. This was eventually to become *The Tale of Peter Rabbit*, published privately at her own expense in 1901. The next year saw *The Tailor of Gloucester* and by 1903 her work was being published by Frederick Warne, who continued to publish her work throughout her life.

In 1905 she purchased Hill Top Farm in Sawrey, mainly from the royalties earned from her by now immensely successful books. Whilst her parents were tolerant about the enterprise, she was still expected to live for most of the time in London but she visited the farm as often as possible. To provide sufficient accommodation for the manager and

John Ruskin's gravestone, Coniston

Bust of William Wordsworth, Cockermouth

his family, Beatrix had the farmhouse extended whilst retaining a sufficient living area for herself.

Throughout this period she wrote more of the little books, finding inspiration in the animals, buildings, and countryside of Sawrey and Hawkshead. In *The Pie and the Patty-pan* the cat Ribby and the small dog Duchess were owned by people in Sawrey, the story being set in cottages in the village. The tales of Tom Kitten, Jemima Puddleduck, and Tabitha Twitchet, are similarly set in Sawrey, Hawkshead, and the lakes, fields and lanes within a few miles of Hill Top Farm.

Increasing popularity and sales of the books enabled Beatrix to acquire more farms and land. Through these negotiations she met William Heelis, a local solicitor. From a business-based relationship a friendship developed and they married in 1913. The couple started their married life in another property owned by Beatrix in Sawrey.

Hill Top Farm

William would ride his motor-bike to and from his office in Hawkshead (the building is now The Beatrix Potter Gallery owned by the National Trust and open to the public). For Beatrix, life changed considerably following her

The World of Beatrix Potter attraction

171

marriage; she now lived permanently in the Lake District. Writing books became less important to her – perhaps because she was now surrounded by live animals she felt less need to fantasise about them. However, farming, rural life, and land management became more time absorbing and demanding.

Some years before her marriage Beatrix had been introduced by her father to Canon Hardwick Rawnsley, one of the three eminent people who founded the National Trust. Beatrix shared the Canon's ideals for preservation and conservation of the countryside. The friendship between Canon Rawnsley and Beatrix continued until his death shortly after the end of the First World War. His opinions were to bear on Beatrix for the remainder of her life and to have far-reaching influence in perpetuity.

Mrs Heelis was a shrewd business woman. With her husband's undoubted local knowledge and assistance, she purchased property and land in the locality; this helped to ensure that farms and estates were not broken down into units too small to remain viable. At the time of her death in 1943 she owned over 4,000 acres of land, 15 farms, large flocks of Herdwick sheep (a breed she particularly wished to conserve because of their hardiness in the severity of the fells), and numerous houses and cottages. This vast estate was bequeathed to the National Trust, showing that Beatrix Potter believed that the protection and conservation of parts of the Lake District could be safely left in the care of this relatively new organisation.

Many visitors ask where to find the grave of Beatrix Potter – it does nor exist. She was cremated, her ashes scattered in an unknown place by Tom Storey, her faithful servant and farm manager at Hill Top.

This very brief biography of Beatrix Potter may tempt the visitor to explore the settings for her books and the land and farms she owned – but do remember that many are private residences – and the lovely villages of Sawrey and Hawkshead. Hill Top Farm is a justifiably popular place to visit (owned by the National Trust).

William Wordsworth

Ask any visitor the name of a famous poet associated with the Lake District and, even from those who have never read a poem in their lives, there is only one possible answer, William Wordsworth. Indeed, there is no other name in any walk of life which is so indivisible with the District; Beatrix Potter, John Ruskin, Canon Rawnsley and A. Wainwright must all compete for second place in public recognition.

Childhood

Wordsworth was born in 1770 at Cockermouth where his father John was lawyer and agent to Sir James Lowther of Lowther Castle, who became the first Earl Lonsdale in 1784. The Lowther family was long established and immensely powerful throughout Wesrmorland and Cumberland and Sir James was largely responsible for the profitable development of the rich iron and coal deposits of West Cumberland. Despite the family wealth, Sir James owed a considerable sum of money to John Wordsworth for many years, recovered by William after the death of his father in 1783.

Of the four other Wordsworth children, William's sister Dorothy, 21 months his junior, was much the most significant. The family home in Cockermouth is a handsome Georgian house of modest size in the main street, now in the care of the National Trust. As small children, whilst living with relatives in Penrith, William and Dorothy attended Mrs. Birkett's dame school, beside the churchyard; Mary (later to marry William) and Sara Hutchinson were fellow pupils. The building is still in existence as a coffee shop.

Schooldays & Cambridge

In 1778 his mother died and William's education continued at Hawkshead Grammar School where, with his brothers, he was a pupil from 1778-87. Dorothy was sent to live with relatives in Yorkshire. The grammar school, for about 100 boys, had been founded in 1585 by Edwin Sandys, Archbishop of York, who had strong Hawkshead connections. The school is open to visitors, its prime exhibit being the desk upon which Wordsworth carved his initials. Whilst at school here William lodged with Ann Tyson whose cottage in the village centre can still be seen, although it is not open to the public.

Outside school hours young William took to roaming around the surrounding countryside and fells, often well into the night, absorbing the sights, the sounds and the smells, his sensitive character deeply appreciating the wholeness of nature, storing up a vast well of experience from which he would draw for inspiration for the rest of his long creative life.

Works inspired particularly from this period include his autobiographical masterpiece *The Prelude*, and the *Ode on Intimations of Immortality from Recollections of Early Childhood*.

After Hawkshead he went on to study at Cambridge, without in any way distinguishing himself. His father having died in 1783, he was financially supported by two uncles. On leaving Cambridge, William was something of a wanderer, without any clear idea of what he wanted to do in life and with quite radical political opinions. This was, after all, the era of popular revolution in Europe and, after a walking tour in France, for a while he became an admirer of Napoleon.

A second French visit in 1791 – 2 had far more personal significance in that a love affair with Annette Vallon in Orleans resulted in the birth of a daughter, Caroline. Although, mainly because of opposition from Annette's family and the long drawn out Napoleonic War between Britain and France, marriage was not possible, William always acknowledged his responsibility and over the years provided a good deal of financial support for Caroline.

Dorothy & Marriage

On returning to Britain, William was reunited with his devoted sister Dorothy, beginning the lifelong relationship in which her role as his closest friend, soulmate and provider of much of his inspiration has constantly intrigued biographers and others. Dorothy's journals continue to provide the closest insight into William's personality and make fascinating reading, particularly sections such as that describing her reaction to William's marriage. After several years in the West Country, William and Dorothy returned to the Lake District for good in 1799, taking the tenancy of Dove Cottage, a small former inn at Town End, Grasmere. The first poems had been published in 1793 and in the now highly conducive surroundings William was soon in full spate, producing what is widely regarded as his finest work. He married Mary Hutchinson in 1802, producing five children in a comparatively short space of time whilst Dorothy remained as part of a happy triumvirate. Dove Cottage, largely in its original state, and the adjacent barn conversion to form the Wordsworth Museum, are now administered by the Wordsworth Trust as a compelling visitor attraction.

By 1808 the extended family had outgrown the cottage and moved to Allan Bank, a substantial house abo Grasmere village of which, ironcally, Wordsworth had earlier expressed disapproval as being intrusive in the landscape. He did plant some extra screening trees in front of the house. From 1811-13 the Wordsworths lived in the Parsonage opposite Grasmere church. This turned out to be a most unhappy period as the house was dark and damp and two of their children – Thomas (6) and Catherine (4) died. The final move of house was to Rydal Mount which William rented from Lady le Fleming

of nearby Rydal Hall in 1813, living here until his death in 1850. The house is open to visitors.

As his fame spread, so William's youthful ardour mellowed and he became more of an establishment figure, to the dismay of many youthful admirers. The ultimate accolade was the award of the Poet Laureate title in 1843, on the death of his friend Southey. For many years he courted the patronage of the Lowther family, from whom he obtained the moderately lucrative post of Distributor of Stamps for Westmorland, later adding Cumberland. This undemanding job was concerned with the payment of duty on various legal documents. The office in Ambleside which he occasionally used is in Church Street, beside what is now Stampers restaurant.

With the Lakes Poets

Wordsworth's relationships over the years with other poets and writers – The Lakes Poets – are second in importance only to his relationship with Dorothy.

Having met and greatly admired Samuel Taylor Coleridge during his years in the West Country, the two were reunited in Lakeland in a brilliantly creative association until disa-

The gravestone of William Wordsworth

Copper Mines Valley, north of the Walna Scar Road

greement largely over Coleridge's use of drugs and alcohol led to the latter's final departure in 1810. Another acquaintance was Thomas De Quincey, an opium addict who, after admiring Wordsworth from afar for many years eventually succeeded him as tenant of Dove Cottage

Of all the 'Lakes Poets' the most enduring bond was that between Robert Southey and Wordsworth. Southey, with his large family, lived at Greta Hall, Keswick for 40 years until his death in 1843. William often made the long walk from Grasmere or Rydal over to Keswick to visit his old friend. Another regular visitor to the Wordsworths over a period of years was the great Scottish writer, Sir Walter Scott.

Wordsworth's enduring fame is based firmly on his massive output of poetry whether the vast 14-volume work *The Prelude*, or the many shorter, more accessible, pieces such as *I wandered lonely as a cloud* or *Daffodils* (describing the 'host of golden daffodils' by the Ullswater shore at Gowbarrow Park) or *The Rainbow* which includes the immortal line, 'The child is father of the man'.

Guide to the Lakes

However, in his own lifetime, his prose work *Guide to the Lakes* was far more successful from a sales point of view than any of the published poetry. This work started life as an anonymous preface to a volume of sketches of selected views of the Lake District by Rev. Joseph Wilkinson. William did not even like the sketches. Suitably revised and with added chapters on geology and botany (the former by the celebrated Professor Adam Sedgewick of Sedbergh) this preface eventually became a book in its own right.

The fifth edition of 1845, as republished with an introduction and notes by Ernest de Selincourt, is still available. This is very much a guide book of its time. The information which helped visitors to find their way around the district is quite perfunctory, followed by long sections setting out Wordsworth's strong views on matters such as the iniquity of planting foreign species of trees, particularly larches, the colouring of buildings and the inferiority of alpine scenery when compared with the Lake District.

The de Selincourt edition also includes William's eloquent letters to the editor of the *Morning Post* concerning the proposed construction of a railway to Windermere and beyond. Two themes emerge strongly from the guide, including these letters. Firstly, that by today's standards Wordsworth was highly opinionated and had what we would call a snobbish view of the ability of the lower orders of society to appreciate the beauty of the finer things of life such as Lakeland scenery. Secondly, and more to his credit, he emerges as a true, probably the first, Lake District environmentalist, at that early stage recognising the fragility of the local landscape and almost uncannily foreseeing the adverse effects which unsuitable development and mass tourism could have on that landscape. In response to today's environmental problems, over 150 years later the National Park Authority and the many other conservation-orientated bodies are echoing many of Wordsworth's views. A prophet indeed!

Together with several members of his family Wordsworth lies at the far end of the churchyard in Grasmere, where the soothing murmur of the waters of the River Rothay would have pleased him greatly. The headstones on the graves are commendably simple.

Painters

The great surge of poetic writing which played such a prominent part in the Age of English Romanticism was inevitably accompanied by corresponding activity in the visual arts. The 'Discovery of the Landscape' went hand in hand with the 'Discovery of the Lake District', regarded as having the finest scenery in the land.

Painters flocked to observe and to record this unique combination of the picturesque (serene and beautiful) and sublime (horrid and fearful) and, if in their estimation necessary to create a good picture, to rearrange and to exaggerate the various elements. For painters and for some other visitors it was considered to be essential to carry a ' Claude glass', named after the great landscape painter Claude Lorraine. In this glass a 'picture' of any portion of an observed landscape could be composed and framed. These early painters tended to extremes, either picturesque or sublime.

Of the really great artists, **Turner, Constable** and **Joseph Wright** of Derby visited Lakeland. Constable (1776 – 1837) came only once and didn't like the district very much, perhaps not surprisingly in view of his great love of the Essex/Sussex countryside. A pencil drawing of the lower fall at Rydal is at the Abbott Hall, Kendal. Wright (1734 – 97) was rather more active; he, too, visited the fall at Rydal, producing a painting. More significant than either of these was J.M.W. Turner's contribution to Lakeland painting. A near contemporary of Wordsworth, Turner's (1775-1817) genius transcended the picturesque/sublime attitudes which conditioned the work of lesser painters of the time, getting right to the heart of his subject to produce works of timeless appeal.

Of locally born artists, **Romney** (1734 – 1802) born at Dalton in Furness has pride of place, though he was strictly a portrait painter.

Among the many lesser but still important painters working in the district from about the mid-eighteenth century, **Salvator Rosa** was at the forefront of the 'sublime' movement, closely followed by **P.J. de Loutherbourg**, whose *Belle Isle in a Storm* and *Belle Isle in a Calm* may be seen at the Abbot Hall.

A more realistic view of the landscape as inherently friendly, 'a garden where men and nature become one', was depicted by **William Green**, who settled in Ambleside. He is featured at the Armitt Collection. Also living nearby was **Julius Ceasar Ibbotson.** His painting of his home at Clappersgate is one of several attractive and interesting works. Extremely prolific and useful in portraying middle class domesticity of the time was **John Harden**. Other painters of the late eighteenth/early nineteenth centuries who made a significant contribution to the illustration of the district include: William Harrell, James Burrell Smith, William Westall, John 'Warwick' Smith, William

Henry Pyne, John Glover, Thomas Austin, Philip Reinagle, his son Ramsey Richard Reinagle, John Varley, William Collins and Francis Wheatley. Edward Lear, of the mid nineteenth century, is well represented at the Abbott Hall gallery in Kendal.

Later in the nineteenth century, the multi-talented **John Ruskin** promoted Turner and produced many Lakeland paintings of his own, whilst **Beatrix Potter** was, in her early life, a botanical artist of great talent, as can be seen from the Armitt Collection in Ambleside. In her celebrated children's books, the backgrounds in which the animal characters are set all depict local scenes.

In the present century **Kurt Schwitters** was an immigrant, living in Ambleside for many years, producing largely rather avant garde work, but with some local scenes, such as his *Bridge House, Ambleside*. More recently, **Sheila Fell** produced local work of power and originality until her early death in 1980.

The **Heaton Cooper** family have, for many years, been a local institution. Alfred, his son Heaton, and several of the third generation, have produced attractive landscape paintings and other works of art, many being reproduced in large numbers for sale at their Grasmere studios as a commercial operation.

The Abbot Hall Gallery in Kendal has a limited selection of paintings from the 'Romantic' period, Schwitters, and a considerable number of Romney portraits in its permanent collection.

Reaching the Lake District

The Cumbria County Council operates a travelline information and enquiry service for bus, rail and boat timetables at Citadel Chambers, Carlisle, Cumbria CA3 8SG. (Mon to Fri 9.00–17.00, Sat 9.00–12.00).
☎ 0870 6082608
www.cumbria.gov.uk/travtour.htm.

By Road

Despite the restricted car parking and the limited network of predominantly narrow roads, the majority of visitors will arrive in the district by motor car. The M6 motorway is the obvious approach road, either from north or south. From the south, junction 36, followed by the A590 and A591 provides a swift and straightforward approach to destinations in the south of the district. M6 to junction 40, then A66 serves the same purpose for Keswick and other places in the north of the district. From the east, the A66 is the best trans-pennine route, crossing to Penrith from its junction with the A1 at Scots Corner. From the southern part of Yorkshire, the A65 via Skipton (by-passed) is the straightforward route.

By Rail

A good alternative is to travel by rail. There are west coast main line stations at Oxenholme and Penrith. From the former, the Windermere branch line provides a valuable service, generally with connections to and from the London (Euston) services, stopping at Kendal, Burneside, Staveley and Windermere. There are also through trains from Windermere to Manchester and its airport. For the western section of the district, trains to Grange over Sands, Ulverston and Barrow in Furness connect with the London and other main line trains at Lancaster. Again, from Barrow there are through trains to and from Manchester and its airport. From Barrow a rather infrequent service runs north along the coast to Whitehaven and Carlisle; the intermediate stations include Ravenglass, Seascale, St. Bees and Maryport.

By Coach

Another option is to travel by long distance coach, generally less expensive than the railway. Stagecoach and National Express operate services to and from the Lake District from Birmingham, London, Manchester, South Yorkshire and the North-east, some passing through the heart of the district, calling at Kendal, Windermere, Ambleside and Keswick. These coaches serve many intermediate towns and cities thoughout the country. A most useful plan of these, and the local bus services, is available free of charge at Tourist Information Centres.

By Air

By air, the usual approach to the Lake District is by the international air port at Manchester. There are train services from the airport direct to Windermere and to Barrow in Furness

Stagecoach

Stagecoach North West. Traveline 0870 608 2608. The Stagecoach Co. publishes 'The Lakes Rider', a comprehensive guide to bus services throughout the district, with extra information concerning rail routes and steamer services on Windermere. 'Explorer' and other discounted tickets are available. A particularly useful integrated service is provided by the Cross Lakes Shuttle – boat from Bowness to Ferry Nab, bus from Ferry Nab via Sawrey and Hawkshead to Coniston Water, boat across Coniston Water to Coniston village. There is a connection to Grisedale.

Accommodation

Visitors will find accommodation to suit all needs and budgets, ranging from bunk houses and camping barns to luxury hotels; thousands of cottages and apartments are also available to rent. Accommodation can always be booked direct with the establishment or through a Tourist Information Centre on or before arrival in the area. If reserved through a T I C a deposit of 10% will be charged; this will be deducted when paying the final bill. If calling personally, it is quite usual to ask to see the room available at hotels or bed and breakfast houses.

Bunk Houses

Vary in character but offer clean, dry, very basic accommodation, sometimes in dormitories, at low cost. Some are situated in towns, others in rural areas. Current details obtainable from Tourist Information Centres.

Camping Barns

A network of stone barns, usually in remote places, owned by farmers but administered as a scheme by the Lake District National Park Authority (☎ 017687 72803 for reservations).

The barns provide simple overnight shelter for walkers and cyclists, thus avoiding the need to carry tents. The only facilities are a wooden sleeping platform, table, cold water tap, and w.c. Visitors will need to bring sleeping bags, cooking stove and accessories, and a torch. People under eighteen years of age must be accompanied by an adult. Charges are very low.

Camping and Caravan Sites

Because of the impact on the landscape, many restrictions are, quite rightly, imposed by the Lake District National Park Authority. Consequently most sites benefit from seclusion and are well screened from the roads and fells. Generally sites open only from mid-March to mid-November but exceptions do occur. Some sites have large static caravans and/or timber chalets to rent on a weekly (sometimes for even shorter periods) basis, as well as areas for touring caravans, motor caravans, and tents. Other sites will offer pitches exclusively for tourers and tents or one or the other. Farmers sometimes hold a local authority license to use a small field for tents. The larger touring and camping sites are well equipped with showers, laundry, dish-washing and other facilities. Lists of sites can be obtained from Tourist Information Centres.

The two major clubs own and manage sites in the area; in the case of the Caravan Club, with one exception these are for touring caravans and motor caravans only. It is possible for non-members to stay at all of these sites on payment of an increased over-night charge. The smaller certified location sites administered by the Caravan Club or the Camping and Caravanning Club are licensed for members only and are limited to five vans per night; this type of site is frequently found to be a small field on a working farm. Many now have electric hook-ups and/or toilet facilities.

Details of membership, possible reciprocal arrangements with member of clubs in other countries and other information may be obtained from:

The Caravan Club
East Grinstead House, East Grinstead, RG19 1UA
☎0800 3286635

The Camping and Caravanning Club
Greenfields House, Westwood Way, Coventry, CV4 8JH
☎ 024 7669 4995

A 'Camping International Card'; obtainable from caravan and camping clubs in many countries, may be useful.

The National Trust has three sizeable camping sites, at Great Langdale, Low Wray, (Windermere) and Wasdale Head. A descriptive leaflet is available from the Trust or from Tourist Information Offices.

Youth Groups

There are camp sites which cater for youth groups but reservation will need to be made well in advance of the proposed visit. Also some of the churches provide dormitory accommodation in youth centres; again plan well ahead to ensure that the provision is suitable for the group concerned. Contact a tourist information centre for more details.

Youth Hostels

The Youth Hostels Association has excellent coverage throughout the Lake District. The hostels, always very popular, vary from small buildings in the mountains to those of luxurious standard such as the one by the lake at Waterhead, Ambleside. It must be stressed that hostels are for travellers – young, not-so-young, solo, groups, school parties, families – all are welcome. Booking ahead is always adviseable, but is essential for public holidays and in the peak season (July and August). Membership charges are modest – join 'on-the-spot' at any hostel or write in advance to:

YHA

Trevelyan House, Dimple Road, Matlock, Derbyshire, DE4 3YH.
☎ 01629 592600

Included in the membership is a copy of the handbook listing all the hostels in England and Wales with the facilities offered, a location map, and the membership card.

The accommodation offered varies from family rooms to dormitories. Bed linen is provided and included in the modest overnight charge. With few exceptions, all hostels provide meals, usually with a choice of menu and always a vegetarian option. Other diets can be catered for subject to advance notice. Charges for all meals are low and offer good value. All hostels provide a kitchen for those who prefer self-catering and all have a clothes drying facility, especially welcome to walkers and cyclists.

Subject to the availability of beds, there is no maximum or minimum stay in a youth hostel.

Some hostels have a closed period during the day, usually between 10am and 5pm. Doors are locked overnight – usually from 11pm.

In all hostels a friendly and companionable atmosphere prevails – many lone travellers have benefited from this; long-standing friendships frequently develop from a chance meeting in a hostel. Remember! everyone is welcome – from babies to senior citizens.

The majority of hostels (there are only a few exceptions) can be accessed by car.

For those travelling by rail to the Lake District, the YHA run a "shuttle mini-bus" (summer service only) from Windermere Station to local hostels. Please remember that the hostels in this area are very popular – do telephone first for bed availability. For list of YHA Centres see p198.

Hire of Cottages, Flats and Residential Caravans

There are numerous agents who will offer a choice of accommodation to rent on a weekly basis or sometimes for even shorter periods. The size of the property, its facilities, and the cost will vary considerably. It is also possible to rent properties directly from the owner; these are advertised in the weekend newspapers, magazines such as *The Lady*, *Cumbria*, *Cumbria Life*; many are listed in booklets obtainable from tourist information offices.

Bed and Breakfast

Accommodation is offered in private houses or small proprietor-run guest houses in the towns, villages, or rural areas. Standards will vary; this is usually reflected in the price. Most offer at least some rooms with en-suite accommodation and a good standard of cleanliness. The majority do not serve meals other than breakfast but will be able to suggest good local restaurants to suit all budgets. Some of these guest houses will have a residents' lounge; almost all will provide tea and coffee facilities and television in the bedrooms. Look for the sign outside saying "B & B" or "bed and breakfast" – some will quote the price; otherwise inquire at the door. Remember, you can ask to see the room offered before accepting the accommodation.

Farmhouse Accommodation

Generally similar to the type offered above but in houses attached to working farms. Again standards will vary from simple to quite luxurious. Meals, other than breakfast, if available, will sometimes be taken round a large table with the family and other guests. Some farmers will welcome visits to look round the farm and perhaps allow guests to help with the feeding of live-stock.

Country House Hotels

The buildings are usually large houses in extensive grounds. Architecture and decor is frequently de-luxe and service attentive. Such hotels usually have a tranquil setting with attractive views of mountains and/or lakes from the main rooms and from some of the bedrooms. It is customary to reserve a room, breakfast, and evening meal at this type of hotel.

Major and Large Hotels

Throughout the area there are many highly rated hotels. Most offer all the services one could wish for, ranging from shoe-cleaning to fax and internet. There is a wide choice on the menu for all meals and special diets should not cause any problem. As well as the restaurant, less formal eating areas such as the bar will offer meals and by arrangement meals can be served in the bedroom.

In the rooms every facility will be provided – television, radio, telephone, tea and coffee tray, mini-bar, and sometimes even private safes.

Swimming pools and gymnasium facilities are also available in most hotels of this standard and some will cater for private parties and conferences.

Leaflets and brochures with details of all types of accommodation can be obtained from Tourist Information Centres. The English Tourist Board, motoring organisations, and other bodies do have systems of assessing and grading all types of accommodation, with the award of 'stars', 'crowns' and 'keys' as appropriate. The systems are fully explained in the relevant guides.

The following lists include premises within each category of accommodation but inclusion in this book does not imply a recommendation; these hotels and other establishments are merely suggestions from the large numbers available. More comprehensive information is available at Tourist Information Centres.

South Section

Major and Large Hotels

The Castle Green Hotel

Kendal
☎ 01539 734000
Fax 735522

Stonecross Manor Hotel

Kendal
☎ 01539 733559
Fax 736386

Belsfield Hotel

Bowness-on-Windermere
☎ 015394 42448
Fax 46397

Burnside Hotel

Bowness- on-Windermere
☎ 015394 42211
Fax 43824

The Old England Hotel

Bowness-on-Windermere
☎ 015394 42444
Fax 43432

Low Wood Hotel

Ambleside Road, Windermere
☎ 015394 33338
Fax 34072

Rothay Manor Hotel

Ambleside
☎ 015394 33605
Fax 33607

Regent Hotel

Waterhead, Ambleside
☎ 015394 32254

Swan Hotel

Grasmere
☎ 015394 35551
Fax 35741

Wordsworth Hotel

Grasmere
☎ 015394 35592
Fax 35765

Langdale Hotel and Country Club

Elterwater, Ambleside
☎ 015394 37302
Fax 37694

Swan Hotel

Newby Bridge
☎ 015395 31681
Fax 31917

Waterhead Hotel

Waterhead, Ambleside
☎ 015394 32566

Country House, Smaller Hotels and Inns

Garden House Hotel

Fowllng Lane, Kendal
☎ 01539 731131
Fax 740064

Burn How Hotel

Back Belsfield Road, Bowness
☎ 015394 46226
Fax 47000

Fayrer Garden Hotel

Lyth Valley Road, Bowness
☎ 015394 88195
Fax 45986

Linthwaite House Hotel

Crook Road, Bowness
☎ 015394 88600
Fax 88601

Merewood Hotel

Ambleside Road, Windermere
☎ 015394 46484
Fax 42128

Rothay Garth Hotel

Rothay Road, Ambleside
☎ 015394 32217
Fax 34400

Wateredge Hotel

Waterhead, Ambleside
☎ 015394 32332
Fax 31878

Skelwith Bridge Hotel

Skelwith Bridge, Ambleside
☎ 015394 32115
Fax 34254

Gold Rill Hotel

Grasmere
☎/Fax 015394 35486

Grasmere Hotel

Grasmere
☎/Fax 015394 35277

Britannia Inn

Elterwater
☎ 015394 37210 Fax 37311

New Dungeon Ghyll Hotel

Great Langdale
☎ 015394 37213

Old Dungeon Ghyll Hotel

Great Langdale
☎ 015394 37272

Three Shires Inn

Little Langdale
☎ 015394 37215

The Black Bull Inn

Coniston
☎ 015394 41335
Fax 41168

The Sun Hotel

Coniston
☎ 015394 41248

The Waterhead Hotel

Coniston
☎ 015394 41244
Fax 41193

Queen's Head Hotel

Hawkshead
☎ 015394 36271
Fax 36722

Red Lion Inn

Hawkshead
☎ 015394 36213
Fax 36747

Tower Bank Arms

Near Sawrey
☎ 015394 36334

Sawrey Hotel

Far Sawrey
☎ 015394 43425

Langdale Chase Hotel

Ambleside Road, Windermere
☎ 015394 32201

Crag Wood Hotel

Ambleside Road, Windermere
☎ 015394 88177

Briery Wood Hotel

Ambleside Road, Windermere

☎ 015394 33316

Lake House Hotel

Waterhead, Ambleside

☎ 015394 32360

Youth Hostels

YHA Kendal

☎ 01539 724066
Fax 724906

YHA Windermere

Troutbeck, Windermere
☎ 015394 43543
Fax 47165

YHA Ambleside

☎ 015394 31117
Fax 34408

YHA Grasmere, Butterlip How

Easedale Road
☎ 015394 35316
Fax 35798

YHA Grasmere, Thorney How

☎ 015394 35591
Fax 35866

YHA Langdale

Loughrigg, Ambleside
☎ 015394 37579
Fax 37101

YHA Elterwater

☎ 015394 37245
Fax 37120

YHA Coniston

☎ 015394 41323
Fax 41803

**YHA Coniston
(Copper Mines House)**

Coniston
☎/Fax 015394 41261

YHA Hawkshead

☎ 015394 36293
Fax 36720

Caravan and Camping Sites

All club sites are available to non-members.
(C) denotes caravans only
(T) denotes tents only
(C T) denotes caravans and tents

Low Park Wood

Sedgwick, Kendal
(Caravan Club) (C)
☎ 01539 560186

Camping and Caravanning

Club Site, Millcrest, Skelsmergh

Shap Road, Kendal. (C T)
☎ 01539 741363

Ashes Lane Park

Staveley, Kendal (C T)
☎ 01539 821119

Park Cliffe Camping and

Caravan Estate, Birks Road, Newby
Bridge Road, Windermere. (C T)
☎ 015395 31344
Fax 31971

Braithwaite Fold
Bowness-on-Windermere
(Caravan Club) (C)
☎ 015394 42177

Fallbarrow Park
Bowness-on-Windermere.(C)
☎ 015394 44248
Fax 88736

Whitecross Bay Park
Ambleside Road, Windermere (C)
☎ 015394 43937

Limefitt Park
Patterdale Road, Windermere.(C T)
☎ 015394 32300

Skelwith Fold Park
Nr. Ambleside (C)
☎ 015394 32277

National Trust Camp Site
Great Langdale, Ambleside (T)
☎ 015394 37668

Park Coppice
Coniston (Caravan Club) (C T)
☎ 015394 41555

Coniston Hall Camp Site
Coniston (T)
☎ 015394 41223

The Croft
Hawkshead (C T)
☎ 015394 36374
Fax 36544

Hawkshead Hall Farm Camp Site
Hawkshead (C T)
☎ 015394 36221

Grizedale Hall Camping and Caravanning Site
Nr Hawkshead (C T)
☎ 01229 860257

West Section
Major and Large Hotels
There are no hotels in this category
in this section; the nearest is:

The Seacote Hotel
Beach Road, St Bees
☎ 01946 822777

Country House, Smaller Hotels and Inns

Stanley Ghyll House
Boot, Eskdale
☎ 019467 23327

Burnmoor Inn
Boot, Eskdale
☎ 019467 23224
Fax 23337

Woolpack Inn

Nr Boot, Eskdale
☎ 019467 23230

Gosforth Hall Hotel

Gosforth
☎ 019467 25322

Wasdale Head Inn

Wasdale
☎ 019467 26229

Low Wood Hall Hotel

Nether Wasdale
☎/Fax 019467 26100

Ennerdale Country House Hotel

Cleator
☎ 01946 813907

Grange Country House Hotel

Loweswater, Nr. Cockermouth
☎ 01946 861211

Bridge Hotel

Buttermere
☎/Fax 017687 70252

Fish Hotel

Buttermere
☎ 017687 70253

Caravan and Camping Sites

(C) Caravans only, (T) Tents only, (C T) Caravans and tents

Fisherground Farm Holidays

Eskdale (T)
☎ 019467 23319

Hollin Farm Camp Site

Boot (T)
☎ 019467 23253

Seven Acres Caravan Park

Holmrook (C T)
☎ 019467 25480

Dockray Meadow

(Caravan Club Site – non members admitted) (C)

Ennerdale Bridge

☎ 01946 861357

Dalegarth

Buttermere (T)
☎ 017687 70233

Youth Hostels

YHA Black Sail

Ennerdale
☎ 07711 108450

YHA Ennerdale

Cat Crag
☎ 0870 770 5820

YHA Eskdale

Boot, Holmrook
☎ 0870 770 5824

YHA Wastwater

Wasdale Hall
☎ 0870 770 6082

YHA Cockermouth

Double Mills, Cockermouth
☎ 0870 770 5769

YHA Buttermere

Cockermouth
☎ 0870 770 5736

North Section

Major and Large Hotels

Keswick Hotel
Station Road, Keswick
☎ 017687 72020
Fax71300

Trout Hotel
Crown Street, Cockermouth
☎ 01900 823591
Fax 827514

Shepherd's Hotel
Lakeland Sheep and Wool Centre,
Egremont Road, Cockermouth
☎ 01900 822673

Pheasant Inn
Bassenthwaite Lake,
Nr Cockermouth
☎ 017687 76234

Castle Inn Hotel
Bassenthwaite, Nr Keswick
☎ 017687 76401

Ivy House Hotel
Braithwaite, Keswick
☎ 017687 78338

Applethwaite Country
House Hotel, Applethwaite,
Keswick
☎ 017687 72413

Borrowdale Hotel
Borrowdale, Keswick
☎ 017687 77224

Greenbank Countryhouse Hotel
Borrowdale
☎ 017687 77215

Leathes Head Hotel
Borrowdale
☎ 017687 77247

Hazelbank
Rosthwaite, Borrowdale
☎ 017687 77248

Scafell Hotel
Rosthwaite, Borrowdale
☎ 017687 77208

Kings Head Inn
Thirlspot, Thirlmere, Keswick
☎ 017687 71312

Near Howe Hotel
Mungrisdale
☎ 017687 77907

Youth Hostels

YHA Cockermouth
Double Mills
☎ 01900 822561

YHA Keswick
Station Road
☎ 017687 72484
Fax 74129

YHA Derwentwater
Barrow House, Borrowdale
☎ 017687 77246
Fax 77396

YHA Borrowdale
☎ 017687 77257
Fax 77393

YHA Honister Hause

Seatoller, Borrowdale
☎ 0870 770 5870

YHA Skiddaw House

Bassenthwaite, Keswick
☎ 07747 174293

Caravan and Camping Sites

(C) denotes caravans only
(T) denotes tents only
(C T) denotes caravans and tents

Wyndham Caravan Park

Old Keswick Road, Cockermouth
(C T)
☎ 01900 822571

Robin Hood Caravan Park

Bassenthwaite (C T)
☎ 017687 76334

Braithwaite Bridges Camp Site

Braithwaite (T)
☎ 017687 78343

Burnside Caravan Park

Underskiddaw, Keswick (C)
☎ 017687 72950

Camping and Caravanning Club Site Derwentwater

Keswick (C T)
☎ 017687 72392

Castlerigg Hall Caravan and Camping Park

Keswick (C T)
☎ 017687 72437

Low Manesty Caravan Club Site

Borrowdale (non-members admitted)
(C)
☎ 017687 77275

Ashness Farm Camp Site

Borrowdale (T)
☎ 017687 77361

Hollows Farm

Grange-in-Borrowdale (T)
☎ 017687 77298

Burns Farm Caravan and Camping Site

St John's in the Vale, Keswick (C T)
☎ 017687 79225

Gill Head Caravan and Camping Site

Troutbeck, Penrith (C T)
☎ 017687 79652

Setmabanning Farm

Threlkeld, Keswick (C T)
☎ 017687 79229

East Section

Major and Large Hotels

North Lakes Hotel

Ullswater Road, Penrith

☎ 01768 868111

Fax 868291

Sharrow Bay Hotel

Nr Pooley Bridge

Ullswater

☎ 017684 86301

Glenridding Hotel

Glenridding

☎ 017684 82228

Inn on the Lake

Glenridding

☎ 017684 82444

Leeming House Hotel

Watermillock

☎ 017684 86622

Fax 86443

Shap Wells Hotel

Nr Shap

☎ 01931 716628

Fax 716377

Country House, Smaller Hotels and Inns

George Hotel

Devonshire Street, Penrith

☎ 01768 862696

Brantwood Country Hotel

Stainton, Penrith

☎ 01768 862748

Pooley Bridge Inn

Pooley Bridge

☎/Fax 017684 86215

Haweswater Hotel

Haweswater

☎ 01931 713235

Caravan and Camping Sites

(C) denotes caravans

(T) denotes tents

(CT) denotes caravans and tents

Note: Many of the caravan and camping sites listed above have residential caravans for hire.

Lowther Caravan Park

Eamont Bridge, Penrith (C T)

☎ 01768 863631

Park Foot Caravan and Camping Park

Howtown Road, Pooley Bridge (C T)

☎ 017684 86309

Waterfoot Caravan Park

Pooley Bridge (C)

☎ 017684 86302

Waterside House

Howtown Road, Pooley Bridge (T)

☎ 017684 86332

Ullswater Caravan

Camping and Marine Park

Watermillock, Penrith (C T)

☎ 017684 86666

Fax 86095

The Quiet Camping and Caravan Site

Watermillock (C T)

☎ 017684 86328

Gillside Caravan and Camping Site

Glenridding (C T)

☎ 017684 82346

Sykeside Camping Park

Brotherswater, Patterdale

☎ 017684 82239

Youth Hostels

YHA Hevellyn

Nr Glenridding

☎ 0870 772 5862

YHA Patterdale

☎ 0870 770 5986

Hire of Cottages, Flats & Residential Caravans

Some Agencies and Associations:

Cumbrian Cottages

Windermere

☎ 015394 88772

Fax 88902

Heart of Lakes and Cottage Life

☎ 015394 32321

Fax 33251

Lakelovers

Windermere

☎ 015394 88855

Fax 88857

Windermere Lake Holidays

☎ 015394 47700

Low Briery Holiday Village

☎ 017687 72044

Car Hire

Vickers Self Drive

75, Appleby Road, Kendal

☎ 01539 732643

Lakes Car Hire

New Road, Windermere

☎ 015394 42200

Cycle Hire

Millenium Cycles

Crook Road
Staveley
☎ 01539 821167

Biketreks

Compston Road
Ambleside
☎ 015394 31505

Crook Barn Stables

Torver
Coniston
☎ 015394 41088

Summitreks

Yewdale Road
Coniston
☎ 015394 41212

Keswick Mountain Bikes

Southey Hill
Keswick
☎ 017687 75202

Trackers Cycle Hire

Main Road
Keswick
☎ 017687 71372

Windermere Canoe and Cycle

Bowness
☎ 015394 44451

Country Lanes Cycle Centre

Windermere Station
☎ 015394 44544

Holiday Lakeland

Portinscale and Ireby
Offer organised cycling holidays in addition to cycle hire.
☎ 016973 71811
Fax. 016973 71960

There are waymarked mountain bike routes at Grizedale Forest and Whinlatter Forest. Details at the forest visitor centres.

Note: Byways (usually unsurfaced roads) are open to cyclists, horse rider and walkers; off-road vehicles may also be encountered. Bridleways are open to cyclists but horse riders and walkers have right of way. Footpaths are not available to cyclists. Open land – there is no right of access for cyclists on fells or farmland without the permission of the landowner. Always comply with the Mountain Biking Code of Conduct.

Eating Out

All the large hotels and the majority of the country house and smaller hotels have dining rooms and will provide meals for non-residents, in some cases only during the evening, in other cases also at mid-day. Almost all inns, including those listed in the accommodation chapter, provide bar food both at mid-day and in the evening.

The following list adds further suggestions for each section of the district, ranging from expensive, high quality, restaurants to more simple premises including tea/coffee shops not open in the evening.

Extra special!

The Miller Howe Hotel

Windermere
☎ 015394 42536

Both are also residential hotels

The Sharrow Bay Hotel

Ullswater
☎ 017684 86301

South Section

Waterside Wholefoods

Kent View, Kendal
☎ 01539 729743

Castle Dairy

Wildman Street
Kendal (reservations only)
☎ 01539 721170

Deja Vu

124 Stricklandgate, Kendal
☎ 01539 724843

Farrers Tea and Coffee Shop

13 Stricklandgate, Kendal
☎ 01539 731707

Macdonalds

Stricklandgate, Kendal
☎ 01539 733799

Renoirs Coffee Shop

Main Street, Windermere
☎ 015394 44863

Magic Wok

2 Crescent Road, Windermere
☎ 015394 88668

M & J Fish Restaurant

Birch Street, Windermere
☎ 015394 42522

Rastelli's

Lake Road, Bowness
☎ 015394 44227

Trattoria Ticino

Quarry Rigg, Bowness
☎ 015394 45786

The Porthole

Ash Street, Bowness
☎ 015394 42793

Bowness Kitchen

Lake Road, Bowness
☎ 015394 45529

The Spinnery Restaurant

Kendal Road, Bowness
☎ 015394 42756

Ambles Brasserie

Lake Road, Ambleside
☎ 015394 33970

Dodds Restaurant

Rydal Road, Ambleside
☎ 015394 32134

Bertram's Restaurant

Market Place, Ambleside
☎ 015394 32119

The Cumbria Carvery

Stock Lane, Grasmere
☎ 015394 35005

Newby's Gallery

Stock Lane, Grasmere
☎ 015394 35248

Kirkstone Gallery

Skelwith Bridge
☎ 015394 34711

The Minstrel's Gallery

Hawkshead
☎ 015394 36423

The Cafe

Grizedale Visitor Centre
Grizedale
☎ 01229 860011

Fell Foot Park Cafe

Newby Bridge
☎ 015395 31273

Boater's Restaurant

Lakeside, Newby Bridge
☎ 015395 31381

Lucy's

Church Street, Ambleside
☎ 015394 31191

West Section

Ravenglass and Eskdale Station Buffet

☎ 01229 717171

Brook House

Boot, Eskdale
☎ 019467 23288

North Section

Beatfords Country Restaurant

7 Lowther Went, Cockermouth
☎ 01900 827099

The Norham Coffee House

73 Main Street, Cockermouth
☎ 01900 824330

The Lakeland Sheep and Wool Centre Restaurant

Egremont Road, Cockermouth
☎ 01900 82267

Whinlatter Visitor Centre Cafe

Whinlatter Pass
☎ 017687 78469

The Saw Mill Cafe

Mirehouse, Nr Keswick
☎ 017687 74317

Luca's Ristorante

Greta Bridge, Keswick
☎ 017687 74621

Abrahams Tea Room at George Fisher's

Borrowdale Road, Keswick
☎ 017687 72178

Bryson's Tea Room

Main Street, Keswick
☎ 017687 72257

Honister Yew Tree

Seatoller, Borrowdale
☎ 017687 77634

Priest's Mill Tea Room

Caldbeck
☎ 016974 78267

East Section

Coach House Restaurant

Angel Lane, Penrith
☎ 01768 899544

Cagney's Tandoori

17 King Street, Penrith
☎ 01768 867721

Chataway's Bistro

St Andrew's Churchyard, Penrith
☎ 01768 890233

Arcade Cafe

Devonshire Arcade, Penrith
☎ 01768 891240

Granny Dowbekins Tea Room and Garden

Pooley Bridge
☎ 017684 86453

Aira Force Tea Shop

Aira Force, Ullswater
☎ 017684 82881

Horse Riding

Holmescales Riding Centre

Kendal
☎ 01539 729388

Larkrigg Riding School

Kendal
☎ 015395 60245

Lakeland Equestrian

Windermere
☎ 015394 43811

Crook Barn

Coniston
☎ 015394 41088

Spoon Hall Trekking Centre

Coniston
☎ 015394 44139

Bigland Hall Estate

Newby Bridge
☎ 015395 31728

Park Foot Trekking

Pooley Bridge
017684 86696

Rookin House Farm Equestrian and Activity Centre

Ullswater
☎ 017684 83561

Inglewood Equestrian Centre

Penrith
☎ 01768 86410

Fishing

An Environment Agency rod licence must be purchased by anyone wishing to fish in any water in England. (north west region, north area headquarters, ☎ 01228 25151).

The licence is available from post offices and tourist information centres. In addition, a permit must be obtained from the Angling Association or Riparian owner owning the fishing rights. However, in the Lake District the following lakes and tarns may be fished by rod licence holders without additional permit, either from a shore where there is public access or from a boat on lakes or tarns where launching is permitted:

Windermere

Alcock Tarn, Grasmere.

Easedale Tarn, Grasmere.

Grisedale Tarn, Grasmere.

Codale Tarn, Grasmere.

Coniston Water.

Levers Water, Coniston.

Goats Water Coniston.

High Dam, Finsthwaite.

Blea Tarn, Boot, Eskdale.

Burnmoor Tarn, Boot, Eskdale.

Blea Tarn, Watendlath.

Thirlmere – for bait restrictions, refer to the information board at Armboth car park.

Ullswater.

Brotherswater, Patterdale.

Red Tarn, Helvellyn.

Small Water, near Haweswater.

Blea Water, near Haweswater.

Of the listed, Windermere has the greatest variety of fish, including the rare and highly esteemed char. The smaller tarns are generally limited to brown trout, with perch and schelly present in a minority of cases.

The fishery at Esthwaite Water offers a variety of facilities for visitors, including boat hire and instruction, with facilities for the disabled.

☎ 015394 36541.

A useful leaflet 'Fishing in Lakeland', produced by Windermere, Ambleside and District Angling Association, is available from tourist information offices.

Golf Clubs

Kendal

(pro.) ☎ 01539 723499

Carus Green

Burneside
☎ 01539 721097

Windermere
Crook Road
(pro.) ☎ 015394 43550

Keswick
Threlkeld
☎ 017687 79010

Penrith
☎ 01768 862217

Water Sports and Activities

Lake Holidays Afloat
Glebe Road, Bowness
☎ 015394 43415

Lakes Leisure
Rayrigg Road
☎ 015394 47183

Low Wood water sports centre
South of Waterhead, Windermere
☎ 015394 33338

Coniston Boating Centre
☎ 015394 41366

Summitreks
14, Yewdale Road, Coniston
☎ 015394 41212
Fax. 015394 41089

Howtown Outdoor Centre
Howtown, Ullswater
☎ 01768 486508

Glenridding Sailing Centre
Glenridding, Ullswater
☎ 01768 82541

Balloon Flights

High Adventure
Bowness on Windermere
☎ 015394 46588

Agricultural Shows, Local sports & Festivals

For details ring the local tourist information centre – see pp 219 – 20 or ring the National Park Office on ☎ 015394 45555

Westmorland County Show
Kendal
Lake District Sheepdog Trials
Ings, Staveley
Ambleside Sports
Rydal Sheepdog Trials

Grasmere Sports
Hawkshead Show
Lowick Show
Eskdale Show
Ennerdale Show
Loweswater Show

Cockermouth Show

Hesket Newmarket Show

Patterdale Sheepdog Trials

Penrith Show

Lowther Horse Driving Trials and Game Fair

☎ 01931 712378

Guided Tours

Nearly fifty qualified 'Blue Badge' guides are listed as available to provide a wide variety of guided tours for visitors. All are experienced in general guiding in the district; additionally, many have areas of particular expertise such as local literature, gardens or religious monuments. Mini-buses and/or motor cars may be provided by the guides. Several languages are spoken. For further information, contact Tourist Information Centres.

Tours and Holidays

Mountain Goat

Windermere, Bowness, Ambleside, Grasmere and Keswick
☎ 015394 45161
Fax. 015394 45164

Lakes Supertours

1, High Street, Windermere
☎ 015394 42751

Lakeland Safari Tours

Windermere, Bowness, Ambleside and Grasmere.
☎ 015394 33904

Park Tours and Travel Ltd

Bowness
☎ 015394 48600

Guided Walks

1) Lake District National Park Authority, Brockhole, Windermere

☎ 015394 45555

An extensive programme of guided walks is available throughout the year, from many centres throughout the district. The routes are divided into hill walks, leisurely walks and special interest walks, to suit all categories of walker. Many are free, but in some cases a charge is made and pre-booking is advisable. Walks are graded 'easy, moderate or strenuous'. The full programme is included in the National Park publication 'Out and About', produced annually. Widely available throughout the district.

2) Glaramara, Borrowdale

☎ 017678 77222. A charge is made.

3)Outdoor Centrte, Seatoller

☎ 017687 77222

Lakeland Weather Line

☎08700 550575

Stately Homes open to the public

Sizergh Castle (NT)

Sizergh, nr Kendal, LA8 8AE
☎ 015395 60951
Email: sizergh@nationaltrust.org.uk
(See P81 for details)

Levens Hall

Levens, Kendal, LA8 0PD
☎ 015395 60321
Email houseopening@levenshall.
co.uk
www.levenshall.co.uk
(See P81 for details)

Holker Hall

Cark in Cartmel, Nr Grange-over-
Sands, LA11 7PL
☎ 015395 58328
Email: info@holker.co.uk
www.holker.co.uk
(See P93 for details)

Leighton Hall

Nr Carnforth, LA5 9ST
☎ 01524 734474
www.leightonhall.co.uk
Open from May to Sept, 1400–1700.
Open Sun in Aug and Bank Holiday
Sun & Mon.

Muncaster Castle

Ravenglass, CA18 1RQ
☎ 01229 717614
Email: info@muncaster.co.uk
www.muncaster.co.uk
(See P117 for details)

Mirehouse

Nr Keswick
☎ 017687 72287 (house)
☎ 017687 74317 (tea room)
(See P144)

Dalemain Historic House & Gardens

Nr Pooley Bridge, Dalemain, Penrith,
CA11 0HB
☎ 017684 86450
www.dalemain.com
(See P164 for details)

Hutton in the Forest

Nr Penrith, CA11 9TH
☎ 017684 84449
www.hutton-in-the-forest.co.uk
(See P165 for details)

Smaller Houses

Townend (NT)

Troutbeck, Windermere, LA23 1LB
☎ 015394 32628
(See P86 for details)

Rydal Mount

Rydal, Nr Ambleside, LA22 9LU
☎ 015394 33002
Email: info@rydalmount.co.uk
www.rydalmount.co.uk
(See P87 for details)

Worksworth Museum & Art Gallery (Dove Cottage)

Grasmere LA22 9SH
☎ 015394 35544 (daytime)
www.wordsworth.org.uk
(See P87 for details)

Brantwood

Coniston, LA21 8AD
☎ 015394 41396
Email: enquiries@brantwood.org.uk
www.brantwood.org.uk
(See P90 for details)

Wordsworth House (NT)

Main Street, Cockermouth,
CA13 9RX
☎ 01900 820 884 (Infoline)
☎ 07900 824 805 (Office)
www.wordsworthhouse.org.uk
(See P140 for details)

Farms and other animal-based attractions

Lakes Aquarium

Lakeside, Newby Bridge, LA12 8AS
☎ 015395 30153
Email: info@lakesaquarium.co.
www. lakesaquarium.co.uk
(See P93 for details)

Lakeland Wildlife Oasis

Hale, Milnthorpe, LA7 7FE
☎ 015395 63027
Web: www.wildlifeoasis.co.uk
(See P81 for details)

South Lakes Wild Animal Park

Crossgates, Dalton in Furness, LA15 8JE
☎ 01229 466086
Web: www.wildanimalpark.co.uk
Open daily, 1000–1700 (1630 closing in winter).

Lake District Coast Aquarium

South Quay, Maryport, CA15 8AB
☎ 01900 817760
www.lakedistrict-coastaquarium.
co.uk
Email: info@ld-coastaquarium.co.uk
(See P121 for details)

Lakeland Sheep and Wool Centre

Cockermouth, CA13 0QX
☎ 01900 822673
www.sheep-woolcentre.co.uk
(See P140 for details)

Trotters World of Animals

Coalbeck Farm, Bassenthwaite
☎ 017687 76239
www.trottersworld.com
(See P144 for details)

Nature Reserves

Cumbria Wildlife Trust produce a brochure 'Nature Reserves in Cumbria' listing 32 reserves throughout the county. The majority of these are not in the Lake District but could readily be included in a motor car or cycle tour. Those actually in the district are:

Dubbs Moss

1.5km. (1 mile) south of Cockermouth G.R. 098282.

Haweswater

At head of reservoir
G.R. (car park) 469107.

Rainsbarrow Forest

Ulpha, Duddon Valley
Footpaths start at G.R. 190925 or 198936.

*Roudsea Wood

near Haverthwaite. G.R. 330820.
Ash Landing
close to Far Sawrey. G.R. 386954.

Dorothy Farrers Spring Wood

near Staveley, G.R. 480983.
Hervey Reserve (Whitbarrow) Access at G.R. 436859.

Latterbarrow

near Witherslack village.
G.R. (car park) 441827.
*Permit necessary
(English Nature, Murley Moss Business Park, Kendal).

Tourist Information Centres

*Either closed or limited opening hours out of season.

Alston

☎ 01434 382244

Ambleside

Market Cross
☎ 015394 31576

*Borrowdale

Seatoller Barn
☎ 017687 77294

*Bowness

Bowness Bay
☎ 015394 42895

Brockhole

Windermere (National Park)
☎ 015394 46601

Broughton in Furness

The Square
☎ 01229 716115

Cockermouth

Town Hall
☎ 01900 822634

Coniston

main car park

Ruskin Avenue

☎ 015394 41533

Egremont

☎ 01946 820693

*Glenridding
Ullswater
main car park
☎ 017684 82414

Hawkshead
Main car park
☎ 015394 36525

Kendal
Town Hall
☎ 01539 725758

Keswick
Moot Hall
☎ 017687 72645

Maryport
☎ 01900 812101

Millom
☎ 01229 774819

Penrith
Middlegate
☎ 01768 867466.

*Pooley Bridge
Ullswater, The Square
☎ 017684 86530

Rheged
Near Penrith
☎ 01768 860034

Whitehaven
☎ 01229 774819

Windermere
Victoria Street
☎ 015394 46499

Useful Telephone Numbers

Cumbria Tourist Board
☎ 015394 44444

Cumbria Wildlife Trust
☎ 01539 816300

The Caravan Club
National 'clubline'. ☎ 01342 327410
The Camping and Caravan Club
☎ 01203 856 798.

Index

Index

Index

Published in the UK by
Landmark Publishing Ltd
The Oaks, Moor Farm Road West, Ashbourne, DE6 1HD
☎ (01335) 347349 Fax: (01335) 347303
email: landmark@clara.net website: www.landmarkpublishing.co.uk

4th Edition
ISBN 13: 978-1-84306-436-7

Print: Gutenberg Press, Malta
Cartography: Mark Titterton & Michelle Prost
Design: Michelle Prost

Front cover: A female hiker descending the path from Loughrigg with Grasmere in
the background
Back cover, top: Derwent Water with mountain reflections
Back cover, bottom: Castlerigg, ancient stone circle near Keswick

Picture Credits:
Michelle Prost: 151b, 154 both, 155 both, 158t

The below images are courtesy of www.Shutterstock.com with copyright to:

Dean Mitchell: Back Cover Bottom, 11, 138t; **JP:** 99
Kevin Eaves: Front cover, 6, 31b, 35, 38, 39, 46, 50, 58, 106b, 107b, 138, 146, 158b,
159b, 162b, 162t
Amra Pasic: 99b; **Soca:** Back Cover Top, 107t, 122; **Darren Turner:** 134b;
Peter Brett Charlton: 2; **Peter Guess:** 22, 94

All other images supplied by Norman Buckley and Lindsey Porter